THE THIRTEEN COLONIES

Louis B. Wright

AMERICAN HERITAGE • NEW WORD CITY

Published by New Word City, Inc.

For more information about New Word City, visit our Web site at
NewWordCity.com

INTRODUCTION

It began in 1492 when Christopher Columbus sailed west to find a new route to the Indies and stumbled onto an unknown continent. But if the origin of the colonial period was accidental, the ending was not. The representatives of the thirteen colonies who approved the Declaration of Independence in 1776 charted a collision course, aware of the obstacles in their path and the risks they were taking.

The events that led to their decision took place over a period of nearly 300 years. Looking back, the wonder is that it culminated so quickly. For a century after its discovery, the New World was little more than a lode to be mined by adventurers seeking profits. It wasn't until the end of the sixteenth century that serious efforts were made to establish permanent colonies. Even then, the perils of the journey and the threats of starvation and Indian attack inhibited settlement. Many colonists turned back when they discovered life in America wasn't what land developers promised.

But settlers gradually came, spurred, in part, by the fear of religious persecution, but above all, drawn by the hope of owning land. They were a mixed lot: English Separatists from Leiden, French Huguenots, Dutch burghers, Mennonite peasants from the Rhine Valley, and a few gentleman Anglicans. But they shared a quality of toughness.

America was not a tranquil place to establish a home. Settlers found themselves immersed in continuous conflict as European nations maneuvered for power in the New World. Foreign policy made in London, Madrid, Paris, and The Hague turned America into a battleground for more than a century.

The English colonies were the underdogs in these frontier extensions of dynastic wars. Although English land claims stretched to the Pacific, the thirteen colonies occupied a narrow, vulnerable strip of land along the Atlantic seaboard. For the most part, colonists fended for themselves against the imperial troops of France and Spain. The Spanish were drawn to the New World in search of gold and silver, the French to the fur trade. The people who settled the English colonies understood these attractions, but most came determined to stay.

This tenacity enabled them to endure, but not to prevail. That required a sense of common purpose - and not surprisingly, it was a long time coming. The colonists differed enormously in nationality, religion, and language. They were a fragmented group more apt to pursue independence in diversity than in union. Eventually, a time came when colonists began to consider themselves not English or Dutch, not Virginians or New Yorkers, but Americans. As Americans, they were willing to sacrifice regional interests to serve common goals. As John Adams observed, there had been a "change in the principles, opinions, sentiments, and affections of the people," and this was "the real American Revolution."

When colonists came to grips with their destiny, it was because they had realized liberty and responsibility go together. No single event brought about that awareness. No single reason - the struggle for survival or the search for identity - can explain it. If we are to understand how the colonies became one nation and the colonists one people, we must examine their story from beginning to end.

1
A WORLD TO TAKE

When Christopher Columbus set out from Palos, Spain, on August 3, 1492, Western Europe had changed little since the age of Dante and Chaucer. An uneasy apathy, characteristic of the late Middle Ages, lay over most of the continent. The Catholic Church still exerted considerable authority, but its strength was uneven and its hold often tenuous as rebellious sovereigns defied popes or as corrupt popes forfeited the respect of the pious. Few states had rulers who sat securely on their thrones. Germany and Italy remained collections of independent or semi-independent cities and principalities. The emperors of the Holy Roman Empire hardly could be said to rule, but they controlled a nebulous portion of Central Europe. The emperor and pope were often at odds and sometimes at war as each contended for dominion over territories in northern Italy and neighboring regions. The continent was poised between two eras, the medieval world, with traditional patterns of thought, and the modern age, with changes that would affect every phase of life within a century.

One of the most powerful influences was the expansion of trade stimulated by demand for commodities from the East. The buying power of most of Europe had built slowly throughout the century as farming and sheep-raising improved, industries expanded, and the silver mines of Eastern Europe poured more bullion into the market. The increasing flow of money initiated an inflationary spiral bolstered by discoveries and conquests of the Spanish conquistadors in the New World that sent another stream of silver and gold to Europe. Money was becoming more plentiful, demand for goods in all the principal markets was strong, and prices were rising.

Trade had long been the lifeblood of many European communities. In the fifteenth century, however, demand for goods that had previously been restricted to the wealthy was increasing. More people could buy more goods, and merchants and ship owners struggled to meet demand.

The consequences of the Crusades went beyond the rescue of the holy places from the

Muslims - or the Saracens, as they were called in those days. They exposed Europeans to Eastern cultures and made them aware of luxuries little known in their home countries. The Venetians, in particular, profited from the Crusades. They exacted high prices for warring knights to the East, and they loaded their returning galleys with expensive products collected from Alexandria, Cairo, and other Mediterranean ports. The Republic of Genoa, on the west coast of Italy, developed into a great seaport and a rival of the Queen of the Adriatic. Venice and Genoa established bases and imposed their rule at various points in the Mediterranean as they expanded trade between the Near East and distant European markets.

By the end of the fifteenth century, Venice and Genoa were in decline. The Ottoman Turks, who had supplanted the Seljuk Turks, the Arabs, and the Moors as the bearers of the banners of Islam, threatened their traditional trading routes. Previously, the leaders of Venice had reached an accommodation with the Seljuk Turks of Asia Minor and negotiated terms with the Mamelukes of Egypt. Genoa also had made favorable trade agreements in the Mediterranean before the rise of the Ottoman Turks. By the end of the century, however, the situation had changed. The Ottoman Turks, a warlike, organized military power, swept into Egypt and Asia Minor. They were diverted temporarily in 1402 by the attack on their rear from other Asiatic invaders under Tamerlane, but their power was short-lived, and the Ottoman Turks managed to take Constantinople in 1453. Moving into Europe, they marched to the walls of Vienna before they were stopped, and none knew when they might resume their advance.

The Turks developed sea power. Before this time, they had been an army of horsemen, but after they captured Constantinople, their naval prowess increased. Privateers flying the Turkish flag lurked in all principal seaports of North Africa. Many bases and colonies of Venice and Genoa surrendered to Turkish naval commanders. A crowning insult to the incumbent European powers occurred in 1480, when Muhammad II captured the Italian town of Otranto and set up a market for the sale of Christian slaves. By 1565, the Turks attacked Malta and nearly captured it. The days when the Venetians ruled the Mediterranean and Venetian merchants held a monopoly of the trade in Eastern luxuries ended before Columbus set sail.

Venice and Genoa managed to bring in some luxury goods and even traded with the Turks - on their terms. But cost of Eastern products became exorbitant. Merchants across Europe hoped to discover new routes to India, the Spice Islands, and other lands in the Far East.

For generations, Europeans had depended upon the East for spices and comestibles. The Crusaders had acquired a taste for dates, raisins, preserved fruits, candied melons, and other delicacies enjoyed by their enemies, the Saracens. The Moors in Spain had introduced many products of the East, and Spaniards had learned from their conquerors about a life more civilized than northern Europeans had known.

Although Turks in the eastern Mediterranean were a considerable force in the fifteenth century, the power of Islam as represented by the Moors, an Arabic-speaking people of Muslim faith in North Africa, was declining. A small Moorish kingdom still held power in Spain, but ten years before Columbus' first voyage, Christian Spain began its final war against the Moors, which ended in 1492 with the surrender of Granada, the last Muslim stronghold.

At the same time, Portugal was at war against the Moors in Africa. In 1415, the Portuguese captured Ceuta on the African mainland and used it as a base. This was an important step in Portugal's development as a maritime, trading nation. The man who raised the Christian standard over the walls of Ceuta was Prince Henry, later to be called by the English - somewhat erroneously, for he made no voyages – "Prince Henry the Navigator," because of his encouragement of maritime affairs.

The Portuguese, who had developed a mercantile society, were eager to expand their commercial ventures. With a foothold on the shores of Africa, it was natural for them to consider expanding into that continent. The Portuguese believed they had a mission to convert the heathen - especially when their missionary effort would produce material rewards. If God permitted the Portuguese to capture unbaptized Africans who could be sold into Christian bondage, loss of liberty was a small price for these heathens to pay for salvation. Thus, the Portuguese - and the slave traders who came after them – eased their consciences.

In 1418, Prince Henry established a residence overlooking the sea on Sagres Point, near Cape St. Vincent. Sailors were welcome at Sagres, which became a combination of religious order and school of navigation. As Grand Master of the Order of Christ, Prince Henry sent expeditions that annexed the Madeira, the Azores, and the Cape Verde Islands to Portugal. Expeditions under his sponsorship sailed down the African coast, and before his death in 1460, his captains had gone as far south as Senegal and had brought back gold, ivory, and slaves.

Africa was promising, but neither the defeat of Islam nor the conversion of the Senegalese nor the trade in pepper, ivory, and slaves was enough to satisfy the Portuguese. Stories of the riches of the East prompted them to find a way to India. Prince Henry's explorers had gone far enough around the western hump of Africa to convince themselves they might reach India by rounding that continent, and the opening of that route became their goal. A Portuguese traveller, Pero de Covilhã, set out in 1487 on a journey that eventually took him from Cairo to Aden and across the Arabian Sea to Calicut on the coast of India. He was the first Portuguese to visit Goa. Although Covilhã settled in Abyssinia, he sent back a report of the opportunities for trade with India.

In the same year Covilhã departed, Bartholomeu Dias sailed from Lisbon on a voyage that took him around Africa to the east coast near the Great Fish River and Mossel Bay. What Dias learned strengthened his belief that India could be reached by sea, but lack of provisions made it impossible for him to test his theories. In December 1488, he returned by way of the cape on the tip of Africa, which he called the Cape of Storms and King John II of Portugal renamed the Cape of Good Hope.

When Dias docked at Lisbon, the Genoese navigator Christopher Columbus was there and made notes concerning the voyage. In 1485, Columbus made a proposal to King John II to reach the East by sailing west. John, more keenly than Prince Henry before him, was concerned with maritime exploration and trade. He encouraged chart makers, seamen, and pilots until Portugal became the foremost center in Europe for maritime enterprise. King John put off

Columbus in 1485 because two of his captains had a project for sailing westward that cost less than the Italian's proposal. When nothing came of this endeavor, he revisited Columbus' proposal. But when Dias returned with news that India could be reached without sailing west, King John lost interest in the Genoese's plans.

Since Portugal had a monopoly of African commerce and the Cape of Good Hope route, Columbus realized Spain might be more receptive to exploring what he called "the Great Ocean Sea." He returned to Spain, where he earlier had appealed to Ferdinand II of Aragon and Isabella of Castile. At the same time, he sent his brother Bartholomew to London to make his proposal before King Henry VII.

In 1488, as Columbus struggled to gain a new hearing from the Spanish sovereigns, Bartholomew tried to interest the Tudor monarch in a western voyage of discovery. Although no direct evidence remains of Henry's dealings with Bartholomew, Columbus' son Ferdinand later wrote that the English king was sufficiently interested to continue negotiations. Spanish historian Gonzalo Fernàndez de Oviedo, asserted that Henry's counselors ridiculed Bartholomew's idea of sailing west to the Indies and that Henry declined to support the project.

Until 1492, Columbus met with no more encouragement from the Spanish rulers than

Bartholomew had received in England. Ferdinand and Isabella were preoccupied with the last crusade against the Moors, and Isabella was more concerned with driving the last of the Muslim warriors out of Spain than with unknown lands. In the meantime, scholars appointed by the sovereigns reported that Columbus' plan was not feasible, and if he ever reached the other side of the Western Sea, as the Atlantic was called, he would never return.

His patience drained, Columbus applied to the king of France for help. But before he had crossed the Spanish border, friends interceded with Queen Isabella, who again sent for the would-be explorer. He found the queen preoccupied with the siege of the Moors in Granada and had to wait for an audience. When Granada fell on January 2, 1492, Columbus carried a banner in the procession that celebrated the final victory over the Muslims in Spain. Still, the queen refused to back the Enterprise of the Indies, and it was not until April 1492, that the two sovereigns finally gave Columbus three ships and permission to make his voyage.

On August 3, 1492, Columbus, with ninety men in three ships, the *Santa María,* the *Pinta,* and the *Nina,* sailed from the port of Palos. Columbus and his men took Holy Communion in the gray dawn, asked God's blessing on their enterprise, and sailed away. Queen Isabella had seized an opportunity that John of Portugal, Henry of England, and

Charles of France had rejected, and for this, she would gain for Spain an empire that would be the envy of the world.

After a long voyage, the ships made landfall on October 12, 1492, probably at San Salvador (Watling's Island) in the Bahamas. Columbus believed he had reached one of the outermost islands of Asia and that Japan (then known as Zipangu) was near. He had read his Marco Polo and studied a letter and chart by Italian Paolo Toscanelli, which showed the land mass of Asia reasonably close. He believed the geographical lore of his day that proclaimed the Western Ocean was much narrower than it is, and that Japan was much nearer to Europe than the Atlantic seaboard of North America. When his voyage ended in the Bahamas, he was certain he had found the western route to the Indies, a belief he held through three more voyages.

When Columbus returned to Spain after exploring Cuba, Hispaniola, and other islands, he reported to his sovereigns he had found the westerly route to the Indies and had discovered islands with gold mines. He had collected gold nose plugs, a few pearls, and stories of vast quantities of gold on the next island. The search for that precious metal, just beyond the next inlet, just over the next mountain, was to be a lure that would attract men to fateful destinations for generations. The news of Columbus' return to

Palos in March 1493, carried by letter to the rulers of Spain, brought an invitation from the king and queen to Barcelona, where they were holding court. Columbus journeyed triumphantly across Spain in April, and the king and queen received him with great pomp. He drew up a plan for colonizing the new territories and began preparations for a second expedition. The age of western discovery had begun.

So accustomed are we today to instant dissemination of news that we find it difficult to realize that Europe did not learn of Columbus' voyage immediately. Many parts of Europe had to wait months and even years to hear about the discovery. In the ports of Spain and Portugal, sailors and ship captains did talk of the western voyage. Italian merchants, eager for news that would affect commerce, wrote home of the return of Columbus from exploring islands off Asia, and the Portuguese, in particular, renewed their maritime activities. But outside the Iberian Peninsula and Italy, news of Columbus' first voyage traveled slowly.

In the meantime, Spain took steps to ensure possession of the lands Columbus discovered in the West. The reigning pope, Alexander VI, was a Spaniard, born Rodrigo Borgia. The Spanish sovereigns sent a delegation to persuade him to issue a bull favorable to Spanish interests. The bull, called *Inter Caetera* (1493), drew a line from pole to pole 100 leagues west of the Cape Verde Islands. It gave Spain all lands beyond the line and left to Portugal lands to the east. Portugal complained that its interests were damaged, and successfully negotiated with Spain the Treaty of Tordesillas (1494), which shifted the line to 370 leagues west of the Cape Verde Islands. This new boundary ran through eastern South America, giving Brazil to Portugal. The rest of the world was thus excluded by papal decree from sharing the discovery; eventually French, Dutch, and English explorers ignored the line of demarcation and began exploring the coastline of the New World.

Portugal aimed to exploit the Africa-to-India route. On July 8, 1497, ten years after Bartholomeu Dias had demonstrated that ships could reach India by sailing around the tip of Africa, Vasco da Gama sailed from Lisbon with four vessels, bound for India. Da Gama's voyage, the theme of one of the greatest of Portuguese epics, Luiz Vaz de Camões' *Os Lusiadas,* took two years and established not only the sailing route for future voyages to India, but also the essential trading plan the Portuguese were to follow. Da Gama made contacts in Calicut, an important spice port. He learned that trading with India would have to be more sophisticated than bartering the trinkets that African natives desired and returned with a cargo of cinnamon and pepper. Trade with the East via the Cape of Good Hope had begun, and the Portuguese began establishing naval bases to protect their interests. Portugal's attempt to monopolize the Indian trade, especially in spices, succeeded until the rise of the English and Dutch East India companies in the early seventeenth century.

Other European powers envied the Portuguese for their monopoly of the eastern trade and hoped to find another route to the wealth of Asia. For many years after Columbus' journeys, even after it was clear a land mass blocked the way to the East, explorers continued to search for some strait that would lead into the Great South Sea and then to Japan and China. Explorers became professional adventurers willing to serve under any ruler with the means to hire them. Geographers, navigators, pilots, map makers, and other maritime specialists came from Italy and Portugal, ready to offer their skills.

One such geographer was Amerigo Vespucci, who gave his name to the New World. Vespucci began his career as a commercial agent working for the Medici of Florence. In 1492, he was sent to Seville on business concerning ships supplies. Vespucci became a proficient observer on four voyages, in which he served as a specialist in geography rather than a commanding officer. He was the first who realized the new discoveries were an unknown continent and not part of Asia.

After his second voyage with Alonso de Ojeda in 1499, an expedition that discovered the pearl fisheries off the coast of Venezuela, Vespucci returned and entered the service of Portugal. In 1501, he went with Nuño Manoel's expedition that explored the coast south of Brazil. Their findings led experts to believe that a passage to the ocean beyond might be discovered at the tip of South America, just as a passage had been found around Africa. Vespucci accompanied a fourth voyage to Brazil and finally returned to Spain, where he received an appointment in 1508 from the Casa de Contratación (or India House) in Seville as pilot major, that is, chief pilot and instructor in navigation, a post he retained until he died in 1512 of malaria.

Vespucci's reports secured his reputation. Although some of his claims were exaggerated, he was an accurate observer, and he wrote well. His descriptions of the coasts provided information other explorers could use, and these reports, in the form of letters, were published. They formed part of Fracanzano de Montalboddo's *Paesi Novamente Retrovati* ("The Newly Discovered Lands") in 1507, a popular work that was subsequently translated into Italian, French, and German.

In that same year, German geographer and mapmaker Martin Waldseemüller of the College of St. Dié in Lorraine published two maps, with an introduction entitled *Cosmographiae Introductio,* which included Vespucci's letters. Waldseemüller tentatively named the southern part of the new lands, shown on his map as an island, "America" for Amerigo Vespucci. Waldseemüller's work became popular throughout Europe. The name he had given South America at length attached itself to the entire New World.

Ferdinand Magellan, a Portuguese nobleman who had served in India under the viceroy Affonso de Albuquerque, was the first explorer to circumnavigate the globe. In disfavor in Portugal, Magellan offered his services to Spain's King Charles V, whom he persuaded to outfit an expedition under his command to seek the spice islands of the East by sailing around South America. A fleet of five ships with some 270 men sailed from Sanlúcar on September 20, 1519. More than a year later, on October 21, 1520, after exploring the coastline of South America, Magellan discovered the strait named for him.

The wind and currents in this strait are notorious among sailors, and Magellan spent nearly forty days trying to make the passage. Finally, with three ships surviving, he reached the Pacific on November 28, 1520. He was the first European to emerge in "the Great South Sea," an expanse of water that would have terrified him had he known its extent. Sailing northwest, he found only an endless sea until on March 6, 1521, he reached the Marianas islands. Food and water were nearly gone, but, after refreshing themselves, the expedition pushed on to the Philippines. Intervening in a tribal war, Magellan was killed there on April 27, 1521, and Juan Sebastián del Cano took command.

One of the three surviving ships proved unseaworthy and was burned. The explorers used the remaining two to sail to Borneo and the Moluccas, where they loaded a cargo of spices. One vessel turned and sailed for Panama; it ultimately wrecked. In the other, the *Victoria,* Cano sailed across the Indian Ocean, rounded the Cape of Good Hope, made a landfall on the Cape Verde Islands, where the Portuguese intercepted him and removed thirteen men. He ultimately reached Sanlúcar on September 7, 1522, with eighteen survivors out of 270 who had sailed three years before. Though Magellan did not live to see it, his voyage demonstrated the possibility of sailing around the earth. (This circumnavigation also proved the oceans were larger than Columbus and most contemporaries had dreamed.) Spain had found a route to the Spice Islands and had established a claim to an empire in the Pacific. The way to Asia around South America proved too hazardous and costly to make it practicable for the spice trade, but Spain developed commercial routes between the Philippines and the west coast of America. For many years, vessels from Manila brought cargoes to Mexico, where they were distributed to other markets.

With the circumnavigation of the globe begun by

Magellan, the extent of the world was established, and cartographers could make accurate maps. People finally realized the nature of the great land mass between the Atlantic and the Pacific. Though explorers continued to seek a northwest passage to Asia, they knew that a long voyage separated them from Japan and China. The New World was known to be two vast continents, although their extent and treasures remained unknown.

Even before Magellan's expedition, Spanish adventurers heard rumors about gold and pearls on the coasts of the new lands. Although few had reached the mainland and islands of the Caribbean, some who had landed on the Isthmus of Darien (now Panama) heard stories of a people to the west so rich in gold they stored it in baskets. Vasco Nunez de Balboa, who organized an expedition to seek this wealth, verified the tales. Beating his way through the underbrush of the Isthmus on September 25, 1513, he came upon and climbed a small hill. Stretching endlessly before him was the Pacific Ocean. Thus from "a peak in Darien" the first white man saw the ocean Magellan's expedition would cross seven years later.

Francisco Pizarro was with Balboa on this expedition. On that September day he stood with Balboa, looked at the Pacific, and considered tales of a people to the west whose utensils were said to be made of gold. Balboa did not reap this wealth. He was executed on a charge of treason in January 1517.

In 1519, two years after Balboa's execution, Hernan Cortes marched from the coast of Mexico to Tenochtitlán (now Mexico City), capital of the Aztecs and located on an island in Lake Texcoco. The city, ruled by the emperor Montezuma and resplendent with flowers, gold, silver, and temples where gods required human sacrifices, astonished the Spaniards.

At first welcomed as gods by the Aztecs, the Spaniards soon earned their hatred. On the night of June 20, 1520, the Aztecs drove them out of Tenochtitlán. Many Spanish soldiers were so burdened with gold they fell from the causeway leading to the mainland and drowned.

Eventually, Cortes recaptured the city and sent most of its gold to Spain. In 1528, he went to receive the thanks of Spanish Emperor Charles V. The capture of Montezuma's treasure, greater than any previously found, spread throughout Spain and Europe. Soon adventurers were pouring into Mexico. Cortes had laid the foundation of the Spanish empire in America, and Mexico became its most valued region. Spain would reap a golden harvest from Mexican mines, and bullion from the New World would maintain its armies and support its economy.

The known sources of gold, silver, and pearls

in Central America and Mexico concentrated Spanish attention upon the Caribbean and adjacent regions. But the Spaniards did not neglect the rest of America. In 1513, Juan Ponce de Leon, who had made a fortune in gold and slaves as governor of Puerto Rico, explored the mainland of Florida. He is best- remembered for his search for a fountain of youth, but he had more realistic aims. In 1521, he attempted to settle a colony in Florida, but Indians forced the expedition to retreat to Cuba, where Ponce de Léon died.

Embarking in 1539, Hernando de Soto, who had been in Peru with Pizarro, led an expedition across Florida and into the future states of Alabama, Georgia, the Carolinas, Tennessee, and Mississippi. Crossing the Mississippi River, his group went as far west as present-day Arkansas before returning to the Mississippi. At this point de Soto died. Luis de Moscoso took command of the expedition, which wandered into Texas, returned to the Mississippi, made its way to the river's mouth, then sailed around the coast to Vera Cruz, reaching it in 1543.

De Soto's expedition was remarkable in distance covered and hardships endured, but Francisco Vásquez de Coronado made a more astonishing trip that began in 1540. Coronado went in search of the Seven Cities of Gold and of an Indian city called Quivira. This expedition pushed north from Mexico and into what is now Arizona, New Mexico, Texas,

Oklahoma, and western Kansas. One of Coronado's lieutenants discovered the Grand Canyon, and the expedition made contacts with the Zuñi, Pueblo, and Plains Indians. Indeed, it was a Plains Indian, given to telling tales about the rich city of Quivira, who led the Spaniards to continue traveling until they reached a point near modern Wichita, Kansas, to find only villages of seminomadic Indians. The Seven Cities of Gold turned out to be Indian pueblos near present-day Santa Fe, New Mexico. Coronado returned to Mexico, disappointed and ruined. Although he had found no gold, he had shown the extent of the vast land, for secondary expeditions had explored the west as far as Southern California.

The lure of treasure hunting, which had become a Spanish mania soon after Columbus reported gold and pearls on the islands he had discovered, affected Spanish activities in the New World. The evidence of the wealth of Mexico that Cortes brought to Spain inspired eager adventurers to set sail. Every swordsman from Andalusia to Estremadura believed he could make his fortune in the newly discovered territories. Such news was not confined to Spain, and soon other countries were eying Spain's monopoly and plotting how to circumvent the line of demarcation set by Pope Alexander VI, dividing the heathen world between Spain and Portugal. Ultimately these two countries would have to recognize, begrudgingly, the rights of other countries.

Although news of Columbus' first voyage initially may have had small repercussions in northern Europe, the most knowledgeable seafaring people were aware of its implication. During the fifteenth and sixteenth centuries, trained pilots, geographers, and navigators, particularly from Italy and Portugal, followed news of maritime events. These men were constantly hatching new schemes of exploration and eager to enter the service of whichever monarch would support them. Thus, John Cabot of Genoa, a merchant naturalized in Venice, went to Bristol in 1496 to offer his services to Henry VII of England. Later, his son Sebastian served England and then Spain, where he was pilot major for years before finally returning to England.

It is significant that Cabot went to Bristol, for the city counted among its populous the most daring English mariners. For years they had been sailing around Ireland to Iceland for fish, and they had reached the seas of the northwest, perhaps as far as the fishing banks off Newfoundland. Since they were intent upon keeping trade secrets, no one can be sure how far they sailed. Some scholars believe they may have reached the shores of Newfoundland and the mainland of North America before Columbus' first voyage. Other fishermen from Brittany and the Bay of Biscay also may have discovered the Newfoundland banks and adjacent regions. They certainly were active in the decade after 1492, and by the early sixteenth century, Portuguese, English,

French, and Spanish fishermen were swarming to Newfoundland, which became a neutral ground for fishermen of all countries.

Stories of two mysterious islands to the west of Ireland had circulated in northern Europe. The nearest of these mythical islands, Antilia, was the Island of the Seven Cities that appeared in medieval legend. The other, the island of Brasil, lay farther west, and it was this island that discoverers of Newfoundland thought they had found.

Medieval legends told of voyages to islands in the West by St. Brendan. The only historically verifiable voyages, however, are those made by Irish monks to Iceland and by the Norsemen, who superseded the Irish on Iceland and continued on to Greenland, where they settled. Norse sagas tell of Vikings going to the mainland of America. That Norsemen reached North America at intervals after the occupation of Iceland and Greenland in the tenth century is well-proven, but they did little with their discovery except to procure timber.

The stories of lands in the Western Sea spurred Bristol explorers around 1480 and possibly before. John Day, an English merchant trading in Spain, wrote in 1498, possibly to Columbus, that men from Bristol had found the island of Brasil before Cabot's first voyage. This letter, found in the archives at Simancas, Spain, in 1956, reinforces the belief that Bristol men discovered lands in the northwest probably as early as 1480, when other records show voyages of discovery were going out of Bristol.

Since the Bristol men were concerned with fisheries and not with trying to find the Spice Islands and a short route to Asia, only fishermen were interested in discovering Brasil or Newfoundland. It took John Cabot, with his dream of finding a quick north-westerly passage to China, to interest King Henry VII. Exactly when Cabot reached Bristol has not been determined, but John Day's letter indicates that Cabot made an unsuccessful voyage of reconnaissance in 1496, soon after he received a patent from the king. This patent, granted "to our well-beloved John Cabot, citizen of Venice, and to Lewis, Sebastian and Sancio, sons of the said John," authorized them "to sail to all parts, regions and coasts of the eastern, western and northern sea, under our banners, flags and ensigns, with five ships or vessels of whatsoever burden . . . to find, discover and investigate whatsoever islands, countries, regions or provinces of heathens and infidels, in whatsoever part of the world placed, which before this time were unknown to all Christians."

The king gave Cabot, his sons, and their heirs the right to seize and govern such lands as they could conquer, but he required them to acknowledge themselves servants of the king of England and to pay him one-fifth of the profits from each voyage.

Cabot thought Asia lay before him in the northwest, and he envisioned several profitable voyages that would follow the opening of the route.

Little is known about the 1496 voyage except that it failed. Of the second voyage, in 1497, Cabot sailed in May from Bristol in a small bark, the *Matthew*, with some twenty men. At least two were Bristol merchants who may have sailed in northern waters before. Since this was to be a voyage of reconnaissance rather than of trade, a small craft and crew of experienced seamen sufficed. After clearing Ireland, Cabot first sailed north, then turned west, and on June 24, made landfall, naming the spot Prima Tierra Vista. The precise location remains a mystery, but historians believe it may have been on the coast of Maine. Cabot and his men claimed the land for King Henry VII of England, planting a cross and the banners of England, the pope, and St. Mark, the patron saint of Venice, thus honoring God, his royal patron, the head of the church, and his adopted city. Vague as the geographical details are, this voyage was critical to England, for it was upon Cabot's taking possession of the land that England later based its claim, by right of discovery, to North America.

Cabot made a rapid, fifteen-day passage from the easternmost cape of the mainland to Bristol and arrived about August 6. Few Atlantic crossings for the next century exceeded this in speed, and it renewed hope of a short route to the East.

The success of Cabot's voyage roused mercantile circles, and he became famous, considering "himself at least a prince," according to a letter from the Milanese ambassador in London, Raimondo de Raimondi de Soncino, to Lodovico il Moro, Duke of Milan, dated December 18, 1497. "Perhaps . . . your Excellency, it may not weary you, Soncino wrote, "to hear how his Majesty here has gained a part of Asia, without a stroke of the sword. There is in this Kingdom a man of the people, Messer Zoane Caboto [John Cabot] by name, of kindly wit and a most expert mariner. Having observed that the sovereigns first of Portugal and then of Spain had occupied unknown islands, he decided to make a similar acquisition for his Majesty."

Another voyage to build on the discovery Cabot had made already was being planned, Soncino reported. "Before very long they say that his Majesty will equip some ships, and in addition he will give them all the malefactors, and they will go to that country and form a colony. By means of this they hope to make London a more important mart for spices than Alexandria. The leading men in this enterprise are from Bristol, and great seamen, and now they know where to go, say that the voyage will not take more than a fortnight, if they have good fortune after leaving Ireland."

In 1497, excitement about discovery had spread to

Bristol and London as it had in Spain and Portugal. Soon, mariners in every Western European port wanted to sail across the Atlantic.

Cabot's voyage began in the spring of 1498, when a fleet of four or five ships, provisioned for a year and containing articles of trade, sailed from Bristol. Somewhere in the ocean, Cabot and his ships were lost. The fate of the vessels is unknown. Some evidence points to English ships as far south as the Caribbean in 1498, but records of Cabot's last voyage are scarce. His voyage of 1497, however, had done enough to give England a claim to a portion of the New World it would one day assert. That time, however, was far away.

England had not heard the last of the Cabots. John Cabot's son, Sebastian, made a voyage in 1508. Little about it is known. He was seeking the elusive Northwest passage that for years would attract many seamen. He may have reached Hudson Bay, but the voyage failed. In 1512, while serving in Spain with Lord Dorset, who was leading an army allied with King Ferdinand, Sebastian obtained permission to enter the service of Spain, and four years later he became pilot major of Spain. After a long career, part of which he spent exploring the South Atlantic, he returned to England in 1548. In 1553, he was one of the organizers of a joint stock company designed to find a northeast passage to India and Cathay. In that year, Cabot planned the voyage of Stephen

Borough (or Burrough) that rounded the North Cape and reached Russia. Cabot became governor of the company formed by Borough, which developed trade with Russia and for that reason came to be known as the Muscovy Company.

With Henry VII's interest in exploration, it is surprising England waited nearly a century before attempting to establish a colony. Although Henry had promised John Cabot some convicts to serve as colonists, no evidence exists that he made any attempt at settlement. Bristol fishermen did become more active on the Newfoundland banks, but that was common ground for all Europeans. English colonization was secondary to other political events in Europe.

Because England's break with Spain late in the reign of Queen Elizabeth was so dramatic, we think of England and Spain as enemies during the centuries of expansion overseas. Actually, for long periods in the sixteenth century, England and Spain were allies. Henry VII dared to encroach on what Spain claimed as its rights in the Western Sea only because, at the time, Spain was trying to induce England to assist in a war against France.

Henry VIII was not ready to compete with Spain for America. He was occupied building a navy for protection closer to home, and only occasionally would a merchant vessel venture into Spanish waters overseas. The brief Protestant reign of

Edward VI came before the reign of Mary, who married Prince Philip, later Philip II of Spain. She would not challenge Catholic Spain and did not wish to encroach on Spanish rights on the other side of the Atlantic. If Mary and Philip had had an heir, England might never have colonized any portion of North America, and Latin America might have extended to Canada.

Soon after Elizabeth's accession in 1558, she began to play Spain against France. Faced with domestic problems and critical diplomacy in Europe, she could not afford to expend energy to overseas expansion. But its merchant marine was growing, and its sailors were becoming more enterprising. The day was not far when they would reach Spanish waters on the western side of the Atlantic Ocean.

In the meantime, the leaders of France pondered opportunities overseas. Since France and Spain were frequently at war during the sixteenth century, France was not concerned with challenging Spanish rights in America. Seamen from Normandy and Brittany already were traversing the North Atlantic for Newfoundland fisheries; early in the sixteenth century, some had ventured as far as the mainland.

Florentine navigator Giovanni da Verrazano took service with Francis I in 1524 and made an extensive reconnaissance of the Atlantic seaboard from North Carolina to Maine. He was probably the first European to sail into New York Harbor.

Verrazano continued to sail for the French, but in 1526–27, while exploring the West Indies, he was killed - and probably eaten - by Carib Indians. Verrazano's investigation of the North Atlantic coast provoked French exploration of that region.

The ancient walled city of St.-Malo in Brittany had become a nest of pirate ships, and its seamen were among the most daring in France. In 1534, one of its leaders, Jacques Cartier, led an expedition to the shores of Newfoundland and continued on through the Strait of Belle Isle into the Gulf of St. Lawrence. Landing on the Gaspé Peninsula, Cartier claimed the land for France. After reaching Anticosti Island, he sailed back to France and reported he had discovered a fertile land, suitable for colonists, and he had found an estuary, which he believed might open a sea route to Cathay. With this news, the king authorized - and paid for - a second expedition of three ships that sailed in May 1535.

This time, Cartier sailed up the St. Lawrence as far as the Lachine Rapids and the site of Montreal. To his disappointment, he found he was exploring a river that continually narrowed, not an estuary that led to the China Sea. A long winter spent near present-day Quebec nearly ended the expedition, for many died of scurvy until friendly Indians taught them to drink a tea made from spruce needles. When warm weather returned, Cartier kidnapped some Indians and sailed for St.-Malo, which he reached in July 1536.

In 1541, Cartier led a third expedition to Canada, with colonization as its purpose. Sailing in May with five ships, he landed near Quebec, where settlers built their camp, planted turnips, searched for gold and diamonds, and prepared for the winter, which nearly proved disastrous. Cartier was disgusted because Sieur de Roberval, a nobleman from Picardy who had been appointed viceroy, had failed to appear with additional men and supplies. When spring came, he and his colonists sailed for France. Reaching St. John's Harbor, Newfoundland, on June 8, he met Roberval with his ships, bound for the Canadian colony. Cartier had no intention of turning back and slipped away in the night, leaving Roberval to find his way to the deserted site where colonists had wintered. Without experience or supplies for establishing a colony in the wilderness, Roberval's people suffered like previous settlers, and a third died during their winter in Canada. Finally, in 1543, the king ordered ships to bring back the survivors. Thus ended the earliest French efforts to claim Canada for France.

A few years later, French Huguenots attempted to gain a foothold in America, this time in Florida. Under Jean Ribaut, a Huguenot sea captain from Dieppe, two ships of colonists sailed from Le Havre on February 18, 1562, and on May 1, they landed at the mouth of a river they called the

River of May, now the St. Johns. A stone inscribed with the royal arms was installed to claim the land for the king of France. Ribaut pushed farther north and settled on present-day Parris Island, South Carolina. He called the harbor Port Royal and built a stockade named Charlesfort in honor of the new king, Charles IX. Leaving a garrison of thirty men, Ribaut sailed home. After a few difficult months, the members of the garrison built a vessel and left for France.

French Huguenots were determined to colonize Florida where they could practice their religion free of controversy and persecution. Two years after Ribaut's expedition to Port Royal, René de Laudonnière, a nobleman from Poitou who had been with Ribaut, led a second group of Huguenot settlers to Florida. They landed on the south bank of the St. Johns River and established Fort Caroline. Like previous French colonial ventures, Laudonnière's settlement was soon on the verge of starvation, and by 1565, the hungry settlers were planning to build a vessel to escape.

At this point, English explorer John Hawkins sailed into the St. Johns River with a flotilla of four vessels. He sold one to Laudonnière, whose men were clamoring to return to France. Before they could sail, Ribaut reached the St. Johns with seven ships and reinforcements. In the meantime, Pedro Menéndez de Avilés, named *adelantado* (governor) of Florida by Philip II, was ordered to sail for that land and drive out the Huguenots. He arrived off the mouth of a small river he named St. Augustine in late August 1565, and in early September, he began to fortify a Spanish settlement. After failing to force Ribaut to a fight, he marched overland, destroyed Fort Caroline, and killed every Frenchman he captured. Over some, hanged from trees, he placed the inscription: I do this, not as to Frenchmen, but as to Lutherans."

Ribaut, who had sailed with his fleet to attack the Spaniards at St. Augustine, met disaster. A September hurricane wrecked his ships, and the Spaniards murdered him and his men. Out of the carnage, Laudonnière and Jacques Le Moyne, an artist who painted pictures of Florida life, escaped and ultimately reached France.

Menéndez, a ruthless soldier, successfully founded a colony at St. Augustine. He was instrumental in sending an expedition to establish an outpost at St. Helena in South Carolina and a short-lived settlement on Chesapeake Bay. The French had been rebuffed, and Spanish influence extended, but France had served notice it would claim a portion of the New World.

John Hawkins' appearance on the Florida coast in 1565 was symbolic of the growing activity of English seamen in western waters. For this, England could thank the Hawkins family, for they had been pioneers in attempts to profit from America. William Hawkins, a seaman and merchant from Plymouth, was said to revere Henry VIII because of his knowledge of "sea causes." In 1530, he sailed to Guinea, on the West African coast, where he traded for ivory and slaves. He sold the slaves in Brazil, thus initiating a future profitable venture. He made two other voyages to Brazil with slaves and set an example for his son John, who developed the slave trade with America.

Before 1560, John Hawkins engaged in the Spanish trade and sailed to the Canary Islands, where he discovered the demand for slaves in Spanish lands. In 1562, he organized an expedition of three ships that loaded slaves in Senegal and continued to Hispaniola, where he sold slaves and received a cargo of hides, sugar, gold, and pearls. Taking Spanish largesse for granted, he loaded an additional hulk with hides and sugar and shipped it to Spain. But Hawkins was a foreigner and an unlicensed trader in Spanish dominions. The Spanish government refused to ignore Hawkins' activities and confiscated the ship. Even so, the voyage was so profitable from the sale of slaves that, with support of Robert Dudley (later the Earl of Leicester) and the Earl of Pembroke, among others, he organized a second expedition in 1564. He obtained the loan of a royal ship, the *Jesus of Lübeck*. With four ships, Hawkins collected more slaves in Africa and sold them on the Venezuelan coast. He continued up the coast of Florida until he found Laudonnière at Fort Caroline. Hawkins recognized the value of Florida as a land for raising cattle and producing other commodities.

Although this voyage was profitable, and Hawkins was granted a coat of arms, the queen and Privy Council disavowed responsibility for him after the Spanish ambassador protested. The council even prohibited him from making another voyage he was planning. By 1567, however, Hawkins circumvented the council's prohibition and was preparing another slave and trading expedition. This time he had two royal ships, the *Jesus of Lübeck* and the *Minion,* and four other vessels. One was the *Judith,* commanded later in the voyage by Francis Drake, Hawkins' distant kinsman. While collecting slaves at Sierra Leone, the expedition plundered Portuguese vessels and secured more than 70,000 gold pieces. Hawkins sold most of his slaves in the West Indies and at Cartagena. Soon after, his fleet took refuge from a storm in the harbor of San Juan de Ulúa, (modern Veracruz), port of entry to Mexico.

It was bad luck for the English that a convoy of thirteen ships of Spain arrived at this moment bearing the new viceroy of Mexico. Hawkins could have used his weapons to blockade the harbor, but he would have been cornered. Therefore, after securing a promise of peace from the Spaniards, he permitted the convoy to anchor. On September 23, 1568, despite the truce, the Spaniards attacked the outnumbered English. Only two ships escaped, the *Minion,* crowded with 200 men, and Drake's *Judith,* which sailed away without helping the *Minion.*

Lacking food and space for so many men, Hawkins was forced to put half of his company ashore on a desolate beach 200 miles north of Veracruz. Some marched into the wilderness and died at the hands of Indians or from starvation. Others found a Spanish settlement, surrendered, and were taken as prisoners to Mexico City, where they came before the Inquisition.

Three men claimed they reached Nova Scotia, where a French fishing vessel rescued them. Their narrative, printed by Richard Hakluyt in the first edition of his *Principall Navigations* (1589), was omitted in later editions because of "certain incredibilities." Hawkins returned to England in the *Minion* on January 25, 1569. Many of his men, half-starved, had died on the voyage home. Drake in the *Judith* had arrived three days before him.

The disaster at San Juan de Ulúa marked a turning point in English-Spanish relations, which previously had been relatively peaceful. Although English corsairs occasionally had plundered Spanish ships, as they had Portuguese craft, England had recognized Spain's rights in America and had made little effort to stop them. But after

San Juan, English seamen despised Spain. In addition, Mexican authorities held several English as prisoners. Hawkins was determined to release them. Although the queen could take no action, she, too, was displeased. From this time forward, English corsairs multiplied, and though the queen condemned their actions, she encouraged them secretly and shared in the spoils.

The experience that Drake gained at San Juan made him, like Hawkins, an enemy of Spain. Revenge gilded with Spanish gold was behind the voyage he made in 1572 to Panama and the adjacent region. For months, during the late summer, fall, and winter, Drake terrorized the coast of Spain. He pillaged towns and captured and destroyed shipping. In February 1573, he marched across the Isthmus of Darien and saw the Pacific, which prompted him to pray he might sail an English ship in that sea. When he returned to England in August 1573, he had burned Puerto Bello on the Panama coast, destroyed many Spanish ships, spread terror throughout the West Indies and Central America, and made a fortune. Few voyages against the Spaniards could have been more satisfying.

But Drake dreamed of greater things, as the queen encouraged him. He confided in her a plan to sail around the tip of South America, following Magellan's track, and attack the Spanish possessions in the rear. He had observed enough to know Spain was filling its ships with gold and silver on the west coast of South America, and its towns were unprotected. The queen could not openly participate in this scheme, nor did she share the news with her trusted minister, Lord Burghley, for Burghley intended to keep peace with Spain.

But Drake's description of the treasure awaiting English ships was too alluring. With its real purpose kept secret, the expedition was organized. Drake went in a ship of his own, the *Pelican;* Captain John Winter commanded the *Elizabeth*; three smaller vessels sailed, too. On December 13, 1577, the squadron left Plymouth. Only Drake and the queen knew its destination. Spanish spies had reported it, but they thought Drake was heading for the Spanish Main. His men had been told they were going on a Mediterranean expedition, but after they had left the Cape Verde Islands, they learned the squadron was bound for the River Plate. There, they captured two Portuguese vessels, kidnapping a pilot, Nuño da Silva.

On the south coast of what is now Argentina, at Port St. Julian, Drake's squadron stopped for two months. There, Drake executed Thomas Doughty, after he charged him with mutiny. Two small vessels, no longer seaworthy, were broken up, and the *Pelican,* the *Elizabeth,* and the *Marigold* sailed for the Strait of Magellan. In honor of Sir Christopher Hatton, an investor in the voyage, Drake changed the name of the *Pelican* to the *Golden Hind*.

After making a fast passage of only sixteen days through the strait and entering the Pacific on September 6, 1578, Drake encountered violent storms. He lost *Marigold* and all its crew; later *Elizabeth* eventually returned to England. At the beginning of November, the *Golden Hind* was in smooth seas and turned north to seek the gold Drake had promised his men.

Carefully, Drake made his way up the coast, searching for Spanish vessels as he went, plundering and taking what he wanted but refusing to harm the ships' crewmen. At Callao, in Peru, where he arrived on February 13, 1579, he heard about a treasure ship, the *Cacafuego,* bound for Panama, which he captured. It was a rich prize, loaded with gold, silver, jewels, and precious stones. A few weeks later, off Acapulco, he captured another Spanish ship with its owner, Don Francisco de Xarate, who, after being freed, reported to the viceroy.

Drake, Xarate asserted, lived lavishly, his food served on a silver plate bearing his crest, his cabin sweet with perfumes given him by the queen, and his meals enlivened by the music of violins. His council of men dined with him and showed him great respect. The sailors and men-at-arms, around 100, kept their weapons polished and clean. In short, Xarate gave an almost idyllic - and exaggerated - picture of life aboard Drake's ship and described Drake as one of the greatest seamen alive.

With his vessel so heavy with treasure that he dared take no more, Drake sailed north and made a reconnaissance of the California coast. At a bay, likely north of San Francisco, he mounted a brass plate claiming the land for Queen Elizabeth and naming it New Albion.

Drake had hoped to find a passage in the north back to the Atlantic, but having failed, he set his course across the Pacific. During the long and dangerous voyage, he demonstrated exceptional skill as a commander and brought his ship safely home through the Cape of Good Hope. In the East Indies, he managed to find space for a quantity of highly prized cloves that added to the value of his cargo.

On September 26, 1580, the *Golden Hind* anchored at its home port of Plymouth. Drake sent his trumpeter to London to report to the queen the ship's safe arrival after a prosperous voyage, and the news quickly spread. The Spanish ambassador complained vigorously to Queen Elizabeth, who promised an investigation. She ordered Drake to report to her, and sent a messenger to Plymouth to inventory the treasure and see it was secured in the Tower of London. But Drake first was allowed to remove 10,000 pounds' worth for himself.

The crew of the *Golden Hind* testified that no Spaniard had been killed and none injured in the capture of ships and the plundering of towns. As to the amount of treasure taken, all involved, including the royal messenger sent to list it, were vague. It was a huge amount, and investors in the voyage stood to make a considerable profit. But first the queen had to answer the charges of the Spanish ambassador.

Elizabeth guessed that Philip II was not ready for war with England. He didn't support papal attacks on the British monarch, designed to remove her from her throne, for the likeliest heir was Mary, Queen of Scots, widow of a French king and closely allied with France. Philip wouldn't want an alliance of France and England under Mary, and he was willing to forgive attacks such as Drake's rather than start a costly war that would end poorly. So Philip let his ambassador bluster, while he sat in the Escorial thinking of some other plan to thwart Elizabeth the Heretic.

For her part, Elizabeth told the Spanish ambassador she already had endured much from Spain. Spanish and Italian troops had initiated a rebellion in Ireland, and Spanish interference in English affairs had cost her more than all the treasure Drake had taken in America. By refusing to allow trade with colonists in the New World, Spain and Portugal had brought upon themselves attacks by privateers. Furthermore, the queen refuted Spanish and Portuguese claims to the entire New World by reason of any papal decree, and she asserted English rights to territory not occupied by any Christian prince. She clearly did not intend to punish Drake, and she was unlikely to return to Spain the treasure she had stored in the Tower.

As if to emphasize her reply to Spain, Elizabeth ordered Drake to bring his ship to the Thames, and on the deck of the *Golden Hind* at Deptford on April 4, 1581, she dubbed him a knight, publicly demonstrating her support of Drake's attacks on the Spanish empire. From this time forward, England knew that the wealth of the New World no longer was exclusively Spain's. Her men had brought back stories of the riches Spain had found across the Atlantic, and now Drake had returned with treasure taken from Spanish ships and towns, tangible evidence of the prizes the new land offered. In this way, Drake's expedition stimulated a movement, already being encouraged by Richard Hakluyt and Walter Raleigh, to colonize a portion of America.

2
ENGLAND STAKES A CLAIM

Although the English were slow to challenge Spain's claims to the New World, a few Englishmen argued as early as the 1560s that England must seize a portion of America before it was too late. Jean Ribaut, the Huguenot sea captain from Dieppe, shaped their thinking. When Ribaut came home in 1562 after establishing a French colony in Florida, he found the civil war between Catholics and Protestants raging and fled to England. There in 1563, he published a treatise on Florida that stimulated interest in America and caught the attention of Queen Elizabeth, who began to support a joint Anglo-Huguenot effort to aid the colony at Fort Caroline. She lent one ship to a fleet of six under the command of Thomas Stukeley. Stukeley was a rogue who immediately turned a pirate. He used his flotilla to prey on shipping in the channel and elsewhere with little thought of colonizing, and the project became an embarrassment to the queen.

Despite this, the fact the expedition could be organized indicates the growing English interest in colonial enterprises. Indeed, when John Hawkins sailed up the coast of Florida in 1565, he may have considered planting a colony. Laudonnière, who was there, certainly feared the English might prove competitors, and as much as he needed help, he didn't want Hawkins to linger too long on that coast.

John Sparke, who accompanied Hawkins on this voyage, wrote an account that Richard Hakluyt published in his *Principall Navigations* (1589). In it, Sparke described the fertility of Florida and its promise as a place for raising cattle. (Hawkins had discovered in the West Indies that trade in cattle hides could be extremely profitable.) But because investors in the New World expected immediate profits, he thought colonization of Florida was "more requisit for a prince, who is of power able to go thorow with the same, rather than for any subject." Elizabeth was not ready to enter the cattle business in Florida, and ignored Sparke's hint.

Nevertheless, word was circulating among mercantile and shipping men in England that money could be made in the New World and that the time was ripe for England to assert its rights to land overseas by taking over unoccupied areas.

The pioneer in English colonial ventures was Sir Humphrey Gilbert, a Devonshire man associated with the merchants and seamen of the West Country, and a half-brother of Sir Walter Raleigh. If Gilbert's success was small, his arguments and propaganda were important in influencing opinion in the latter part of the sixteenth century, and he helped shape the views of imperialist Raleigh.

About 1566, Gilbert wrote his views of the advantages of seeking a northwest passage to China. His treatise was published ten years later as *A Discourse of a discoverie for a new passage to Cataia* (1576). Although his purpose was to advocate the advantages of a short trade route to the East, which Gilbert maintained could be found in the northern waters of America, he emphasized the advantages of founding colonies in the new land along the passage to China. Not only would trading posts with Indians be profitable, but colonies in North America would provide opportunities for "such needie people of our Countrie, which now trouble the common welth, and through want here at home, are inforced to commit outragious offenses, whereby they are dayly consumed with the Gallowes." The notion that American colonies would serve as a place for the growing population would increase, and the idea of shipping English convicts overseas would continue to entice authorities at home. Long before Gilbert, Henry VII had promised John Cabot some "malefactors" if he needed settlers for the lands he had discovered.

Before Gilbert could continue to promote the search for a northwest passage to China, he, along with Walter Raleigh, Sir Richard Grenville, and others, worked to pacify the rebellious Irish and to establish English colonies and plantations in Ireland. That experience helped him develop ideas about American colonization. Sir Henry Sidney, Lord Deputy of Ireland, wrote to Lord Burghley that it would be costly for the government to foster a settlement in Ulster, but private speculators might be convinced to try it. They would have to come "well-prepared," he warned, and "they must be so furnished with mony, apparell, victualle, and meanes to tyll the grounde, and seede for the same, as if they should imagine to finde nothinge here but earthe. And in dede Littell els shall they finde savinge only fleshe, and some beastes for careing of the grounde."

The proposals and efforts to establish English colonies in Ireland in the late 1560s and early 1570s kept alive the idea of colonies overseas and prompted Englishmen to consider similar undertakings in America. The Indians would be no greater hazard, some thought, than the Irish, and prospects for wealth across the Atlantic were greater. Colonial efforts in Ireland or America would not involve the government but would be made by private enterprise.

Gilbert left Ireland in 1570, and although he pursued other activities for the next several years, he remained interested in exploration and expansion. He was a shareholder in the Cathay Company, organized by Michael Lok, a London merchant, and Martin Frobisher, a sea captain who was convinced of the existence of a northwest passage to China. In his first voyage in 1576, Frobisher discovered a gulf he thought might be the passage to the Pacific. Of more interest to some London promoters was a rock he brought home, for they mistakenly thought it contained gold. A rumor spread that Frobisher had found a gold mine, and when the queen granted a patent to the Cathay Company, Lok and Frobisher had no trouble selling the stock.

On a second voyage in 1577, Frobisher loaded his ship with ore that proved worthless, but before that was known, he had departed in May 1578 on a third expedition. For a brief period, speculative fever swept London, and the stock of the Cathay Company rose spectacularly as investors dreamed of gold mines in North America, with colonies working to remove the ore. When the truth leaked out that Frobisher had brought back worthless iron pyrites, "fool's gold," the Cathay Company went bankrupt. Frobisher returned from the third voyage with more worthless ore and news of the discovery of a strait later to be named after Henry Hudson.

While London's mercantile circles were excited about the expeditions of the Cathay Company, Humphrey Gilbert received a patent for a colonial venture in America. His charter gave him the right to settle, fortify, and govern any land unoccupied by a Christian prince. It did not limit him to any specific region. Furthermore, his claim would extend for 200 leagues - about 600 miles - in every direction from the point of settlement. He would rule any such land as a liege of the English sovereign, and such laws as he would impose would be consistent with English common law. The sovereign claimed a fifth of all precious metals discovered. If Gilbert did not make a settlement within six years, the patent lapsed.

Gilbert's first effort under this patent was made in the autumn of 1578, when he collected an imposing fleet of nearly a dozen vessels, one of which was commanded by Walter Raleigh. The expedition sailed in November for an unknown destination and returned in the spring of 1579 with a story of hardships, bad weather, and desertions of some vessels, with nothing to show for the endeavor. The enterprise is shrouded in mystery. Some of the fleet apparently strayed off and became pirates - buccaneering always seemed more enticing than settling the wilderness. In 1579, when Gilbert was planning a second expedition, the Privy Council required him to put up sureties for the behavior of his seamen.

But Gilbert believed settlements overseas were vital if England expected to protect itself from Spanish might. On November 6, 1577, before he had launched his first expedition, Gilbert had presented to the queen two discourses headed "How Hir Majestie May Annoy the King of Spayne." In one, he offered to lead an expedition that would capture the foreign fishing fleet in Newfoundland and bring home the best ships loaded with fish, which could be sold in Holland. Gilbert suggested this could be done under the ruse of a colonizing expedition, and that the queen could disavow responsibility by asserting it was the work of pirates. The second discourse recommended an attack on the Spanish West Indies. Again a colonizing expedition, ostensibly headed for the St. Lawrence region, could rendezvous in Bermuda and establish a base there, from which it could attack Hispaniola and Cuba. Gilbert clearly planned to use colonization as a means to weaken Spain's power in America and its potential for attacking England at home.

In defense of his plans, he says in his first "Discourse": "I hold it as lawfull in Christen pollicie, to prevent a mischief betime[s]: as to revenge it to late, especiallie seing that god him selfe is a party in the common quarrells now a foote, and his ennemy['s] malitiouse disposition towardes your highnes, and his church manifestlie seen, although by godes mercifull providence not yet throughly felt."

Eager as Gilbert was to set his schemes into motion, he had to be content with activities nearer home. In the summer of 1579, several of his ships tried to keep Spanish reinforcements from reaching Irish rebels. When his sailors did not receive their pay, they seized his ships and turned pirate. Eventually, he recovered one small vessel, a frigate of eight tons called the *Squirrel*. The next spring, Gilbert placed a Portuguese pilot, Simon Fernandez, in charge of the *Squirrel* and sent it exploring the North American coast. It made a landfall somewhere on the coast of New England and returned with a report on the Indians and other useful information.

The speed of the *Squirrel's* trip and the information it gathered encouraged Gilbert, but he was so financially strapped he had to make assignments under his patent to other individuals, including Dr. John Dee, a geographer, scholar, and astrologer interested in exploration. Dee wanted to pursue the Northwest Passage project, and he received from Gilbert the privilege of making discoveries and settlements above the fiftieth parallel of latitude, a privilege Dee could not to immediately use.

Though Gilbert was unable to send colonists to America at once, he hoped to license others to make settlements he eventually could combine under his governorship. They would in effect hold land under him as tenants and pay rent in lieu of the services he could otherwise require. He encouraged two Catholic leaders, Sir George Peckham and Sir Thomas Gerard, to organize a project to establish a haven in America for loyal English Catholics who wished to worship without restrictive laws. Sir Francis Walsingham, an expansionist as well as a leader of the reformed faith, approved this plan to rid the kingdom of troublesome Catholics and at the same time further the development of English colonies overseas.

By summer of 1583, after much negotiation, Gilbert organized a joint stock company known as the "Merchant Adventurers with Sir Humphrey Gilbert," financed chiefly by the merchants of Southampton, who received a promise that colonists would use that port exclusively for trade. Peckham and Gerard, unable to organize a separate venture, partnered with Gilbert. On June 11, the expedition of five vessels sailed from Southampton. Gilbert sailed in the 120-ton *Delight,* captained by William Wynter. Raleigh had contributed a vessel, the *Bark Raleigh*, although he was not aboard, and his vessel deserted two days out of port. Edward

Hayes, chronicler of the voyage, commanded the *Golden Hind,* named after Drake's famous craft; the other two vessels were the *Swallow,* which later turned pirate, and Gilbert's frigate, the *Squirrel.*

The fleet headed for Newfoundland, where it arrived in early August. It was the height of the fishing season, and thirty-six fishing craft were in St. John's Harbor when Gilbert arrived. There, on August 5, 1583, he went ashore, claimed the land in the name of the queen of England, set up a post upon which he nailed the royal arms in lead, announced himself as governor of the land for 200 leagues around, and leased ground to fishermen for drying their catch. He declared a number of laws: The religion of the territory was to be that of the Church of England, no one should dispute the rights of the English to claim the land under Gilbert's patent without risking the penalty of trial under the queen's law, and anyone who spoke to the dishonor of the queen should suffer losing his ears and, if he were a shipowner, his ship.

Gilbert proposed sailing to the mainland, where he planned to establish his colony, but some men, including Captain Wynter of the *Delight* and the captain of the *Squirrel,* refused to go any farther. After some wrangling, Gilbert let them leave in the *Swallow,* which had been an embarrassment because of its pirating. He took command of the *Squirrel,* leaving his papers and documents in the

Delight. The three ships made for the mainland, but somewhere on the coast of Nova Scotia, probably south of the site of Louisbourg on Cape Breton Island, the *Delight* ran aground and sank with all hands except for sixteen men who escaped in the ship's dinghy. All of Gilbert's maps and papers went down in the *Delight.*

Short of supplies and with crews discouraged, the two remaining vessels headed for England. The sea was rough, and the *Squirrel* was not seaworthy, yet Gilbert refused Captain Edward Hayes' advice to come aboard the *Golden Hind.* On September 9, Hayes again hailed the *Squirrel* and repeated his advice, but Gilbert replied, "We are as neere to heaven by sea as by land." That night the crew on the *Golden Hind* saw the lights of the *Squirrel* vanish. The ship and those aboard were never seen again.

Gilbert had paved the way, however, for further efforts to establish colonies by an expansionist group headed by Walsingham, Raleigh, Edward Dyer, and other prominent figures. Their propagandists were the two Richard Hakluyts: the elder a lawyer who was influential with the London merchants, and his cousin, a preacher and historian of voyages.

For years, the two Hakluyts had been collecting information and making reports that would be useful to explorers and colonists. For Gilbert, in 1578, Richard Hakluyt the lawyer had written notes on what an expedition ought to look for in a new country and the kind of place that ought to be chosen for a settlement. Hakluyt made it clear Englishmen should seek a climate that would yield those products being bought from England's enemies. If inhabitants of the new country would not allow the English to occupy the land, then an effort should be made to establish a base for trade. "But if we may injoy any large Territorie of apt soyle, he adds, "we might so use the matter, as we should not depende upon Spaine for oyls, sacks [sherry], resignes [raisins], orenges, lemons, Spanish skinnes, etc. Nor uppon Fraunce for woad, baysalt, and gascoyne wines, nor on Estland [Eastland, or the Baltic] for flaxe, pitch, tarre, mastes, etc. So we shoulde not so exhaust our treasure, and so exceedingly inrich our doubtfull friendes as we doe." Hakluyt thus expressed a doctrine that would prevail for years: England must find sources for products not obtainable within its closed system of trade.

In 1579, while the fate of Drake's voyage around the world was unknown, the younger Hakluyt submitted to the queen a plan headed, "A Discourse of the Commoditie of the Taking of the Straight of Magellanus." He recommended seizing and fortifying the entrance to that gateway to the Spanish possessions on the Pacific side of America. A base should be seized at Cape St. Vincent in Brazil. If the queen should find it inexpedient to send an expedition to do this, a notorious pirate, Thomas

Clark, might be induced to do it, taking convicts and other undesirables as settlers for new bases. Two years after this report was submitted, Hakluyt the younger assembled his first compilation of travel narratives, his *Dicers Voyages to America* (1582), dedicated to Sir Francis Walsingham's son-in-law, Sir Philip Sidney, who was interested in westward expansion. In his preface, which was a plea for colonization overseas, Hakluyt commented: "I marvail not a little (right worshipfull) that since the first discoverie of America . . . after so great conquest and plantings of the Spaniards & Portingales there, that we of England could never have the grace to set fast footing in such fertill and temperate places, as are left as yet unpossessed by them." But, he continued, since Spain had taken over Portugal, and Spain's secrets uncovered by Englishmen such as Drake, Hakluyt hoped the "time approchéth and nowe is, that we of England may share . . . both with the Spaniarde and the Portingale in part of America, and other regions as yet undiscovered." The compilation provided not only narratives but also a documented argument of the rights of Englishmen to America, based on Cabot's discoveries and other voyages.

A more eloquent statement about colonization came from the younger Hakluyt two years after the *Divers Voyages*, when he presented to the queen a document headed, "A particular discourse Concerninge the greate necessitie and manifolde commodyties that are like to growe to this Realme of Englande by the Westerne discoveries lately attempted, Written in the yere 1584 by Richard Hackluyt of Oxforde at the requeste and direction of the righte Worshipfull Mr. Walter Raghly nowe Knight, before the Comynge home of his Twoo Barkes." This treatise, called *A Discourse of Westerne Planting*, was a pamphlet summarizing the reasons of state that required England to seize and settle a portion of the New World. Written at the behest of Raleigh, it was designed to convince the queen and to provide Walsingham with all the facts he might need to defend expansion overseas before skeptical members of the government. The *Discourse* was Hakluyt's most complete statement of the value and necessity of colonization. He proved that the economic, political, and spiritual welfare of England demanded settlements overseas.

As the heading of Hakluyt's *Discourse* indicated, Raleigh sent two ships to America sometime before the document was completed. In March 1584, he received a patent similar to Gilbert's, except that Newfoundland, already claimed by Gilbert the previous year, was excluded from lands Raleigh might occupy. On April 27, he dispatched two vessels under the command of Philip Amadas and Arthur Barlowe. They spent two months exploring the coast of what is now North Carolina and returned to Plymouth by mid-September. The explorers claimed the land for England, and in honor of the virgin queen, Raleigh named it Virginia. Pleased with his exploit - and the compliment - Queen Elizabeth dubbed Raleigh a knight early the next year.

Barlowe wrote an account of the land between Cape Hatteras and Cape Lookout. Grapes, he observed, grew in abundance. The land was well-wooded, game was plentiful, and the soil produced excellent corn, peas, melons, cucumbers, and gourds. The Indians were friendly and hospitable. So pleased was Barlowe with their entertainment and the fruitfulness of the country that he commented: "Wee found the people most gentle, loving, and faith-full, void of all guile, and treason, and such as lived after the manner of the golden age."

This notion of the New World as a land where crops grew easily, and one could live off the land with little effort quickly gained traction. It aligned with what early promoters hoped to find and exempted adventurers from tedious labor. It also helped doom many early settlers, who came unprepared and ill-equipped, mentally or materially, to deal with the wilderness.

Amadas and Barlowe brought two Indians back from Virginia, Manteo and Wanchese, who created a sensation in London. After they had learned English, they were used to promote Raleigh's plan for a colonizing expedition. Raleigh would have gone himself, but the queen refused permission, and he had to give the command to his cousin, Sir Richard Grenville, who had a reputation in privateering voyages against the Spaniards. With seven ships and a complement of nearly 600 men, 100 of whom were settlers, Grenville began in April 1585. Ralph Lane, a professional soldier, went along as governor of the colony. John White, an artist, and Thomas Hariot, a scientific observer, were among the group.

Grenville's fleet took the southern route by the West Indies. In Puerto Rico and Hispaniola, they traded with the Spaniards for supplies and livestock, seized a few Spanish vessels, and stole other commodities before heading north. One of the purposes of the colony was to establish a base for raiding Spanish shipping, and Grenville intended to maintain that practice.

On June 26, the expedition reached Ocracoke Island on the North Carolina coast, but it took them a month to explore the rivers and sounds in the region. On July 29, they decided to settle on Roanoke Island, and for the next several weeks they were busy unloading vessels, collecting information about the country, erecting huts, and preparing a settlement for the 108 people who were to remain. Grenville sailed away on August 25, leaving Lane in charge with a small vessel and a few boats to use in further exploration.

John White's watercolors have survived, but the

man is shrouded in mystery. Nothing is known of him before 1585 or after 1593, and it is possible two John Whites existed. In 1585, he appears accompanying the first Roanoke colonists, commissioned by Sir Walter Raleigh to make drawings to use in stimulating settlement. It is generally accepted - though not proved - that he was the same John White whom Raleigh sent in 1587 to establish what became the Lost Colony. Among the colonists who disappeared without a trace while White was in England were his daughter and his granddaughter, Virginia Dare, the first English child born in America. After 1593, when White, then in retirement, sent Richard Hakluyt an account of his last voyage, he disappears from history. But his pictures remain; his Indian drawings are among the few realistic portrayals of natives of the region.

Lane and his colonists, despite Hakluyt's advice, were ill-prepared as settlers. They were more eager to search for gold, silver, and pearls than to cut trees or plant crops. Furthermore, the season was too far advanced to hope for food crops until another year. They had to depend on Indians for corn and game, and already the English had created acrimony with the Indians by burning one of their villages in retaliation for the theft of a silver cup. Neither the site chosen nor the actions of the settlers promised success. Furthermore, the colony was essentially a military base, and its inhabitants were men manning a garrison rather than settlers intending to make a life in a new land.

As proof that privateering was more profitable than colonizing, Grenville successfully seized a Spanish ship on his way home, the *Santa Maria de San Vicente,* loaded with sugar, hides, cochineal, ginger, pearls, silver, and gold. The Spanish complained about the loss, which amounted, they claimed, to a million ducats. To Sir Francis Walsingham, one of the investors, Grenville admitted that adventurers not only would get back the money they had risked, but they also would make "some gain." Queen Elizabeth is said to have received from this prize a casket of pearls. As backer of the expedition to Roanoke, Raleigh recouped his investment with money to spare, thanks to Grenville's audacity at sea.

While Grenville searched for Spanish prizes, members of the colony on Roanoke Island set about building a fort for defense against both Indians and Spaniards. John White made maps and drawings of plant, animal, and human life. Thomas Hariot busied himself with scientific observations and notes for *A Briefe and True Report of the New Found Land of Virginia,* which he published in London in 1588. Ralph Lane, the governor, led expeditions he hoped might find a gold mine or a passage to the South Sea.

By the summer of 1586, the Indians, having decided the white settlers whom they had at first welcomed were a threat to their security, plotted to starve them by denying them food. In the warfare that developed, Lane's men killed the chief of the Roanoke Indians and a number of his tribe. For the time, the danger from the Indians was lessened, but the garrison had to live in a state of siege, and food was scarce.

Just when the colonists' morale reached its lowest ebb, a party stationed at Croatoan Island, on June 8, 1586, spied English ships offshore. These were vessels commanded by Sir Francis Drake, who had successfully pillaged Spanish towns and shipping in the West Indies and Central America and had destroyed St. Augustine. On his way back to England, he had orders to check on Raleigh's colony. Finding the settlers ill-furnished and discouraged, he initially offered them a ship but later agreed to take them home. Since supplies had not arrived, Lane decided to embark, and he sailed on June 18 or 19. A short time after, supplies that Raleigh had sent arrived at Roanoke, but when its crew could find no settlers, they returned to England. Later Grenville arrived with supplies and new recruits, but finding the colony deserted, he left fifteen men on Roanoke and departed in search of Spanish prizes. Indians later killed the unfortunate men, or they may have perished while trying to escape by boat.

Although most of the garrison who returned from Roanoke could not say a good word for Virginia,

John White and Thomas Hariot remained strong supporters of colonization. Raleigh was determined to establish a permanent settlement, not just a military garrison. To that end he planned an expedition that sailed on May 8, 1587, with John White as governor. Settlers were to receive a minimum of 500 acres, which they would hold as Raleigh's tenants. Included in this expedition were women, wives of settlers, for this colony was intended to perpetuate itself.

White, captain of the *Lion,* the largest of the three vessels, had Simon Fernandez, the Portuguese pilot who had been on the previous voyages, as master and pilot. White complained that Fernandez displayed carelessness and ignorance in guiding them through islands in the West Indies while trying to find the North Carolina colony. White hoped to stop at Roanoke, which he planned to leave in charge of Manteo, the Indian who had been taken to England by Amadas and Barlowe in 1584, while he would sail to Chesapeake Bay, where he expected to establish a new City of Raleigh. But Fernandez was more intent on privateering than getting settlers to Chesapeake Bay, a fact that may account for landing on Roanoke despite White's protest. At any rate, in late July, they found themselves on Roanoke, where they began to repair the houses of the previous settlers. White had Manteo baptized a Christian and established friendly relations with his band, the Croatoans, who were hostile to the Roanoke Indians who had given Lane trouble. On August 18, John White's daughter Eleanor, wife of Ananias Dare, gave birth to a daughter, named Virginia. She was the first child born to English parents in America.

Supplies were so scarce and the prospects at Roanoke so bleak that colonists begged White to return to England to procure reinforcements and aid. Accordingly, with a certificate that proclaimed this the wish of the colonists, White set sail in a flyboat, while Fernandez left in the *Lion* to look for prey that would be more profitable than lumber and sassafras (then valued as a drug), the only cargo visible on the coast of North Carolina. Left behind on Roanoke Island were 112 colonists - eighty-four men, seventeen women, and eleven children.

White did not reach England until early November, but at once he began trying to help the colony. Raleigh provided a dinghy, which White was to use for taking supplies to Roanoke while a larger expedition was being organized. But the dinghy did not sail, and in the spring of 1588, when Grenville assembled a small relief expedition, the Privy Council refused to let him sail because of the threat of invasion from Spain. White finally was allowed two pinnaces, but he could not control his seamen, who turned to privateering as soon as they were out of sight of land. A French privateer severely damaged White's vessel, and he had to return to port. White was wounded. Once again, privateering thwarted colonial enterprise. By this time, the threat of the Spanish Armada forced England to employ its maritime resources for defense.

Early in 1589, after the danger from the Armada was past, Raleigh resumed his efforts to help his colony in Virginia. He authorized a small stock company, chiefly of London merchants but including Richard Hakluyt the younger, to trade with the colony tax-free and to have rights of tenancy like those offered White's colonists under Raleigh's charter. The company would have the responsibility of sending reinforcements to Roanoke. William Sanderson, one of Raleigh's men, purchased a ship to go to America, but the effort stalled until the spring of 1590, when White was permitted to go with a privateering expedition that promised to get him to Roanoke.

In mid-August, two vessels anchored off Oregon Inlet, not far from Roanoke Island. White and some of the ships' company went in small boats to seek the colony. When they reached the site, they discovered the houses had been dismantled but that the barrier around the settlement was standing. Some heavy guns remained, but smaller cannon had been removed. Chests that the settlers had buried had been dug up and pillaged by Indians.

The settlers had agreed to leave an inscribed cross as a sign of distress if they had to leave under dangerous conditions. No cross was found, and no trace of any person was discovered, although White and his companions marched through the island while their trumpeter played English tunes to assure any hiding Englishman that they were friends. But no person, white or Indian, appeared. Because of stormy weather, the search had to be abandoned without visiting Croatoan Island, and the two vessels eventually sailed for England. White hoped the colonists were living on Croatoan with Manteo, but he never again would return to America to search for them.

Nor did Raleigh push to find the settlers. Raleigh's patent would expire on March 24, 1591, if he had not established a colony by then, but as long as the colony in Roanoke was lost and not destroyed, his patent would remain valid. For this reason, Raleigh may have been reluctant to discover his outpost had been wiped out. He let the matter remain unsolved and during the 1590s failed to invest additional funds in colonial enterprise.

The fate of the lost colony has remained a mystery and the theme of numerous legends. One of the most persistent is that the settlers were absorbed into the Croatoan band. Long after, the Hatteras Indians, who may have been the same band, showed evidence of Caucasian ancestry and told of white ancestors. Another theory, supported by reports of the early settlers at Jamestown, is that some colonists reached the Chesapeake Bay region and were killed there by the Powhatan tribe about the time Jamestown settlers arrived in 1607. Another possibility is that the colonists sailed away in their ship and were lost at sea. Whatever their fate, they have made a lasting impression upon American folklore.

If Raleigh's colony served no other purpose, it provided John White with an opportunity to make drawings and watercolors of American life that influenced his contemporaries, and it induced Thomas Hariot to write a descriptive account of the settlement that served as promotional material for years. In 1590, Theodor de Bry, a Flemish engraver, published *America, Part I*, an edition of Hariot's *A Briefe and True Report of the New Found Land of Virginia,* illustrated with engravings based on White's drawings. These engravings helped to stimulate the imagination of Europeans for generations.

Raleigh did not abandon his colonial ambitions, but he never understood that the establishment of permanent colonies required more capital than he was willing to invest. To him, colonies would mean personal aggrandizement and glory. He expected them to pay their way as a source of valuable commodities, and they also were designed to serve as bases for attacking their bitter enemy, Spain.

The expansionists never stopped their propaganda promoting colonization. Richard Hakluyt the younger continued his collection and publication of expeditionary reports. To him, colonization was a religion, and he and others continued to advocate overseas expansion. They were convinced colonization would be for the glory of God and the benefit of the nation. The need to Christianize the heathen, before Spain made them all papists, was a constant theme, and it was combined with the promise that this pious enterprise would return handsome profits. Hakluyt and his colleagues emphasized the value of trade and the useful commodities certain to be found in the New World, citing as proof Raleigh's expeditions in the early 1600s to the coast of North Carolina to load timber, sassafras, and other medicinal plants, which were profitable on the London market.

Raleigh was beginning to sense that the products of the soil in the new territory might be a money-making enterprise, but before he could make any serious effort at renewing his colonial ventures in North America, Queen Elizabeth died in 1603, and King James I, at the behest of Spain, had Raleigh imprisoned in the Tower of London on a charge of treason. Raleigh's activities in the colonization of North America had ended. But the experiments he had fostered were soon to bear fruit.

3
ATLANTIC FOOTHOLD

The later years of Elizabeth's reign saw an acceleration of mercantile activity in London and other ports, with renewed efforts to extend English trade to the distant parts of the earth. The merchants of London, Bristol, Southampton, Exeter, Norwich, and other towns had grown rich from trade across the English Channel, and with increasing prosperity came more demand for an extension of trade. The Muscovy Company, which before the accession of Elizabeth had opened commerce with Russia, continued to explore the possibilities of trade with Eastern countries. In 1592, the Levant Company received a charter to trade with countries of the eastern Mediterranean and established its main base at Aleppo, in northern Syria. Using Aleppo as a jumping-off point, Levant traders reached Persia and brought home the fabulous products of the East, from raisins to rugs. On December 31, 1600, the British East India Company received its charter and began operations that were to influence the course of British expansion for more than two-and-a-half centuries.

America seemed another logical area for the trading companies to extend their activities. The merchants were eager, enterprising, and had money to invest. Although they were not always certain what opportunities America had to present, Hakluyt, Hariot, and others indicated that a fruitful and undeveloped land awaited conquest by English masters, and they were convinced products of value would be found, products they previously had obtained from what Richard Hakluyt the elder called their "doubtful friends." Particularly, they hoped to obtain commodities that normally came from the Mediterranean basin and the East: olive oil, dates, raisins, dyestuffs, silks, drugs, and spices. England also needed naval stores - timber, masts, rosin, turpentine, and pitch - items it had traditionally traded for in the Baltic region. And the lure of gold, silver, copper, and pearls remained, for the hope of finding rich mines never completely died. Gradually, however, merchants came to realize that fish from the waters of the New World might be more profitable than elusive gold mines.

In the last decade of the sixteenth century, London and Bristol shipmasters were competing against French, Spanish, and Portuguese skippers for fish and whales in the waters off Nova Scotia and in the Gulf of St. Lawrence. Whale oil and oil and ivory from walruses were in demand, and furs obtained from the Indians opened new possibilities for trade.

Although privateering continued to excite English seamen, they were learning that America offered more reliable sources of income. Even Raleigh had discovered that importing sassafras and sarsaparilla, believed to have curative powers, could be extremely profitable. During the last years of Queen Elizabeth's reign, Raleigh was not the only explorer to send trading expeditions to North America. In 1602, Bartholomew Gosnold led an expedition that sailed from Falmouth in the *Concord*, a vessel of about thirty tons. Gosnold explored the coast from southern Maine to Martha's Vineyard and built a fort on nearby Cuttyhunk Island (which they named Elizabeth's Isle).

Gosnold's voyage was more than a trading venture. He intended to leave twenty men at the post he established on Cuttyhunk Island and trade with the Indians. Among them: Bartholomew Gilbert, who served as sailing master and John Brereton, a preacher, wrote a narrative of the voyage. They traded for skins and furs, established relations with the Indians, loaded a ton of sassafras roots and a quantity of cedar logs, and observed vast schools of fish. However, because of the shortage of supplies and objections of Gosnold's intended colonists to being left on Cuttyhunk, his plan failed. The expedition returned to England in July, after a voyage of seventeen weeks.

Whether this expedition had Raleigh's permission to make the voyage is moot, for Raleigh, who still held a patent that gave him the right to license voyages to North America, attempted to have the *Concord's* cargo impounded to prevent a glut in the market. One of Raleigh's vessels had made port shortly before the *Concord* with a cargo of sassafras, and he was interested in maintaining a high price. The parties apparently worked out an amicable agreement, for Brereton later dedicated his report on the expedition - the *Briefe and True Relation of the Discoverie of the North Part of Virginia in 1602* to Raleigh.

Although Gosnold failed to make a settlement, his expedition buttressed the argument for colonization, since it brought back proof of the fertility of the land across the ocean and the value of commodities. Brereton's description of the voyage induced other adventurers to attempt trading expeditions to the North Atlantic coast. Gosnold later became one of the first settlers in Virginia.

In the spring of 1603, a group of Bristol merchants

organized an expedition to the northern coast of America. After obtaining Raleigh's permission, the merchants fitted two small vessels, the *Speedwell* of fifty tons, under Martin Pring, the overall commander; and the *Discoverer*, with William Browne as captain. They went supplied with trading goods, enumerated in an account printed by Samuel Purchas, a compiler of travel books: "slight Merchandizes thought fit to trade with the people of the Countrey, as Hats of divers colours, greene, blue and yellow, apparell of coarse Kersie and Canvasse readie made, Stockings and Shooes, Sawes, Pick-axes, Spades and Shovels, Axes, Hatchets, Hookes, Knives, Sizzers, Hammers, Nailes, Chissels, Fish-hookes, Bels, Beades, Bugles, Looking-glasses, Thimbles, Pinnes, Needles, Threed, and such like." Leaving Milford Haven on April 10, they made a quick crossing directly to the coast of Maine. They explored the coastline to the south, entered Massachusetts Bay, and anchored in Plymouth Harbor.

Like Gosnold, they were seeking, and found, sassafras. Along the coast they noted the fish, "better than those of New-found-land," and observed that the rocky coast made a good place to dry their catch. They could "see no reason to the contrary, but that Salt may bee made in these parts," an important matter. They believed the mainland of what we call Massachusetts was a promising country. "The Land is full of Gods good blessings," they reported, and "so is the Sea replenished with great abundance of excellent fish, as Cods sufficient to lade many ships, which we found upon the Coast in the moneth of June, Seales to make Oile withall, Mullets, Turbuts, Mackerels, Herrings, Crabs, Lobsters, Crevises, and Muscels with ragged Pearles in them."

Although the Indians were eager to trade, they were ruthless. Pring's sassafras gatherers avoided attacks, partly because they had two English mastiffs named Fool and Gallant, who terrified the Indians (one dog was trained to carry a half-pike in his mouth, to the astonishment of the natives). Having loaded the *Discoverer* with sassafras and furs, Pring dispatched the ship in late July "to give some speedie contentment to the Adventurers," and about two weeks later he departed in the *Speedwell*. The two vessels reached Bristol after absences of five and a half and six months respectively, and their cargoes were sold easily.

The Earl of Southampton and his Roman Catholic son-in-law, Thomas Arundell, sponsored an expedition in 1605, commanded by George Weymouth in the *Archangel*. This, too, was a trading venture, but Arundell was eager to find a suitable site for a Catholic colony. Weymouth sailed at the end of March, and on May 14 he made a landfall on an island off the Maine coast, probably Monhegan. The ship's company marveled at the ease with which they caught fish of many sorts, and James Rosier, who wrote an account of the voyage, enumerated many varieties of sea life he considered commercially valuable, including whales, seals, and porpoises.

Weymouth explored the coast and found a great river (not definitely identified, but either the Penobscot or the Kennebec), which interested him. He thought mines of precious metals might be on its shores, and he examined enough mussels to convince him they produced valuable pearls. The summer climate pleased the explorers; tall evergreens, oaks, and other trees held promise for shipbuilding.

Leaving the American coast on June 16, Weymouth made the return trip to Dartmouth in one month and two days, a quick crossing. Besides a profitable cargo of furs obtained in trade, Weymouth brought back five Indians whom he had kidnapped. They proved to be willing captives and were a sensation in England. Sir Ferdinando Gorges, the military governor of Plymouth and Dartmouth, already nursing a scheme for colonizing in America, commandeered the Indians, kept three and sent the other two to a friend, Sir John Popham, the Lord Chief Justice. Gorges and Popham made sure the Indians were taught English (the Indians adopted British habits and developed a taste for beer). What made them particularly valuable was their willingness to learn and recite speeches promoting their native land as a paradise for English settlers. Gorges and Popham had found a way of dramatizing the propaganda that Richard Hakluyt and his expansionist colleagues had been disseminating for nearly a generation, and the land boom was on. All over England, especially in London and in the port towns of the West Country and East Anglia, men were talking about the possibilities of trade in North America.

King James' accession in 1603 gave the movement further stimulus. The years of uncertainty about the succession had ended. Businessmen could breathe easier now that the threat of civil disturbance had passed. More than that, James, a man of peace, set about ending the long conflict with Spain, which he accomplished in 1604. No longer were Englishmen privileged to capture Spanish and Portuguese vessels on the high seas; they would have to look elsewhere for quick riches. Although Spain formally did not admit England's right to colonize lands in America, no overt action was taken against English trading expeditions to unsettled regions of the North, and it was understood that settlements might be made there.

The increased concern over colonization reached its peak when a charter was issued on April 10, 1606, providing for two colonies in North America between the thirty-fourth and forty-fifth parallels of latitude. The charter, issued on petition of

Sir Thomas Gates, Sir George Somers, Richard Hakluyt, Edward Maria Wingfield, Thomas Hanham, Raleigh Gilbert, William Parker, George Popham, and others, established a royal Council of Virginia that would have overall supervision of colonial activities. The charter granted the petitioners rights to establish "two several colonies and companies; the one consisting of certain knights, gentlemen, merchants, and adventurers, of our city of London and elsewhere" who would settle anywhere between the thirty-fourth and the forty-first parallel, and "the other consisting of sundry knights, gentlemen, merchants, and other adventurers of our cities of Bristol and Exeter, and of our town of Plimouth, and of other places" who were permitted to settle between the thirty-eighth and the forty-fifth parallel, providing the last colony to plant itself should not choose a location within 100 English miles of the first.

Two stock companies established the colonies: the Virginia Company of London, or simply the London Company, and the Plymouth Company. On November 20, 1606, the king issued "Articles, Instructions, and Orders" that included names of fourteen individuals who "shall be our councel for all matters which shall happen in Virginia or any [of] the territories of America." The royal Council of Virginia was empowered to appoint for each of the separate colonies resident councils that would elect one of their number to be president for a one-year term. These resident councils would govern the colonies "as neer to the common lawes of England, and the equity thereof, as may be."

With a charter and a plan of government, albeit a plan that proved almost unworkable, the next problem was raising capital and finding willing settlers. By December 1606, more than 100 potential settlers were enlisted and embarked in three vessels, the *Susan Constant,* the *Godspeed,* and the *Discovery.* Under the command of Captain Christopher Newport, an experienced officer who had served in the Muscovy Company and had led privateering expeditions to the West Indies, the three vessels sailed from their Thames dock at Blackwall on December 19, 1606. The weather proved unpredictable, and they had to anchor in the Downs for more than a month. They did not clear the coast of England until January 29, 1607.

Following a southerly route, they sailed for the West Indies and made their first landfall at Martinique on March 23. Slowly they proceeded north until on April 26, they reached the Chesapeake Bay, where they went ashore at what is now Old Point Comfort and at an Indian settlement called Kecoughtan. After two weeks of exploration that took them up a river, which they named the James, they chose a peninsula far enough inland to be out of danger from sea marauders. In water deep enough to moor their vessels to the trees, they tied up on

May 13 and began unloading supplies. This site, named Jamestown in honor of their sovereign, was destined to become the first permanent English settlement in North America.

But for several years, the survival of Jamestown would be in doubt, for rarely had so incompetent a group of colonists arrived in a foreign land. Even before they arrived, the leaders were quarreling, and the rank and file were sea-weary and discouraged. On the way over, enemies of Captain John Smith, one of seven named to the council in Virginia, had him "restrained" - a form of arrest - on the grounds he planned to murder the rest of the council and make himself king in Virginia. The charge was without foundation, but Smith was not released until they landed and was not admitted to the council until June 10.

Edward Maria Wingfield, chosen the first president of the council, disliked Smith profoundly, and the feeling was mutual. Wingfield, an Elizabethan "gentleman" aware of the prerogatives of his class, looked down upon Smith, of less imposing social rank. On his part, Smith, who let nobody forget he had been a captain in the armies of the Holy Roman Empire, was not beyond showing his contempt for some of his colleagues, including Wingfield.

Discipline was lacking in the colony. Of ninety-three men, fifty-nine were classified as gentlemen, and they regarded the manual labor of digging, cutting trees, and planting crops as beneath their dignity, if, indeed, these labors were not beyond their skills. They had come to fight the heathen, search for mines, and get rich. The class consciousness of these early gentlemen-adventurers is considered a primary reasons for the incompetence of the Jamestown settlers. After two months, the men had planted little and had built no houses or permanent shelters.

Though Smith blamed Wingfield's lack of leadership, the group was responsible for its indolence. The settlers had no incentive to work. A few were shareholders, but most were poorly paid employees of the Virginia Company of London. Since initiative was lacking, only a disciplinarian with the authority to enforce his commands could have driven the ill-fed, dispirited, inexperienced colonists to work. But the gentlemen refused to build houses for themselves; they were waiting for Captain Newport to return to England for laborers and carpenters to do this work.

Although the accounts of the fruitfulness of the country published by propagandists convinced many would-be colonists they could live off the land, the Jamestown settlers were too inexperienced. The James River swarmed with fish. A few years later, a parson, the Reverend Alexander Whitaker, wrote in his 1613 *Good News from Virginia* about the abundance of fish, many of which he had caught with his hook and line. But the first settlers had neither the gear nor the skill to catch fish. In the surrounding woods, deer, bears, squirrels, and turkeys abounded, but the Jamestown colonists had little knowledge of how to hunt them. Furthermore, they were terrified of the Indians who roamed the woods. Hence, the settlers huddled together on their peninsula and consumed peas, meal, and ships' biscuits from Captain Newport's stores. They supplemented this diet with game and corn bartered from the Indians. Indeed, they soon came to depend upon the Indians for their subsistence. But before the first summer had ended, poor diet, contaminated water, mosquitoes, and the hot climate had taken their toll, and Jamestown's graveyard was growing.

The gentlemen still hoped to find gold and other valuable minerals. Newport, who sailed for England on June 22, had explored as far as the falls of the James, the present site of Richmond, and was convinced the country contained mineral wealth. He had picked a few pieces of "ore" that looked promising. Much more certain that he had found gold-bearing earth was Captain John Martin, a member of the Jamestown council and son of a London goldsmith, who had some of his ore loaded on Newport's vessel. When Newport returned to Plymouth, England, in late July, he sent a letter to Robert Cecil, Earl of Salisbury, to tell him, "The contrie is excellent and very rich in gold and Copper. Of the gould we have brought a say [an assay] and hope to be with your Lordship shortlie to show it to his Majesty and the rest of the Lords." Fortunately, Newport also brought back a cargo of timber and sassafras that helped to pay the expense of the voyage, for the ore proved to be rocks containing mica.

Newport returned to the colony in January 1608, bringing the first supply of recruits, including two refiners and two goldsmiths, competent, presumably, to examine ore and evaluate its mineral contents. In 1624, Smith published *The Generall Historie of Virginia* in which he complained there was "no talke, no hope, nor worke, but dig gold, wash gold, refine gold, load gold - all to no avail, for glittering earth and ore were worthless." Quick wealth was not destined for the Virginia Company of London and its men whom it sent to Virginia as settlers.

The colony had continued to decline. Soon after Newport's return, fire destroyed most of the shacks the colonists had built. The winter was cold, the Indians were wary of trading, food was scarce, and sickness and death stalked the settlement. Although Newport's sailors worked to erect shelters for the men and their supplies, the outlook was dismal.

Before Newport's return from England, tribesmen of Powhatan, the overlord of several Indian tribes, captured Smith, who was conducting an exploring and trading expedition from Jamestown. According to Smith's account, Powhatan's daughter Pocahontas, a girl of eleven or twelve, saved his life by placing her head next to his when Powhatan's warriors had him stretched on the ground with his head between two stones, ready to crush his skull. Powhatan released Smith, who returned to Jamestown with a tale of an alliance with this Indian potentate, who was described as king or emperor of the Indians of the region.

Perhaps, as one historian suggests, this experience, later embellished by Smith, was a ritual, and his reprieve was a symbol of his acceptance into the tribe. At any rate, Powhatan declared Smith a chief, and the curious and fickle friendship between Powhatan and Smith enabled the English to barter with the Indians for corn. And without corn and occasional deer and turkeys obtained from the natives, colonists would have perished.

Leaders of the colony quarreled constantly. In September 1607, only a few months after the settlers had established themselves, the council posed absurd charges against Wingfield (one accusation was that he was conspiring with the Spaniards to destroy the colony). Robert Hunt, the chaplain, tried to make peace between the squabbling factions, but his efforts were unsuccessful. The council arrested and deposed Wingfield and put in his place Captain John Ratcliffe, who was as vain as he was incompetent. For his aggrandizement, he ordered a presidential palace constructed, a folly never completed.

While Ratcliffe was finding ways to satisfy his vanity at Jamestown, Smith took a barge and a party of men and again went exploring. He found the entrance to the Potomac and believed it might lead to Asia, the eternal dream of seventeenth-century explorers. In July 1608, Smith and his party pushed their barge through marshes that one day would be the site of the State Department in Washington. A little later, they reached the Potomac rapids above Georgetown - a sign the Potomac would not lead to the South Sea. Smith turned back and made his way to Jamestown. There, he found colonists rebelling against Ratcliffe, and in September 1608, he was installed as president of the Virginia council.

Smith realized that food, shelter, and security from Indian attack were more important than the search for gold, and he made those necessities his priority. Death had silenced many of the rebellious and indolent gentlemen-adventurers, and the rest had come to grips with the harsh realities of colonial life. Smith put everyone to work. Gentlemen whose soft hands blistered easily swore at their pain, but Smith kept them cutting timber, sawing boards, digging drains, preparing fields for crops, and improving their buildings. Furthermore, not to offend the Almighty, whose presence Smith felt acutely, he penalized each man who uttered a profanity by pouring a cup of cold water down his sleeve. For the first time since the settlers landed at Jamestown, a disciplinarian was in charge.

In October 1608, Newport again sailed into the James River with the second supply of recruits, seventy in number, including the first women to arrive, a Mistress Forrest and her maid, Ann Burras. In this group were four Dutchmen (probably meaning Germans), one Swiss, and three Poles who were to teach the colonists various industrial skills, including the manufacture of glass, the making of pitch, and the smelting of iron and other ores. The Virginia Council in London was determined to find a profitable source of wealth in America. Smith established a glassworks and began several construction projects, but the Dutchmen defected to Powhatan. They plotted to lure other dissidents from Jamestown and, with the help of the Indians, overtake the colony. The plot failed, but Smith was unable to recapture them for punishment.

A report of Powhatan's importance in Virginia, given by Newport to the Virginia Council in London, had induced those diplomatic planners to devise a ceremony to draw Powhatan to the English cause and make him a staunch feudal lord of King James. They would have him crowned as emperor of the Indians, with all the trappings of royalty. Newport had brought the regalia. The only problem was to get Powhatan to participate in the ceremony.

Smith took on this task and sought to persuade Powhatan to come to Jamestown for a coronation. Powhatan, asserting his royal prerogatives, replied that if he was a great king, the English should come and crown him in his territory. Thus, it was that Captain Newport began one of the most bizarre expeditions of his varied career. Wearing his full-dress uniform as captain of the king's ship, he and his retinue journeyed to Powhatan's village in what is now Gloucester County with the imperial regalia, consisting of a gilt crown, a bowl and pitcher, an English bed, and a scarlet cloak.

Powhatan was ready to receive the gifts but uncertain about some elements of the coronation ceremony. Kneeling was new to him, even to be crowned, and it took physical force to complete this portion of the ceremony. "He, neither knowing the majesty nor meaning of a Crowne," Smith later wrote, "nor bending of the knee, indured so many perswasions, examples, and instructions as tired them all. At last, by leaning hard on his shoulders, he a little stooped, and *Newport* put the Crowne on his head; when, by the warning of a pistoll, the boates were prepared with such a volly of shot, that the king start[ed] up in a horrible feare till he saw all was well. Then remembering himselfe, to congratulate their kindnesse, he gave his old shoes and his mantle to Captain *Newport*." But crowning Powhatan a king in the service of King James had little effect on his relationship with the settlers. From time to time, he continued to withhold corn and devise other ways to discourage the settlers.

If the colony did not flourish under Smith, it at least survived, and Smith's gentlemen-axemen cut enough timber and made enough clapboard to give Newport a comfortable cargo for his return to London. During Smith's presidency, in 1609, the London merchants and investors procured another charter that gave direct control of the Jamestown colony to the Virginia Company of London instead of vesting control in the royal Council of Virginia. Under this second charter, the London Company was empowered to select a governor and give him administrative power. Although Smith was keeping the colony away from disaster, the history of bickering and near-mutiny was such that authorities in London appointed Lord De La Warr, a man of impeccable character, as lord governor and captain general. Since he could not leave immediately, the company chose Sir Thomas Gates to be deputy governor pending De La Warr's arrival. Gates sailed in June 1609, in the largest expedition yet organized for Virginia - seven ships and two small pinnaces under the command of Sir George Somers, bearing some 600 men, women, and children.

The fleet encountered a hurricane, and on July 25, the *Sea Venture,* commanded by Newport and bearing Gates and Somers, foundered on a reef off Bermuda. Fortunately, the boat wedged on the reef, and the ship's company with their supplies and tools got ashore. They remained there for eleven months while they constructed two pinnaces that eventually carried them to Virginia. Accounts of this shipwreck furnished Shakespeare with details used in *The Tempest.*

Seven of the vessels rode out the hurricane and in early August limped into the James River. Shortly afterward, John Smith was badly burned in a powder explosion and returned to England on one of the vessels. Pending the arrival of the new deputy governor, George Percy, brother of the Earl of Northumberland, was named president of the council.

The winter that followed Smith's departure was the worst that the colony had endured. Percy was far less competent and showed little of Smith's capacity for making colonists work and trade with the Indians. Disease and malnutrition took their toll. During this time, settlers devoured every living animal they had brought, even dogs and cats, and such rats and mice as they could catch. Reduced to cannibalism, one man murdered his wife and salted her corpse for food. Despite their fear of local tribes, some men, crazed for food, ran to the

Indians and were never seen again. When spring came, sixty survivors remained of nearly 500.

At length, on May 23, 1610, Gates, Somers, and Newport arrived from Bermuda in their two pinnaces, bringing just enough food for their crews and passengers. Discouraged at the state of the colony and thinking it hopeless, Gates agreed to take the survivors in his two pinnaces and in two the colony owned. He planned to land in Newfoundland, where they might find passage back to England in the fishing fleet. Accordingly, they abandoned Jamestown on June 7 and set sail. The next morning, while lying off Mulberry Island, they saw a longboat approaching and were told that Lord De La Warr had arrived in the mouth of Chesapeake Bay with three ships, 300 men, and a "great store of provisions." Upon hearing this, Gates returned to Jamestown and took his disconsolate settlers ashore again.

De La Warr's ships arrived at Jamestown on June 10, and he came ashore and took possession with considerable pomp and circumstance. After a sermon by the minister, De La Warr delivered a stern speech warning the colonists of their vanities and idleness, which might cause him to "draw the sword of justice." Finding the town a "very noisome and unwholesome place," he ordered his sailors to clean it. He restored the palisades around the fort and rebuilt the church, where he went each Sunday to worship, accompanied by a group of soldiers in red cloaks. The Jamestown populace understood they had a governor who knew his dignity and would not tolerate idleness or mutiny.

But not even the rule of De La Warr could stop disease or keep the Indians from picking off the colonists when they strayed beyond the palisade. Death from malaria and typhoid fever and from the arrows and tomahawks of the Indians took a toll on colonists. De La Warr contracted a fever and eventually returned to England, leaving George Percy in charge as deputy governor. The population was less than 150.

Investors in the Virginia Company of London were discouraged over the failure of the colony to show a profit. Some favored taking their losses and abandoning the colony permanently, but the leadership in the company refused to admit defeat. Pamphlets and sermons inspired by the company praised Virginia and its products and held out promise of unbounded prosperity just around the corner. A few realists, however, privately gave sound advice. De La Warr reported that a better quality of colonist was needed, and John Smith had made similar recommendations. The Virginia Company began a more careful system of recruiting, but for years governors complained about unruly, indolent rogues who came to Virginia as colonists.

But if stern rule could transform the Jamestown

colonists into a civilized society, the governors who came after De La Warr were determined to provide it. Two veteran soldiers, Sir Thomas Dale (deputy governor on two occasions, from May to August 1611 and from March 1614 to April 1616) and Sir Thomas Gates (lieutenant governor from August 1611 to March 1614), worked to govern the colony under martial rule. The laws they enacted and that William Strachey, secretary of the colony, compiled and published in 1612 under the title *For the Colony in Virginea Britannia, Lawes Divine, Morall and Martiall, Etc.* were harsh but necessary to keep the colony from chaos. In this respect, they were successful, but they had little effect on the prosperity of the settlement or morale of the colonists. The truth is that a settlement of recalcitrant, unruly, untrained people, living under martial law, never could become more than a military garrison. The London Company's dream of prosperity for such a colony was fantasy.

A development occurred in 1612, however, that eventually transformed the economy of Virginia and neighboring regions and assured prosperity to the planters. In this year, one of them, John Rolfe, began to experiment with raising tobacco. Rolfe was a smoker, and his interest began with a desire to ensure a supply suitable for his pipe. The tobacco used by the Indians of Virginia and other parts of North America was a bitter variety known as *Nicotiana rustica*. Spaniards had taken a sweeter variety to Europe that smokers preferred, called *Nicotiana tabacum,* which was grown in the West Indies and South America.

Rolfe got seed for this sweet tobacco, and by 1614, he had grown enough to send a shipment to England in the ship *Elizabeth.* At last, the settlers had found a commodity they could produce with a minimum of skill and that would command a ready and seemingly inexhaustible market in England. Tobacco production increased rapidly. Three years after Rolfe's first shipment, Virginia settlers sent nearly 20,000 pounds of this crop to England. Tobacco became the one product they could depend upon for ready money. In time, it became so important that all values, even to the parson's pay, were calculated in pounds of tobacco.

Rolfe appears again in the history of the colony. In April 1614, he married Powhatan's favorite daughter, Pocahontas. The charms of Pocahontas were known to the colonists, for she had visited Jamestown often and turned handsprings while nude in the streets. On one occasion, she provided Englishmen, who came to visit Powhatan, with thirty unclad Indian women who invited them to their wigwams.

The appeal of Pocahontas was such that Rolfe found himself captivated, but he convinced himself - according to his letter to Sir Thomas Dale - he ought to marry Pocahontas to save her soul. No Puritan ever wrote with more passion than Rolfe on this occasion. He declared his love was motivated "but for the good of this plantation, for the honour of our countrie, for the glory of God, for my owne salvation, and for the converting to the true knowledge of God and Jesus Christ, an unbeleeving creature, namely Pokahuntas." In 1616, Rolfe took Pocahontas (now christened Rebecca) to London, where she became a sensation, was introduced at court, and had her portrait painted. King James is said to have been displeased that Rolfe, a commoner, had married into a royal family without his permission, but he later forgave him. A year later, in March 1617, when Rolfe and Pocahontas were about to sail for Virginia, she died at age twenty-two and was buried, it is believed, in the parish church of St. George, Gravesend. She left an infant son, Thomas, who survived to become the progenitor of a long line of Virginians.

Though tobacco quickly proved to be a profitable commodity, the colony in Virginia continued its struggle until the Virginia Company at last realized no substantial progress could be expected from gentlemen-adventurers, convicts, and ruffians plucked from the streets of London. Dale had the wisdom to allot three acres of land to old settlers, which they could plant as they saw fit. The company soon began offering fifty acres of land to everyone who would pay twelve pounds, ten shillings. An individual emigrating at his expense would receive fifty acres for himself and fifty acres for each person he brought with him. This "headright system" of granting land improved the ambition and energy of the emigrants, for Englishmen of the seventeenth century yearned to own land. The mark of prestige and status, land was available in Virginia for anyone with enough capital to cross the Atlantic. With a staple crop such as tobacco that would turn a profit, doubt about the means of earning a livelihood was gone. Men could establish themselves as landed proprietors with certainty of improving their prospects. Gradually, small groups pushed out from Jamestown, up and down the James River. A small settlement was established at Henrico, near the present-day Richmond, and other farming communities even more distant began to develop.

Nearly every colonist was attempting to grow tobacco, even in the streets of Jamestown, for it brought a high price, and ship captains were eager for cargoes. The ease with which tobacco could be grown carried with it one hazard for the future of the colony: Tobacco production overwhelmed other crops and industries. King James and other planners in London were hoping to develop a silk industry in Virginia, and silkworms, sent over as early as 1614, flourished on Virginia mulberry leaves, but labor proved too scarce for silk making. French *vignerons* were sent to start a wine industry, but this also failed, as did other enterprises. Virginia and the tidewater region were soon in the grip of a one-crop system.

The fact that unskilled labor could raise tobacco helped to initiate another evil on the Chesapeake Bay region. In 1619, a Dutch ship brought twenty Africans to Virginia, and small numbers of slaves were imported throughout the seventeenth century. In time, African slave-labor became the mainstay of tobacco production. During most of the seventeenth century, however, white indentured servants - those who signed a bond to pay their passage over by working from four to seven years - provided most of the labor.

Small as the colony was, its government remained burdensome to the Virginia Company and to inhabitants as well. Governors might be good or bad, and no one in the colony had much influence. But in November 1618, the company drew up another charter - the fourth - known as the Great Charter, which established several reforms, including a more liberal provision for land grants and a commission for setting up a legislative assembly. To carry out these provisions, the company in April 1619, sent Sir George Yeardley as governor. Sir Edwin Sandys, who succeeded Sir Thomas Smythe as treasurer of the company, began a vigorous effort to improve the colony. Lands were set aside for the establishment of a university in Virginia at Henrico, and funds were collected for the purpose.

The legislative assembly, the first in English America, met on July 30, 1619, in the church at Jamestown. Twenty-two burgesses, two each elected by popular vote of the citizens of the eleven districts, met with the governor and council to consider the problem of the colony's government. The assembly lasted for a week or two and disbanded because of the intemperate heat and the illness of several members. But in that time, it had enacted new laws, recommended changes in laws sent over by the company, and ruled on judicial matters.

Popular government in the English colonies had begun. It is true that the Virginia Company could veto any laws passed in Virginia, but the first assembly began a procedure that would be followed in the future: Laws enacted would become operative at once; if later they were vetoed, they could be modified and sent back for approval. Thus, owing to the time required for communication, it was possible to enact and retain a law that eventually might be vetoed.

By 1622, Virginia seemed to be on the way to prosperity. During the three preceding years, forty-two ships had brought in more than 3,500 settlers. The Virginia Company, to care for the lonely men in the colony, sent women of good character to be their wives. The settlers had lost their fear of Indians and no longer carried weapons except when hunting. Throughout the colony, peace prevailed. But the Indians secretly resented the continuing expansion of the white population.

Powhatan, who died in 1618, was succeeded by his half-brother, Opechancanough, who kept up a façade of friendship with the English while plotting their destruction. In March 1622, on Good Friday, he signaled an attack. In all the outlying settlements in Virginia, the Indians slaughtered white men, women, and children. A warning from a Christian Indian saved Jamestown and a few other communities, but before the day was over, between 300 and 400 settlers were dead. Quickly the news was carried to London, with a request for armor and weapons, which were sent. In time, colonists wreaked such vengeance on the Indians that they made only one other significant attack, in 1644. But the massacre of 1622 forever ended any peaceful relations between the Virginians and the natives. After this, the colonists were determined to annihilate Indians as a threat to their expansion.

The Virginia Company of London, despite Herculean efforts, had not made a success of its stock-company venture in colonization. Political factions inside the company created dissension. Finally, in 1624, King James intervened, dissolved the company, and transformed Virginia into a crown colony. Henceforth, the king would appoint a governor to rule the province. But the king allowed the continuance of the general assembly, which ensured some local autonomy.

Virginia was firmly established under the royal authority. Since land was available to emigrants, men with a little capital and ambition could come to Virginia and found estates for themselves and their heirs. No longer were the dwellers in Jamestown and other settlements mere laborers working for a stock company. They were free citizens in a venture that promised great rewards. Furthermore, a commodity had been found that ensured a source of money. Tobacco continued to increase in economic importance.

If, in 1624, Virginia had much to accomplish, it was well on its way to prosperity. Years of tribulation had at last brought forth a permanent colony. The English were in North America to stay.

4
RELIGIOUS HAVENS

While the Virginia Company of London was struggling to settle a colony in the southern part of Virginia - the great sweep of the Atlantic coast between Cape Fear River and Bangor, Maine - the Plymouth Company and other venturers were attempting to exploit the northern portion of this territory. Sir Ferdinando Gorges and Chief Justice Sir John Popham, both representative of the land-hungry Englishmen of the day, became prominent in the Plymouth Company. Popham already had been interested in Irish colonization and in draining the marshes in East Anglia. North America offered greater prospects for the acquisition of land and bases for trade.

After sending two exploratory voyages to the New England coast, the Plymouth Company sent ninety colonists in two ships, the *Gift of God,* commanded by George Popham, a nephew of the chief justice, and the *Mary and John,* under Raleigh Gilbert, son of Sir Humphrey Gilbert. Sailing separately on May 1 and June 1, 1607, they reached the Kennebec River, then called the Sagadahoc, in early August and chose a site for settlement not far from the mouth. At the end of two months, colonists had built a fort and some houses inside the palisades.

The same troubles that nearly had destroyed Jamestown hindered the settlement at Sagadahoc. George Popham, elected governor, was fifty-three years old, timid, and incompetent; Gilbert, twenty-four years old, was headstrong and arrogant. A clash between the leaders and their partisans was inevitable. Furthermore, as in Jamestown, the colonists were undisciplined, lawless, lazy, and quarrelsome. Again, like the first Jamestown settlers, they had no personal stake in the success of the venture. Even so, the group contained a few skilled workers and at least enough shipwrights and carpenters to make a pinnace of thirty tons, named the *Virginia*, which later sailed to Jamestown and proved useful in that colony.

It was inevitable that the colony at Sagadahoc would fail. Half of the potential settlers returned. During the winter, some of the buildings, with the colonists' essential supplies, burned. One piece of bad luck followed another. In England, Sir John Popham, who had dreamed of getting rich by settling Maine with England's surplus population, especially paupers, died suddenly. Before the winter ended, his nephew at Sagadahoc was also dead. Raleigh Gilbert received news of the death of his older brother and had to return to England to look after his inheritance. Since the settlers at Sagadahoc were weary of Maine and eager to leave, colonists abandoned the site early in 1608. No further effort would be made to colonize New England for more than a decade.

But interest in the region did not die. Reports of its rich fisheries had reached Europe, and Spanish, Portuguese, and French frequented the coast and set up temporary bases where they could salt their catch and dry their nets. Sir Francis Popham, another son of the chief justice, sent several expeditions to fish and trade for furs. In 1614, Captain John Smith led an expedition, underwritten by certain London merchants, to the coast of Maine to hunt for gold and copper mines, catch whales, fish, and trade for furs. Captain Thomas Hunt accompanied him in a second ship. They made a landfall at Monhegan Island and attempted to hunt whales, but to no avail - the cetaceans were too elusive for their unskilled harpooners. The expedition could find no gold or copper deposits, but fish were abundant, and Smith knew the Indians would part with skins and furs for trinkets. Leaving Hunt and his own ship at anchor off Monhegan while their crews fished from small boats, Smith and a party of eight or nine set out in another boat to explore the coastline and trade. Before he returned to the ship, he had visited the shores of Massachusetts Bay, including Plymouth harbor, skirted Cape Cod Bay, landed at Provincetown harbor, and rounded the cape before sailing back north. Smith mapped the region as he went, and the details he captured were so exact that sites he described can be recognized to this day. Smith returned to England with two convictions: that here was a region suitable for another English colony, and that fishing and fur trading would be more profitable than mining. Although he managed to interest Ferdinando Gorges in an attempt at colonization, a series of mishaps thwarted their hopes.

One result of Smith's expedition of 1614 was the publication in 1616 of his *A Description of New England,* together with a map, dedicated to Prince Charles (later Charles I). At Smith's request, the prince examined the map and suggested names in place of those supplied by Smith, but the name New England, first used by Smith, remained unchanged. "Of all the foure parts of the world that I have yet seene not inhabited," Smith declared in his *Description*, "could I have but meanes to transport a Colonie, I would rather live here then any where: and if it did not maintaine it selfe, were wee but once indifferently well fitted, let us starve." He emphasized the value of fish, which had made the Hollanders rich, the vast quantity of timber and naval stores, the profits from furs, and the fertility of the soil.

Thomas Hunt, who commanded the second ship in Smith's expedition of 1614, was an unsavory character who not only tried to steal Smith's maps and readings but, when left in New England to fish, also kidnapped twenty-four Indians in the Cape Cod region with the intention of selling them as slaves in Spain. One of the Indians, named Tisquantum, or Squanto, eventually returned to New England, where he befriended the Pilgrims.

John Smith's dreams of founding a prosperous and profitable colony in New England never were realized, but a few years later, New England would become a refuge for groups who sought a haven from religious persecution, as well as a means of livelihood.

Beginning with Humphrey Gilbert's explorations of Newfoundland and Nova Scotia, some Englishmen thought of the New World as a place where those who dissented from the established religion might find a refuge. Later, Weymouth's voyage of exploration had as one of its objectives the search for a place where Catholics might settle. But the revelations of the 1605 Gunpowder Plot to blow up the Houses of Parliament temporarily halted plans of Catholics to emigrate to America with the government's blessing.

In the early seventeenth century, others besides Catholics found it difficult to reconcile their beliefs with those of the established Anglican Church. The term Puritan generally is used to describe a variety of dissenting sectarians who objected to the polity and ritualism of the English church as smacking too much of "popery." Great differences existed among the sects. Some merely wished to purify the ritual of elaborate ceremonies; others objected to bishops and hierarchical control; many found the use of the prayer book distasteful; some objected to the clergy wearing vestments, or the requirement to kneel at altar rails. The more extreme dissenters objected to all these traditions and others in their quest for simplicity. Although the majority of Puritans wanted to stay within the fabric of the established church if they could remodel or purify it to their taste, others gave up hope of improving it and sought to withdraw. They were Separatists. The Protestant doctrine that every man had the right to read the Bible and interpret it as he believed prompted fractionalization.

One group of Separatists from the neighborhood of Scrooby Manor in Nottinghamshire suffered so much persecution from church authorities that they decided to emigrate to Holland, then the most tolerant country in Europe. A few left secretly in

1607, and a larger group got away in 1608. The Scrooby Separatists, eventually to be known in American history as the Pilgrims, first settled in Amsterdam, but disturbed by the quarrels of religious groups there and confused by so large a city, they decided to move to the university town of Leiden. There, they established a church and found employment as weavers, cloth workers, tailors, bakers, and artisans of various sorts. Their pastor was John Robinson, and their lay leader, an elder in their church, was William Brewster, who, like his father of the same name, had been bailiff and postmaster at Scrooby Manor.

After more than a decade in Holland, some Separatists became restless. Their children were learning the Dutch language and customs. Their labor was extremely hard, and many were worried whether war with Spain would break out at the expiration of the truce made in 1609. They had heard of opportunities in America, and some began to propose to move to the New World. Although a majority voted to remain in Holland, something fewer than 100 agreed to attempt the American venture and petitioned the Virginia Company of London in 1617 for permission to settle in Virginia. Negotiations dragged on for two years, until finally, in June 1619, they received a patent for a plantation.

King James had been asked to approve their request for freedom to worship according to the doctrine of the Leiden congregation. Although he refused them explicit approval, he promised they would not be harassed. In the meantime, another group of Amsterdam Separatists under Francis Blackwell, who had received a patent and had sailed for Virginia in 1618, met with disaster. Of 180 who embarked, 131 died on the voyage. When news of this calamity reached Leiden, it dampened enthusiasm for emigration, but a hardy few continued their plans.

The cost of outfitting a colonial expedition was greater than the Leiden Separatists had anticipated, and they made arrangements with a group of London promoters headed by Thomas Weston and known as John Pierce and his Associates, which had a patent for a plantation in Virginia. The Pilgrims joined forces with Weston's fellow merchants and formed a stock company, under the terms of which each investor of ten pounds would have one share; an emigrant who contributed only his labor for seven years would have one share. If an emigrant had capital enough to put up ten pounds and his labor, he would receive two shares. All profits and capital would go into a common fund, and at the end of seven years, shareholders would divide everything in proportion to their investment. London and Virginia were to share control of the colony. Weston and the associates would conduct business affairs from London. The government of the colony would be in the hands of the emigrants, who would choose a governor. This arrangement proved unfortunate, but at the time it seemed the best the Pilgrims could make.

The Leiden emigrants bought a small boat called the *Speedwell,* a vessel that belied its name. It left Delfshaven on July 22, 1620, and was joined at Southampton near the end of July by the *Mayflower* from London, a ship carrying some eighty passengers, including Separatists, laborers, and others Weston recruited in London. After clearing Southampton, the vessels got only 300 miles west of Land's End when the *Speedwell* proved so unseaworthy the *Mayflower* took aboard as many of that ship's passengers as it could accommodate and finally set sail from Plymouth on September 16, 1620. Besides officers and crew, the emigrants numbered 101, only thirty-five of whom had come from Leiden. The other sixty-six were from London and Southampton.

After a long and tedious voyage, they made a landfall on November 9 at Cape Cod, farther north than they intended. They considered sailing south, but after some hesitation, they rounded Cape Cod and entered Provincetown harbor. There, the *Mayflower* anchored while men in the ship's boat explored the coast. On December 11, they discovered Plymouth harbor and decided the land there appeared suitable for a settlement.

Although they did not have a patent for territory so far north, they refused to risk their lives in a longer voyage. The weather was bitter cold (the explorers in the ship's boat had had the spray freeze on their coats), and it was imperative to find a haven where they could find shelter during winter. Returning to the *Mayflower,* the advance party reported they had found a place with a good harbor, "divers cornfields" already cleared, and running brooks. This news, William Bradford wrote in *Of Plimouth Plantation,* "did much comfort their hearts, and the *Mayflower* was brought around to Plymouth.

Bleak though New England is in late December, the land they saw from the deck of the *Mayflower* looked inviting to voyagers who had been on shipboard more than four months. They placed their settlement on the site of an Indian village. Above the beach was a hill they could fortify against Indian attack, and the cornfields waiting to be planted in the spring were an asset. Although they did not know it then, the danger from attack was minimal, for a plague had recently decimated the New England Indians. The emigrants waiting to go ashore numbered 102, one more than had sailed from Plymouth. On the voyage over, one passenger had died, but a boy had been born at sea and christened Oceanus Hopkins. Another boy, Peregrine White, had been born while the *Mayflower* lay at anchor.

Before the emigrants landed, the government of the colony had to be decided, for, according to Bradford, some of the strangers among them (meaning the people Weston recruited) were making "discontented and mutinous speeches," claiming that since they had a patent for Virginia and not New England, no one had any right to exert authority over them. To anticipate such anarchy, on November 21, while the *Mayflower* was still off Cape Cod, forty-one men met in the main cabin and signed a compact calling for a "civil body politic that would rule by "just and equal laws." The Mayflower Compact served as the Pilgrim platform of government. At the same time, it articulated the anxiety for self-government that all emigrants to the New World felt.

Among the signers were some who were not Separatists, including Captain Miles Standish, who had been employed to serve as a military leader, and John Alden, hired at Southampton as a cooper to look after the barreled beer that they brought as safeguard against scurvy. Both Standish and Alden later elected to remain permanently with the Pilgrims. Alden married Priscilla Mullins and during a sixty-three-year marriage fathered eleven children.

With the Mayflower Compact to serve as their constitution, the Pilgrims chose John Carver as governor for the coming year. Although in the ensuing months, Bradford reports, during "these hard and difficulte beginings they found some discontents and murmurings arise amongst some, and mutinous speeches and carriags in other[s]; but they were soone quelled and overcome by the wisdome, patience, and just and equall carrage of things by the Gov and better part, which clave faithfully togeather in the maine."

The winter was miserable, and before spring came, half of the settlers lay in the graveyard; disease and malnutrition were too much even for these stouthearted saints. But the coming of warmer weather at last brought hope. And about the middle of March, an Indian arrived at Plymouth who could speak some English. He was Samoset, from Pemaquid Point, Maine, where English fishermen had taught him their language. He told the Pilgrims of an Indian who had been in England. This was Squanto, whom Hunt had kidnapped in 1614. Through Samoset's intervention, the Pilgrims received a visit from the great sachem of the Wampanoag tribe, which dominated the region, a chief named Massasoit, with whom they made a peace treaty. With Massasoit came Squanto, who joined the Pilgrims because all his own tribe had died in the epidemic three or four years before.

From Squanto, the Pilgrims learned the ways of the country, and Bradford declared he "was a spetiall instrument sent of God for ther good beyond their expectation. He directed them how to set their corne, wher to take fish, and to procure other comodities, and was also their chief pilott to bring them to unknowne places for their profitt, and never left them till he dyed." Squanto taught them to place a herring under each hill of corn for fertilizer and assured them that by mid-April, enough herring would run up their brook to supply their needs.

When Governor Carver died of a stroke in April, the Pilgrims elected William Bradford governor. In his history, Bradford recounts this and remarks he "by renewed election every year, continued sundry years togeather, which I here note once for all."

The Pilgrims, as artisans and farmers, put their first spring and summer to good use. Unlike the indolent settlers at Jamestown, they planted crops, fished, hunted, traded for furs, and improved their housing. When autumn came, they were prepared for their second winter with a comfortable store of supplies. Grateful for a good season, they declared a three-day period of thanksgiving. Massasoit came with ninety of his braves to participate in the festivities. As his contribution, he brought game, including five deer, freshly killed. Bradford sent four men to hunt enough turkeys, ducks, and geese to last a week. With feasting, target shooting, and other sports and pastimes, the settlers passed this thanksgiving period merrily.

Plymouth's legal status was initially precarious because it was on land to which the Pilgrims had no right. To rectify this, on June 1, 1621, the merchants in London who were joint stockholders with the emigrants in the venture obtained a patent from the Council for New England, which had succeeded to the privileges of the Plymouth Company. Another patent, known as "The Old Charter," obtained in 1630, more clearly defined the physical boundaries and confirmed the Pilgrims' title to their lands. But Plymouth was never able to obtain a royal charter to fix territorial boundaries and remained unsanctioned in the eyes of the mother country until it finally was absorbed into the Massachusetts Bay colony in 1691.

The economic condition of Plymouth at first had been as precarious as its legal status, for under the conditions the emigrants made with the London merchants who backed them, they had to pool all profits and assets for seven years, after which time everything would be divided among shareholders. This arrangement was impractical and imposed hardships upon those Pilgrims who could not afford to wait that long. Early in the settlement, each householder had been given a garden plot, and in 1624 each received an acre of land on which he was supposed to raise enough corn for his family. However, it was soon apparent that without the incentive of the ownership of farms, not even the pious and industrious Pilgrims would work as conscientiously as they ought, and by 1632, a division was made so every householder could have his own land, pasturage, and meadow for hay.

The Pilgrims remained unhappy regarding their arrangement with London merchants and arranged to buy them out. Eight of the wealthiest settlers, including Governor Bradford, William Brewster, Miles Standish, and John Alden, formed a holding company to put up the money. After buying the Londoners' shares, the Pilgrims became masters of their economic fate, and they prospered modestly from farming, fishing, and the fur trade. Their friendly relations with the Indians gave them an opportunity to trade for beaver, marten, and other furs, which found a ready market in London.

Plymouth never became a large colony. By 1637, the population was 549, but their numbers gradually increased until the town of Plymouth was able to send groups to settle outlying districts. By 1643, it boasted ten satellite towns, including Duxbury, Scituate, Sandwich, Yarmouth, and Taunton. This growth required some expansion in government, and the colony now had a governor, a deputy governor, and assistants. Each town sent two elected representatives to a general court that made the laws.

One significant effect the Plymouth colony had on the course of English expansion in North America was the contribution it made to religious development. Its congregational system of church government became the characteristic form for New

England churches and ultimately for several large religious groups in the United States, including the Congregational and Baptist denominations. The compact made on the *Mayflower* for the political government of the colony was the forerunner of the covenant that members of each congregation made with one another for the government of its church. Although kindred churches might have some loose association for mutual information and help, the individual congregation was autonomous and owed no allegiance to any other. No central organization, no bishop, no presbytery, nor anyone else had authority over the covenanted group who made up the congregation, which chose its own pastor and went its own way. This plan opened the way for variations in belief, but in practice the congregations clung to a simple theology based on interpreting the Bible as the inspired word of God, which held the answers to problems of morality, ethics, and the conduct of life.

In later American history, Plymouth has loomed much larger than its contemporary importance warrants, largely because it became a theme for poems, plays, and novels. Henry Wadsworth Longfellow's "The Courtship of Miles Standish," published in 1858, with its tale of the captain's courting of Priscilla Mullins by proxy and his loss of the maid to his emissary, John Alden, is only one of many literary treatments of early life at Plymouth. And the story of the first thanksgiving has affected the American imagination profoundly. William Bradford's chronicle *Of Plimouth Plantation*, written in a style of biblical simplicity, is a classic of American literature. But Plymouth produced no learned men, founded no college, nor developed a body of theology. Its people for the most part were farmers, fishermen, traders, and artisans.

While the Pilgrims were creating a tiny commonwealth for themselves, other settlers were arriving on the shores of New England. In 1620, Sir Ferdinando Gorges, who had been a moving spirit in the old Plymouth Company, had obtained a patent for a new group, a proprietary body called the Council for New England, which had among its members a distinguished list of peers and upper class from the west of England. It received proprietary rights to a vast domain between the fortieth and forty-eighth parallels of north latitude and extending from ocean to ocean. For the next fifteen years, until the charter was surrendered to the king in 1635, the Council for New England, a feudal body, tried vainly to stimulate colonial activity by issuing, for a fee, patents to lands within its jurisdiction. Unlike the Virginia Company, it was not a stock company financing and outfitting colonies, but it was merely a lease-granting proprietor. Although several venturers received grants from the council, most settlements made under its patents amounted to little.

In June 1622, a company of "rude and profane fellows (the Pilgrims thought) under the leadership of Andrew Weston landed at Plymouth on its way to the southern shore of Massachusetts Bay. After wearing out their welcome among the Pilgrims, they moved to Wessagusset (now Weymouth), where they set up a base for fishing and trading. Too late to plant corn, and too negligent to store supplies for the winter, they nearly starved during the cold months and scattered the next year.

A year after the collapse of the Wessagusset settlement, a certain Captain Wollaston brought over a large number of servants and established himself at a place he called Mount Wollaston, within the area now surrounded by Braintree. With him came Thomas Morton, one of Weston's associates at Weymouth, who is said to have left England "for his country's good." Wollaston soon tired of New England and departed with a number of his servants to Virginia. But Morton, always generous with his wine, persuaded some of the servants to stay with him at Mount Wollaston, which became known as Merry Mount. Morton's colony soon became a scandal and a disgrace in the eyes of the Pilgrims, soberly watching from a distance of twenty-five miles, for, says Bradford, "they fell to great licenciousnes, and led a dissolute life, powering out them selves into all profanenes. And Morton became lord of misrule, and maintained (as it were) a schoole of Athism."

Morton's lack of Christian faith was not the least of his immoralities. After trading with the Indians, he and his crew invited them to join in drinking "both wine and strong waters in great exsess." One sin led to another, Bradford continues, until "they allso set up a May-pole, drinking and dancing aboute it many days togeather, inviting the Indean women, for their consorts, dancing and frisking togither (like so many fairies, or furies rather), and worse practises."

Such frivolity offended the Pilgrims, but even more serious was selling guns, powder, and shot to the Indians, then teaching them how to use these weapons. At least that was what the Pilgrims accused Morton of. At this point, Captain Miles Standish led troops to Merry Mount to arrest Morton, who barricaded himself in his house with his cronies and threatened to shoot it out with intruders. Morton and his friends were too inebriated to do much damage, Bradford asserts. Fearing that Standish would damage his house, Morton stumbled out "not to yeeld, but to shoote; but they were so steeld with drinke as their peeces were too heavie for them; him-selfe [Morton] with a carbine (over charged and allmost halfe fild with powder and shote, as was after found) had thought to have shot Captaine Standish; but he stept to him, and put by his peece, and tooke him. Neither was ther any hurte done to any of either side, save that one was so drunke that he rane his owne nose upon the pointe of a sword that one held before him as he entred the house; but he lost but litle of his hott blood."

The Pilgrims removed Morton's Maypole and shipped him to England in June 1628. (The main objection was perhaps less to stunt Morton's frivolity than because of his ability to win the friendship of the Indians and cut into the Pilgrims' trade in furs.) But by the summer of 1629, Morton was back at Merry Mount busily trading with his Indian friends, to the chagrin of his pious competitors. This time, settlers in Massachusetts Bay decided to get rid of him for good. After putting him in the stocks and burning down his house, they again sent him to England. His account of life in New England, published in Amsterdam in 1637 with the title *The Mew English Canaan,* lightens the gloom of New England literature with flashes of humor.

While the Pilgrims were getting established - and giving a little help to assorted adventurers who turned up at Plymouth - other plans were being made in England to exploit the resources of New England and its waters. A group of enterprising merchants and shipowners at Dorchester decided to establish a permanent colony in New England where resident fishermen would catch and cure fish for the European market. This would avoid sending fishermen each season from England and save money and time. In March 1624, the Dorchester

Company was organized, with shareholders not only from Dorchester, but from the surrounding counties. One of the leaders in this organization was a Puritan preacher, the Reverend John White, likely the author of a persuasive paper entitled "General Observations for the Plantation of New England." White already was thinking of New England as a place where men who shared his religious beliefs might create a commonwealth of godly folk of their own persuasion. A practical man, White believed that a colony, established under a patent from the Council for New England, could further the work of the Lord at a profit. While these pious colonists went about their daily business of fishing and fur trading, they could set an example of righteous behavior, and their ministers could disseminate the word of God to the Indians and itinerant fishermen who visited that coast. The scheme appeared divinely inspired in both its economic and religious prospects.

A tentative settlement was made at Cape Ann (near today's Gloucester, Massachusetts) by some of the Dorchester promoters in 1623. The next year, another expedition left thirty-two men, but the season was late when they reached Cape Ann, and the catch was small. A third expedition with three vessels in 1625 had similar luck. At this stage, the company found a fisherman living nearby, Roger Conant, who agreed to become resident manager at Cape Ann. Conant had joined the Plymouth colony two years before but left Plymouth for a nearby fishing island (now Hull) to which others unhappy with Pilgrim rule had settled. The Pilgrims made trouble for the Cape Ann fishermen, who, like Morton and his crew, were competitors. Captain Miles Standish marched to Cape Ann and, threatening fire and brimstone, ordered them off, claiming the fishing wharf belonged to Plymouth. Conant quieted the fiery captain and persuaded the Plymouth settlers to move their fishing operations to the Kennebec. But Cape Ann colonists continued to have bad luck. Fishing was poor from their immediate shore, and their trade with the Indians was insufficient to cover their losses. In 1626, the company abandoned the enterprise.

A few of the Cape Ann fishermen and traders decided to stay in New England, and under Conant's leadership they moved south to Naumkeag, soon to be called Salem. Conant wrote to John White of their resolve and received a promise of supplies and help. Even though White's colleagues in the Dorchester Company had lost interest in a colony of religious fishermen and traders, he never wavered. He was soon in contact with Puritans in Lincolnshire and London who had begun to talk about a refuge in New England. The upshot was the organization of the New England Company, designed to take over the old Dorchester Company and utilize Roger Conant's struggling settlement at Salem as the nucleus for a colony of the faithful.

Negotiations of the New England Company with the Council for New England, or with individual members such as the Earl of Warwick, are unclear, but by some means it obtained a patent for a grant of land reaching from three miles south of the Charles River to three miles north of the Merrimac River and extending west to the Pacific. That this grant overlapped territory claimed by Ferdinando Gorges and his associates was overlooked or disregarded.

To begin the occupation, the New England Company in June 1628, dispatched the ship *Abigail* with forty emigrants under the leadership of John Endecott. They were destined for Conant's village of Salem, where Endecott was to become governor. This unsmiling zealot - he had chopped down a second Maypole put up by Morton's men in 1628 - set to work diligently to prepare housing for other emigrants to come. Conant's fishermen might grumble, but Endecott ruthlessly drove them to complete their tasks while assuring them they were doing the Lord's work.

Some leaders in the New England Company, worried over the legality of their title to land claimed by members of the Gorges family and others, petitioned Charles I for a royal charter to their territory, which they received on March 4, 1629. The charter absorbed the old New England Company into the Massachusetts Bay Company, which its letters of incorporation empowered to "govern and rule all His Majesty's subjects that reside within the limits of our plantation." This charter was to be one of the most important legal documents obtained by any colony, for, as it turned out, it made the incorporators self-governing and virtually independent of the government in London. It disregarded previous grants to the Council for New England and to others and thus created future controversy.

The Massachusetts Bay Company immediately began plans to enlarge the colony under Endecott at Salem. In April 1629, the company sent a fleet of vessels with emigrants, supplies, tools, and livestock. As the years passed, the promoters of colonies had learned the kind of people and equipment required. This group made a quick crossing, and some wrote back enthusiastically about the outlook. One minister, the Reverend Francis Higginson, declared in a 1630 pamphlet, *New England's Plantation* that "there is hardly a more healthful place to be found in the world that agreeth better with our English bodies," and "a sup of New England's air is better than a whole draft of old England's ale." A few months after this praise, Higginson died, but most of the newcomers - hardy farmers and skilled artisans - survived and spread out from Salem to form other settlements nearby.

During 1629, a group of Puritans in Suffolk, Lincolnshire, and southern Yorkshire, some related by blood or marriage to the settlers in Massachusetts Bay, began to talk of emigrating to America. Among the leaders of this group were John Winthrop, a country gentleman from the manor Groton in Suffolk; Thomas Dudley, steward to the Earl of Lincoln (a Puritan sympathetic with the prospective emigrants); Isaac Johnson, brother-in-law of the Earl of Lincoln; Emmanuel Downing, Winthrop's brother-in-law; John Humphrey, a son-in-law of Lincoln's and deputy governor; and Sir Richard Saltonstall.

Winthrop, like many fellow Puritans, was discouraged over the state of England, which he believed was ripe for destruction because of corruption and its falling away from the true God. The ascendancy of the high Anglicans, led by William Laud, Bishop of London and later Archbishop of Canterbury, caused more worry. Winthrop was in debt. He, like many landowners, had been caught in a financial squeeze that was particularly hard on those who depended upon regular rents in a period of rising costs. He was seeking a way to recoup his fortune and to improve his estate. The prospect of land in New England, particularly where the owners might establish a godly commonwealth uncontaminated by the corruptions of the Old World, appealed strongly to Winthrop and others fearful of the political and religious trends in England.

Twelve leaders of this Puritan group met at Cambridge on August 26, 1629, and agreed to leave with their families by March 1, 1630, "provided, alwayes that before the last of September next the whole government together with the Patent for the said plantacion bee first by an order of Court legally transferred and established to remayn with us and others which shall inhabite upon the said plantacion." This provision reveals the Puritans' concern for making their position legally secure. At a meeting of the general court of the Massachusetts Bay Company on August 29 - a meeting attended by many Puritans sympathetic to the proposal - the would-be emigrants got their measure approved.

Until this time, management of all companies supporting colonial ventures had been in the hands of individuals who remained in England. Under the provision passed by the Massachusetts Bay Company's general court on August 29, the emigrants would take the charter with them and would assume management and government of the colony. This was a radical departure and perhaps the stay-at-home members of the company had not considered it.

The winter of 1629–30 was spent in orderly but excited preparation for the move to New England. By the end of March, eleven vessels were ready at Southampton. The fleet included the *Arbella*, named for Isaac Johnson's wife, sister of the Earl of Lincoln, and the *Mayflower,* already a veteran of several New England voyages. Four vessels, including the *Arbella,* in which Winthrop, who had been elected governor, embarked with the charter, sailed on March 29, 1630; the other seven were delayed nearly a month loading equipment, supplies, and livestock: forty cows, sixty horses, goats, and poultry.

The more than 700 men, women, and children comprising the body of emigrants represented a cross-section of English society. Among them were a number of learned men, some from Emmanuel College, Cambridge, where Puritan preachers were trained (six years later Emmanuel provided the model for Harvard College); some belonged to the landed gentry; others were members of substantial merchant families. Also included were many yeomen farmers, fishermen, craftsmen, and servants, not all Puritans. A noted Puritan preacher, John Cotton, vicar of St. Botolph's, Boston, in Lincolnshire, came to Southampton to see the first contingent off and send them on with a sermon, "God's Promise to His Plantation." Three years later, Cotton emigrated to New England and became one of its most influential Puritan ministers.

After more than two months at sea, the vessels anchored at Salem, where Endecott had erected a number of houses in anticipation of their arrival.

Since Salem "pleased them not," they moved on to Charlestown, but, the water supply there proving inadequate, some crossed the river to Boston, while others settled in the surrounding villages of Medford, Roxbury, and Watertown.

The region around what is now greater Boston was not entirely unoccupied when the first Puritans arrived. A number of stray settlers, who would be called squatters in later frontier parlance, already were established. Some were individualists who had fled from the regimen of the Pilgrims at Plymouth or the severity of Endecott at Salem. A few had come from England with the fishing fleets, and others were remnants of abortive colonies such as Weston's, and another settled a bit later by Robert Gorges at Weymouth. After nearly starving, Gorges and some of his colonists had returned to England, but others scattered along the coast. Among those who had settled in New England was the Reverend William Blaxton or Blackstone, an Anglican minister of Puritan leanings - but not so much a Puritan as the newcomers of 1629–30. He was living on what is now Beacon Hill, Boston, comfortably surrounded by his garden, orchard, and fields when Winthrop's group settled around him. They proved too stern and intolerant for Parson Blaxton, who in 1635 left for Rhode Island with a parting declaration: "I came from England because I did not like the Lord Bishops, but I cannot join with you because

I would not be under the Lord Brethren."

During the decade that followed the arrival of Winthrop and his group, a period known in New England history as the Great Migration, some 200 ships brought 20,000 settlers to Massachusetts Bay. They were not all Puritans, but the majority were nonconformists of some persuasion. These people funneled through the port of Boston and spread through New England. Boston and the area around it was a hive from which Puritan groups swarmed, usually under the leadership of their minister, who led them as a church unit to some fresh settlement on the frontier. Heavy emigration continued until 1641, when the Puritan Revolution in England for a time caused a sharp drop in the movement of nonconformists to America. But the numbers who arrived in New England between 1629 and 1641 were so large they created a problem when it came to assimilation within the churches of the Puritans. The leaders were determined to retain strict control. They had come to New England to establish a commonwealth where Christians like themselves could remain unsoiled by corruptions that, they believed, plagued England and the English church. Consequently, they directed their efforts toward establishing a form of government pleasing to the heads of each church, lay and clerical. The Puritans of Massachusetts Bay achieved part oligarchy and part theocracy.

The charter provided that the government of the colony should be in the hands of a governor, a deputy governor, and eighteen assistants, also called magistrates. In the future, the freemen (members) of the company were to fill these offices by election at meetings of the General Court, which would make the laws conform with the laws of England, or as nearly so as conditions would warrant. The charter provided for four meetings of the General Court each year. But John Winthrop was governor, and Winthrop's ideas about the unreliability of the people were as dogmatic as those of Alexander Hamilton in a later period.

Though he had fled an England ruled by Stuarts convinced of the divine right of kings, Winthrop firmly believed in the divine right of the inspired leaders of New England to rule the multitude. He had searched the Scriptures and could find nothing to condone democracy. In 1645, after serving many terms as governor, he expressed in his *Journal* his skepticism of liberty that the people insistently demanded, a liberty "incompatible and inconsistent with authority. . . . The exercise and maintaining of this liberty makes men grow more evil and in time to be worse than brute beasts: *omnes sumus licentia deteriores* [we are all worse for liberty]," he wrote. ". . . But if you will be satisfied to enjoy such civil and lawful liberties as Christ allows you, then will you quietly and cheerfully submit unto that authority which is set over you, in all the administrations of it, for your good." Convinced of his own rightness and wisdom to govern, Winthrop hated to delegate authority to the less able.

Nevertheless, the charter decreed a certain amount of popular government in that freemen could hold elections. The problem of the Puritan leaders was to see that freemen were a carefully selected body. At a meeting of freemen, therefore, on May 18, 1631, at which Winthrop was re-elected governor, it was voted that henceforth "noe man shal be admitted to the freedom of this body politicke, but such as are members of some of the churches within the limitts of the same." This was obviously a violation of the charter, but the Puritans were ready to justify the means by the ends, and they asserted the provision was necessary in order to insure a franchised electorate of "honest and good men."

It was not easy to become a church member. One had to testify in open meeting to a conviction he was divinely elected for salvation and allow the minister or elders to interrogate him before being admitted. In this fashion, for many years in the Massachusetts Bay colony, church members retained complete political control and managed to suppress or drive out those who would not conform to their views. Tolerance, in their view, was unchristian, and religious liberty for the individual was unthinkable.

Yet conformity in matters of belief posed many problems, because the creed of the Puritans was based on the Bible as the ultimate authority, and the Bible was sometimes ambiguous. Moreover, not all preachers agreed on interpretations of certain important passages of Scripture. In this dilemma, the best the Puritans could do was to have faith in the wisdom of the most respected of their ministers. John Cotton exerted tremendous power for years after his arrival in 1633. What he uttered in the pulpit, it was said, soon was enacted into law. In fact, the clergy of Massachusetts Bay during the first two generations after settlement served as advisers to the magistrates and exercised almost supreme political influence.

Even so, conformity was difficult to enforce. New England was home to a varied lot of men and women, many strongly individualistic. From the first, the authorities were faced with schism and the threat of political as well as ecclesiastical disintegration. The earliest Puritans in Massachusetts Bay had come not as Separatists but as members of the Church of England. They denied they wished to separate from the mother church; instead they hoped to establish a purer and more ideal version of the church that in England was being transformed by Archbishop Laud and his clergy into an image of Rome.

Once in New England, the Puritans had to decide upon a form of church polity, and they chose that of the Plymouth church. In fact, many came with the notion that bishops were bad and that some non-Episcopal form of church government must be found. They quickly adopted the covenant type of rule, in which individual congregations agreed or covenanted together to form a church and call a minister. This decentralized form of church government contrasted with Winthrop's notion of a strongly centralized civil government, but the Puritans managed to reconcile this inconsistency. They could not reconcile conflicts within church groups, which led to secessions, withdrawals, and sometimes to what the Puritans considered heresy. Many New England towns owed their establishment to discontented groups who withdrew from one church and, under the leadership of a minister, migrated to another locality.

Typical was the case of the Reverend Thomas I. Hooker, pastor of the congregation at Newtown (Cambridge) in 1633. He objected to the way in which Cotton manipulated control, dictated decisions of the magistrates, and insisted upon the clergy's right to advise the civil authorities in matters of law and justice - justice interpreted according to the Mosaic code. In Hooker's opinion, this assumption of clerical authority was dangerously close to tyranny. His congregation was dissatisfied with the land available to them. Hearing about the fertile land of the Connecticut Valley, they determined to move and petitioned the General

Court for permission. This was granted grudgingly, and in 1636 Hooker followed the example of other dissenters and led his congregation to Connecticut. Comparing themselves to the Israelites leaving Egypt, they marched through the wilderness with their cattle and possessions in search of a better land where they would have greater liberty than under the theocratic oligarchy of Massachusetts.

Hooker's congregation settled at Hartford, and two other congregations joined settlements at Windsor and Wethersfield. In 1637, these three towns elected deputies who met at Hartford as a general court to establish a government separate and distinct from control of Massachusetts Bay. Two years later, they adopted a platform of government they called the Fundamental Orders of Connecticut. Although the government established in Connecticut was a far cry from a democracy, it was slightly less oligarchic than that of Massachusetts. In Massachusetts, for instance, John Cotton insisted that magistrates ought to hold office for life; in effect he would have had them a self-perpetuating body. Connecticut prevented this. Yet Connecticut, like Massachusetts, condemned toleration, and Connecticut's chief contribution to liberality in government - if liberality is not too strong a word - was to give more authority to the body of Orthodox Church members instead of letting the clergy and magistrates monopolize power. In both colonies, only the godly according to the Puritan prescription were permitted a voice in government.

In 1638, the Reverend John Davenport and Theophilus Eaton, a London merchant of strict Puritan beliefs, established New Haven, a separate colony later absorbed into Connecticut. Davenport and Eaton permitted no democratic ideas to invade their borders and populated their colony with believers, chiefly from London, who were willing to live under the laws of Moses. Eaton, the first governor, remained in office for twenty years and ruled with the advice of the clergy and the magistrates, who drew wisdom from Scriptures. Because the Bible did not describe any trials by jury, New Haven found no reason to extend this right to citizens, who had to depend upon the magistrates, advised by the clergy, for justice.

The situation in Rhode Island, where Roger Williams had fled in 1635 after he was convicted of holding unsound beliefs, was different. As pastor of the congregation at Salem, Williams had preached doctrines abhorrent to authorities: The magistrates, he declared, had no right to direct a man's conscience; and the New England church should make a formal declaration of separation from the Church of England, for in claiming to remain within the fabric of the English church, it was guilty of pollution. But worst of all, perhaps, Williams questioned the validity of the charter of Massachusetts Bay and the colonists' right to Indian lands.

John Cotton and fellow clergymen were scandalized. Since heresy of this sort struck at the fundamentals of the Puritan commonwealth, it could not be tolerated. Williams was driven from his pulpit, and the court ordered his banishment from Massachusetts Bay.

In Rhode Island, Williams bargained with the Indians for sufficient land to make a settlement for people unhappy under the grim rule of the Puritans and founded a community he called Providence Plantation. There, he and his followers agreed that civil authorities would have no power over any man's conscience and that church and state would be separate. For the first time in America, this fundamental doctrine clearly was enunciated. Tolerance was a new idea in New England, but Williams steadfastly maintained its principles. For example, he condemned the Quakers for refusing to bear arms or to pay taxes, but, unlike the authorities in Massachusetts Bay, he defended them from persecution and let them settle in Providence.

Williams' colony at Providence prospered as a farming community. Land in Rhode Island was more fertile than the uplands of Massachusetts Bay, and colonists grew abundant crops of corn, grain, hay, and tobacco. Their livestock multiplied, and they soon were able to export food, cattle, horses, and hogs. Rhode Island in time achieved an economic and political freedom that was the envy of less well-governed colonists.

Other refugees from Massachusetts Bay filtered into Rhode Island, sometimes individually, sometimes in small groups. The efforts of the Puritan clergy to maintain their particular orthodoxy benefited regions over the Massachusetts border, for many men and women either found it advantageous to migrate or were banished.

The trial of Anne Hutchinson at Cambridge in 1637 ultimately resulted in more than one settlement in Rhode Island. In the eyes of the Puritan hierarchy, Hutchinson's sins were multiple: First, she was a woman with unorthodox ideas she insisted upon expressing; second, she declared a belief in divine love, somewhat similar to Quaker doctrines that were repugnant to Calvinists, a belief that the individual by contemplation and illumination could come into direct contact with the divine; third, despite the duties that bore down upon a mother of fifteen children, she found time to hold meetings in her home to analyze the sermons that the ministers preached on Sundays and lecture days. Much that she believed and said contradicted the legalistic doctrines of the Puritans. Inevitably, she was brought to trial, convicted of heresy, and sentenced to banishment. When she asked why she was being punished, all John Winthrop could respond was, "Say no more, the court knows wherefore and is satisfied."

Anne Hutchinson had many friends and followers, whom the authorities called Antinomian heretics. One of these was William Coddington, who had argued in her defense. Unable any longer to live in peace in Massachusetts, Coddington, with Roger Williams' help, bought land from Indians in Rhode Island and settled at Portsmouth in 1639. His group included Hutchinson and her family. But the settlement had a glut of argumentative and independent philosophers, and its members were soon at such cross-purposes that some began to move out to establish new settlements. Coddington left to found Newport. Another member of the group, Samuel Gorton, lost faith in the strong convictions of the Hutchinsons, departed, and founded Warwick. Although the religious views of dwellers in the four Rhode Island communities varied, they all staunchly defended freedom of conscience, and ultimately, in 1644, they came together in a federated body under a charter obtained by Williams. Controversial and argumentative as the Rhode Islanders were, they created the most democratic commonwealth in British America. Individual liberty was respected and protected under the colony's enlightened laws, which were ahead of their time in many respects. In 1647, for instance, witchcraft was outlawed, and imprisonment for debt was forbidden.

Another fugitive from Massachusetts persecution of the Antinomians, John Wheelright, led a small group of dissenters to New Hampshire and in 1638 founded the town of Exeter. New Hampshire, outside the jurisdiction of Massachusetts Bay, had several towns inhabited by fishermen and farmers. To them the Bay authorities complained they should not have permitted Wheelright to commit so "unneighborly an act as to settle in their midst." Since many earlier inhabitants of New Hampshire were Anglicans, this complaint had little effect.

Despite the flight of occasional heretics, however, the Massachusetts Bay colony prospered. In fact, no other colony in British America displayed greater dynamic energy in the first half of the seventeenth century. Its citizens, confident they were the chosen of the Almighty, were determined to make Massachusetts Bay a garden of the Lord where righteous men might prosper and where the wicked would sin not only at the peril of their souls, but at the risk of incurring the wrath of the magistrates, a more tangible threat. To these people, work was an end in itself, for they feared idleness as they feared the devil. They cultivated diligence, thrift, and sobriety as cardinal virtues, and so great was their application to their vocations that material success was all but inevitable.

As John Smith predicted, the sea proved a source of wealth. As Virginians made their fortunes with tobacco, New Englanders found fish a plentiful and profitable resource. Salted and dried cod became a mainstay of international commerce, eagerly bought in the Catholic lands of the Mediterranean, where the Church often marked days when believers could not consume meat. If any New Englander stopped to consider he was supporting heresy by supplying food for these fasting days, he never let that trouble his conscience or curtail his profitable labor.

Fishing, however, which King James had commended as being the vocation of the Holy Apostles, was only one of the money-making operations of Massachusetts Bay. The forest provided white oak for barrel staves and ships' timbers, spruce and pine for spars, and turpentine, rosin, and tar for ships' stores. Shipbuilders in New England were soon supplying vessels for both colonial and English commerce. Massachusetts farms existed primarily for the subsistence of their owners, but they also produced a surplus of food for shipment to the West Indies and other markets. Through a combination of farming, fishing, industry, and sea-borne commerce, the vision of the New World as a garden of the Lord where the faithful could prosper through their own diligence and thrift was a reality.

The example that New England set as a haven for religious refugees was not lost upon other persecuted groups in England and elsewhere. The fact that thousands of Englishmen had made homes for themselves in New England, where they had established a virtually independent government, encouraged others who looked across the Atlantic for similar opportunities. But the search for religious and political freedom would not be the dominant motive in the settlement of the colonies. Most settlers in British North America - whatever additional motivations they may have had - would come primarily to improve their economic conditions. The eagerness to own land was always the strongest impulse influencing the majority of emigrants. They believed that opportunities in America were unlimited. And they thought if they could obtain land along with freedom from religious or other persecution, they would nearly reach earthly paradise.

5
COMPETITION FOR COLONIES

The ultimate success of the English in establishing themselves in North America was so complete that the early years when the great powers of Spain and France had surrounded the English settlements, threatening to close upon them from the south and north, quickly became a faded memory. Even the Dutch for a time held a domain in the Hudson Valley that split the English colonies into two segments. As it turned out, the Dutch served as a useful buffer at a time when the French might have occupied this region to the destruction of English power in the North Atlantic realm. Only fate - and the vagaries of European politics - can explain the survival of the British colonies during this period.

After the failure of Cartier and Roberval to establish a base in the St. Lawrence Valley in the 1540s, France lost several opportunities to seize Canada, although its kings made sporadic efforts to reinforce settlements in Canada, and French fishermen made yearly voyages to the Newfoundland banks and sometimes to the St. Lawrence and the coast of Nova Scotia to fish and trade for furs. Then, in 1603, Samuel de Champlain sailed to Canada with a trading, exploring, and colonizing expedition. Like John Smith, he became an ardent advocate of settlement in America and a leader in colonial enterprises.

Many French seamen who sailed the Atlantic had been more intent on taking treasure ships than on exploring or trading, but conditions had altered in the more than sixty years since Cartier had embarked from St.-Malo on his Canadian expeditions. Henri IV, now king of France, had made peace with the Spaniards in 1598 and was trying to unite his country. Frenchmen had turned from piracy to trade, and Champlain represented the new type of French seaman-adventurer. He had gone in the service of Spain to the West Indies and on his return had published an account of his observations of Spain's successful exploitation of a rich American empire. Among observations he made was that a canal across the Isthmus of Panama would be a sensible means of reaching the South Sea.

In 1603, the Sieur de Chastes, governor of Dieppe, persuaded Henri IV to give him a monopoly of the fur trade in Canada on condition he establish the Cross of Christ and the flag of France. Allied with De Chastes were several prominent merchants, the best known being Du Pont Grave of St.-Malo, who commanded one of two vessels that sailed for the St. Lawrence in 1603. To bring back exact information about the country, the king appointed Champlain as geographer royal. From this time, Champlain was to devote his energies to colonization.

The expedition of 1603 explored the St. Lawrence as far as the site of Montreal (along the route Cartier had followed in 1535) and proved to the satisfaction of the *voyageurs* that trade with the Indians would be profitable. Champlain mapped both sides of the river and made notes on the Indians, the flora and fauna of the country, and other details that might be useful. The traders returned to Le Havre in September 1603, with a cargo of furs sufficient to interest other merchants. Champlain hurried to complete his report for the king and printed it the next year. With the great North Country christened New France, Champlain was ready to guide his countrymen to that land of promise.

The Sieur de Chastes had died, and the merchants of St.-Malo, who were the principal investors in the voyage, found themselves without a patron at court. The king transferred the monopoly of the fur trade to a friend of Champlain's, a Huguenot nobleman, the Sieur de Monts, with the understanding De Monts admit to his company any merchants and others who wished to invest in the enterprise. To make clear the king contemplated something more than a trading post, the grant to De Monts stipulated the company must send out no more than than 100 settlers each year.

With the high-sounding title Lieutenant General in Acadia, De Monts sailed in April 1604, from Le Havre with two ships. His principal associates on the voyage were Champlain, the merchant-trader Du Pont Gravé, and Baron Jean de Poutrincourt, who came along for adventure and in the end became an ardent colonist. The nobleman was the exception in this expedition, for, unlike the first groups who went to Virginia, the Frenchmen in De Monts' ships were skilled artisans and farmers who had the capacity for hard work. After landing on the coast of Nova Scotia, De Monts sailed around into the Bay of Fundy, and on Champlain's unfortunate advice, chose a site to settle on St. Croix Island in Passamaquoddy Bay. There, they erected houses and laid out gardens, but no sooner had seed sprouted in the sandy soil than the sun burned the young plants. In his choice of the island, Champlain was thinking more of defense than of farming. The soil on the mainland was suitable for grain and garden crops, but fear of Indians, as at Jamestown, confined the settlers to their island.

De Poutrincourt returned to France in one of the vessels, while the remaining colonists prepared for winter, which came sooner than they expected. They had not made sufficient preparations against cold more severe than any had known in France. Without adequate cellars to protect supplies, all their cider and wine, except some Spanish sherry, froze. Lacking fresh food of any kind, living exclusively on bread and salt meat, all but eleven of the colonists had scurvy before winter ended. Drifting ice kept them from going to the mainland for game. The frozen beaches were devoid of shellfish, and fish were scarce. The scurvy, which Champlain described in graphic detail, left those who survived weak and nearly helpless, their mouths swollen and their teeth falling out.

Despite the terrible winter, which, Champlain observed in a understatement, "produced discontent in Sieur de Monts and others of the settlement," the colonists were not ready to desert. But they were eager to find a better place. When a rescue vessel arrived in mid-June, De Monts organized an exploring party that went south as far as Boston harbor and returned in early August. After considering available sites, De Monts moved his colony across the bay to the north side of what is now Annapolis Basin in Nova Scotia, in the harbor the French called Port Royal in the land of Acadia. The colonists transported timbers and clapboards from their buildings at St. Croix and built new houses with better protection against the cold. They had learned from experience to lay in supplies to ensure a variety in their diet and passed the winter of 1605–6 in relative comfort. In the spring, De Monts, who had returned to France on business of the colony, dispatched De Poutrincourt with a cargo of supplies and fresh recruits. In this company came Marc Lescarbot, a lawyer from Paris who wrote an entertaining history of New France. Thanks to the writings of Lescarbot and Champlain, French efforts to establish settlements in Canada are well and wittily documented.

The prospects for a permanent French settlement looked promising. The farmers in the colony at Port Royal produced good crops in the summer of 1606. The Indians were eager to trade beaver, mink, and marten skins for knives and trinkets. But the settlers' success engendered envy among French Catholics, and De Monts, a Huguenot, found himself beset on all sides by enemies who had gained the ear of the king. De Monts' monopoly was canceled, and the company had to go out of business. Since no further support could be expected from France, the colony at Port Royal had to be abandoned.

Champlain, however, was not easily discouraged. The next year he persuaded De Monts to try a trading and colonizing expedition in the St. Lawrence Valley. In the spring of 1608, with a commission from the king giving him a monopoly for one year, De Monts sent two ships to Canada under the command of Du Pont Gravé, who was to trade with the Indians and return in the autumn, leaving Champlain in charge of the settlement. They sailed up the St. Lawrence, and Champlain picked a spot for his colony at the foot of the Quebec cliffs. There, they built houses on the shore and spent a difficult winter. Of twenty-eight men, only eight survived the cold and scurvy. Nevertheless, in June 1609, when a rescue ship came with additional settlers, Champlain was ready for further exploration.

The Huron and Algonquin tribes in the vicinity of Quebec were at war with the Iroquois, who lived farther south. In order to gain a knowledge of the country, Champlain and other Frenchmen agreed to join a war party against the Iroquois. This venture took them across a large lake that Champlain named after himself and as far south as the site of Ticonderoga, where the Algonquins, with the help of Champlain's muskets, routed a party of Iroquois and took a number of prisoners. From this time onward, the French were identified as allies of the Algonquins while the Iroquois were on the side of the English. The expedition gave Champlain some knowledge of the waterways leading to the interior regions and paved the way for expansion west.

Champlain provided one of the earliest descriptions of the cruelty Indians displayed toward their captives. One victim was ordered to sing while his captors danced about, burning him slowly with brands from a fire, tearing out his nails and tendons, scalping him, and piercing him with sharpened sticks, until finally they allowed Champlain to kill him with a musket shot.

Several years later, Champlain was to lead expeditions to explore the western region. Shortly after his return from the foray against the Iroquois, he visited France and had an audience with the king, to whom he showed a girdle of porcupine quills, two birds of the country (scarlet tanagers), and the head of a curious long-snouted fish, all of which caused the king to wonder at the marvels of New France. Of more interest to the sponsors of the colony were the furs the ships brought home, enough to show a profit and to excite other investors.

The fur trade was the immediate objective of the French, for it was clear that in barter with the Indians, they had found a substantial source of revenue. Consequently, investors in colonial enterprises were more concerned with establishing trading posts than developing the country for French inhabitants. Champlain, however, through his writings and by his personal efforts, labored unceasingly to stimulate interest in colonizing New France, to which he returned after his audience with Henri IV. He led small parties of Frenchmen into the interior to bolster the strength of warring groups of Algonquins, thus strengthening the alliance of the French with the Indians, to whom they looked for continuing trade. In 1615–16, he made his most extensive exploration of the interior in a journey with eleven Frenchmen that gave him a view of the Great Lakes and the vision of a vast inland empire that might one day belong to France.

But the political situation in France was not conducive to colonization in America. Henri IV had been assassinated in 1610, and his widow, Marie de Medici, ruled as regent with the aid of an Italian adventurer named Concini. De Monts, or any other Huguenot, could no longer expect favors at court. Various merchants and noblemen received concessions for trade in New France, but little was done to promote colonization. At Quebec, however, Champlain persevered, although less than fifty Frenchmen were to be found in all of New France. Finally, in 1627, after the rise of Cardinal Richelieu as the power behind Louis XIII, the fortunes and future of New France began to improve.

Richelieu reorganized a group of investors into the Company of the Hundred Associates, which excited speculators to such a degree that noblemen, bishops, courtesans, and merchants competed for the privilege of buying stock at 3,000 livres per share. In effect, the company was to be the proprietor of New France and have a perpetual monopoly of the fur trade. But to retain this monopoly, it had to send at least 200 Frenchmen each year to occupy the country, and it was required to encourage missionaries to convert the heathen. Since Richelieu was determined to break the power of the Huguenots, he decreed that no Protestant colonists should be allowed to settle in New France, lest heretics gain a foothold abroad. New France was to be solidly Catholic. To carry on the work of evangelizing the Indians, the Society of Jesus obtained a monopoly of this pious enterprise and established missions that exerted a tremendous influence on Canada for the next century.

To stimulate the colony, the new company sent eighteen vessels loaded with supplies and colonists to the St. Lawrence in the spring of 1628. At that time, however, the English were trying to aid the Huguenots in their struggle against the forces of Louis XIII, and English privateers were free to attack French vessels. English pirate, David Kirke, heard of the rich prizes aboard these ships, headed for the St. Lawrence, and cornered the entire fleet. Only his desire to leave with his gains - combined with the stubborn refusal of Champlain to surrender Quebec - saved the colony from annihilation. A year later, however, Kirke returned and forced Champlain to capitulate. Not until the Treaty of St-Germain-en-Laye in 1632 was Canada restored to France and Champlain permitted to return to Quebec, where a small number of Frenchmen had held the post intact during his absence.

Until his death in 1635, Champlain furiously pursued the cause of French settlements in Canada. He dreamed of pushing west and creating a French domain in the region of the Great Lakes, and although that development did not come until later, Champlain paved the way. To him more than to any other individual, France owed its foothold in North America.

For three decades after Champlain's death, the development of the French settlements in Canada was slow. In 1642, Montreal was founded and became an important trading post, but Canada remained for years little more than an outpost for the fur trade. Despite all the rhetoric about colonization, little was done to establish French residents and to develop agriculture and industries. In 1663, the total French population, including missionaries and itinerant fur traders, barely numbered 2,500.

In that year, Louis XIV dissolved the old Company of One Hundred Associates and declared the country a royal colony, with a sovereign council to rule it. The council was composed of a governor, a bishop, an intendant, and twelve other members. Already the Jesuit missionaries and the secular authorities were competing for power, and for many years they were in constant disagreement. The missionaries, for example, wanted to bar the sale of brandy to the Indians, while traders insisted upon swapping brandy for beaver pelts. This tug of war between religion and trade became one of the facts of provincial life in French Canada.

The transformation of Canada into a royal province did not increase emigration from France, but gradually *habitants* settled farmlands and developed a self-sufficient agriculture. One of the inheritances from the early days that slowed development on the frontier was the incessant war with the Iroquois that resulted from the French alliance with the Algonquins. This affected life on the borders between French Canada and the English settlements until the end of the colonial period. For more than a century, France remained a threat to the stability and security of the English colonies; one of the greatest dangers to the English lay in the Indian policy that the French consistently fostered during the whole colonial period.

While Champlain was struggling to gain and hold New France, another Continental nation, the Netherlands, realized the New World, as well as the Far East, offered sources of wealth. After forty years of war with Spain, the United Provinces in 1609 made a truce set to last twelve years. During this period of peace, the Dutch made enormous efforts to expand commercial activities that were already flourishing. The enterprising Dutch East India Company, incorporated in 1602, was making fortunes for its stockholders. In 1609, eager to find a shorter route to the Spice Islands and to the mainland of Asia, the company employed an experienced English navigator, Henry Hudson, to find a passage either to the east or to the west.

Although Hudson already had made two unsuccessful voyages in search of the Northeast Passage while employed by the Muscovy Company, the Dutch East India Company let him make another attempt. He sailed from the Netherlands in early April in command of the *Half Moon,* with a mixed crew, part English and part Dutch. After trying to pierce the Arctic ice pack in the vicinity of Novaya Zemlya, Hudson gave up the northeast attempt and sail for North America. His men, who had grown mutinous, agreed to search the American coast after Hudson showed them maps and information sent by John Smith, who "indicated to him a sea leading into the western ocean, by the north of the southern English colony."

Hudson made a landfall in Maine, where the ship's carpenter went ashore to fashion a mast, and the crew, having stolen furs from the Indians, quarreled over their spoils. These ill-assorted explorers then sailed south and reached Chesapeake Bay before turning north again. After a brief exploration of Delaware Bay, they moved up the coast until, on September 12, they reached the mouth of the river that now bears Hudson's name.

During the next month, they explored the Hudson River as far as the site of Albany, where the rapids interfered with navigation. "In the lower part of the river they found strong and warlike people," wrote Emanuel Van Meteren, a contemporary historian, "but in the upper part they found friendly and polite people, who had an abundance of provisions, skins, and furs, of martens and foxes, and many other commodities, as birds and fruit, even white and red grapes, and they traded amicably with the people."

Robert Juet, a mate on the *Half Moon,* described a more realistic example of their relations with the Indians: "The people of the Mountaynes came aboord us, wondering at our ship and weapons. We bought some small skinnes of them for Trifles. This after-noone one Canoe kept hanging under our sterne with one man in it, which we could not keepe from thence, who got up by our Rudder to the Cabin window, and stole out my Pillow and two Shirts, and two Bandeleeres. Our Masters Mate shot at him, and strooke him on the brest, and killed him." At intervals, the crew shot other Indians and thus set a course of hatred for future settlers. But despite their ruthless conduct, they succeeded in acquiring furs and obtaining a favorable view of the land.

Hudson wanted to make further explorations, but since his crew again were threatening mutiny, the *Half Moon* sailed for Holland. On November 7, the ship stopped at Dartmouth, where English authorities refused to let him or the Englishmen in his crew accompany the ship to Holland, although Hudson was sailing under the Dutch flag. The next year, 1610, Hudson sailed again to search the coast of the North Atlantic, this time financed by a consortium of London merchants headed by Sir Thomas Smythe. After exploring Hudson Strait and Hudson Bay, Hudson and his crew spent a difficult winter on James Bay. Once more his crew mutinied, and in June 1611, they placed Hudson, his son John, and seven others in an open boat and cast them adrift. They were never seen again, and only a remnant of the mutineers survived to bring their battered vessel back to England.

Henry Hudson made no original discoveries, but his explorations helped to prove that no feasible Northwest Passage existed. However, the report that the *Half Moon's* crew took back to Holland in 1609 convinced the Dutch that the Hudson River Valley offered a profitable region for the development of the fur trade, which soon became an objective of Amsterdam investors. Nor were the prospects for fur trade in the far north, which bordered New France, lost upon English speculators. At a later time, they would realize the opportunities there, and the Hudson's Bay Company would revive the name of an intrepid navigator.

The Dutch laid claim to the Hudson Valley and nearby regions by reason of Hudson's explorations under their flag, but the English never relinquished the claim they made under Cabot's discoveries. The French had overlapping claims, and Spain never had openly conceded that other nations had rights to American territories. Thus, the avenue was open for endless controversies over the possession of one of the most strategic and valuable portions of the North American continent.

After Hudson's voyage, the Dutch began to exploit the fur trade by organizing the New Netherland Company, composed of merchants from Amsterdam and Hoorn. Their High Mightinesses (as the States-General or Dutch parliament was called) granted the New Netherland Company a monopoly of the fur trade for three years. During this period, the company sent a number of ships to the Hudson, established trading posts as far up the river as Albany, and made a handsome profit, causing other merchants to be envious. Consequently, when the monopoly expired in 1618, their High Mightinesses thought it expedient to broaden the base of trade with New Netherland by opening it to other traders.

For many years, Willem Usselincx, an earnest Calvinist fugitive from Antwerp, had been urging the organization of a Dutch West India Company to compete with the Spanish empire. Usselincx's hatred of Catholic Spain motivated him, as well as a patriotic desire to strengthen his country, and the lure of profits, which he foresaw for investors in such a company. During the period of truce after 1609, the Dutch government refused to antagonize Spain unnecessarily, but with the expiration of the truce in 1621 and the prospect of a renewal of war, Usselincx's proposals for the creation of a company that would reap profits while making war on the common enemy received fresh attention.

In June 1621, the States-General granted a charter to the Dutch West India Company, giving it a monopoly of trade between the Netherlands, the west coast of Africa, and the entire coast of North and South America. Five "chambers" or boards of trade from many Dutch localities would govern the company; the most important was the chamber of Amsterdam. Much of the early activity of the West India Company was directed toward wresting a part of Brazil from Portugal and Spain, but it also concerned itself with the settlement of New Netherland and with raiding Spanish settlements in the Caribbean. The first church in New Amsterdam called its worshippers to service with bells pillaged from a Spanish church in Puerto Rico. Off Cuba in 1628, Dutch admiral Piet Pieterszoon Hein with thirty-one vessels, captured an entire Spanish treasure fleet, homeward bound and loaded with gold and silver, a feat Drake and the English buccaneers had dreamed of. From this one stroke of fortune, the West India Company stockholders received a 50-percent dividend. The capture ruined Spanish credit for a time and helped the Dutch achieve greater importance in European finance and trade.

While the West India Company was busy capturing sugar ports and plantations in Brazil and raiding the coasts of the Caribbean, it was trying to gain a foothold on the North Atlantic coast. In March 1624, the company sent thirty families, mostly French-speaking Walloons, Protestant refugees from the southern Netherlands (now Belgium) who were still under Spanish rule. They sailed in the *New Netherland,* commanded by Cornelius May, after whom Cape May is named. He put his passengers ashore at three points: the tip of Manhattan Island, Fort Orange (Albany), and a spot on the Delaware River. Since records of the West India Company were destroyed in 1821, little is known with certainty about the early years of colonization, but it appears that some traders already were established at points where May left settlers. In 1624, Nicolaes van Wassenaer's *Historical Account* observed: "Respecting this colony, it has already a prosperous beginning; and the hope is that it will not fall through provided it be zealously sustained, not only in that place foil [the Hudson] but in the South River [the Delaware]."

Although the Dutch were primarily concerned

with the fur trade, they understood permanent settlement depended upon farmers who would develop land and make colonies self-sustaining. Consequently, in 1625, the West India Company sent additional settlers and a cargo of livestock in three vessels suitably named for the purpose the *Cow,* the *Horse,* and the *Sheep.* The contractor who arranged for shipment took better care of the cattle than most captains did of human passengers. According to Wassenaer's report for that year, "Each animal has its own stall, with a floor of three feet of sand, arranged as comfortably as any stall here. Each animal has its respective servant who attends to it and knows what he is to get if he delivers it there alive. All suitable forage is there, such as oats, hay, and straw, and what else is useful. Country people have also joined the expedition, who take with them all furniture proper for the dairy; all sorts of seeds, ploughs, and agricultural implements are also present, so that nothing is wanting." As the result of this planning, only two animals died on the passage.

While the farmers were getting cattle established in pastures, an engineer, Kryn Frederycks, completed a defense work on the tip of Manhattan before the end of 1626 and named it Fort Amsterdam. The installation was designed to protect the farms in the vicinity from the warlike Manhattan Indians and to safeguard the entrance to the Hudson River (which the Dutch called the North River).

The director of the infant colony, Willem Verhulst, did not live up to the West India Company's expectations as an administrator, and the colony fell into chaos. To improve matters, the company in 1626 sent out a Huguenot, Peter Minuit, to replace Verhulst. A vigorous and intelligent leader, Minuit called in the farmers on the Delaware and at Fort Orange because he feared Indians would attack them. He then assigned the farmers land on Manhattan Island, which he bought from the Indians for sixty guilders' ($24) worth of trinkets, a trade that has gone down in American legend as the greatest real-estate deal in history.

Minuit proved a capable director, but his dictatorial rule was not always popular. Nominally a Huguenot in religion, he was criticized by some of the pious because he made no effort to enforce puritanical laws. Indeed, he failed to heed the words of the first Dutch Reformed minister sent out from Amsterdam, prompting the parson, the Reverend Jonas Michaëlius, to write back that the governor was a liar, a rogue, a profane swearer, a fornicator, and in short, "a slippery fellow who . . . is a compound of all iniquity and wickedness." In 1632, Minuit's enemies finally succeeded in having Sebastiaen Jansen Krol replace him. New Netherland had not seen the last of Minuit, however, for, to the embarrassment of the Dutch, he took service with the Swedes, and a few years later he helped them establish a competing colony on the Delaware.

The West India Company had difficulty recruiting colonists, for Holland in the seventeenth century was both a tolerant and a prosperous country, and its citizens had little incentive to emigrate. The enterprising Dutch would go to the ends of the earth in the pursuit of trade, but few wanted to settle permanently on another continent. For that reason, the West India Company recruited such refugee peoples in the Netherlands as they could persuade to go to America: Walloons from the southern Netherlands; Huguenots from France; a handful of Spaniards, Danes, Italians, and Jews; and some rogue Dutchmen whom their fellow countrymen were glad to see shipped abroad. From the beginning, New Amsterdam was a diverse settlement, intent upon trade and commerce and given over, said preachers, to godless behavior.

The rules of the West India Company prescribed the Calvinistic Dutch Reformed faith as the established religion of the colony, and official oversight of religious affairs in New Netherland was delegated to the classis - the governing body of pastors and elders - of Amsterdam, which supplied ministers. The result: New Netherland was less tolerant than the mother country, and its ministers attempted, usually without great success, to interfere in political affairs of the colony.

The Dutch, like other European nations that sought to exploit the New World, asserted their intention to evangelize the Indians, but they were more interested in trading for furs than saving souls. They soon discovered that the Indians were willing to part with their furs for guns and strong drink but not for Bibles. The pursuit of trade quickly extinguished any zeal for missionary activity, and New Amsterdam promoted commerce to the virtual exclusion of spiritual and intellectual matters.

Since labor was scarce in New Netherland and the Dutch, unlike the Spaniards, were never able to draw upon a reservoir of Indian labor, they began bringing in African slaves in 1625. The Dutch were aggressive slave traders. Their shippers were making considerable profits carrying slaves from Africa to Brazil, where they were essential to the growing sugar industry. They obtained these slaves by bartering with chieftains on the African coast, who in this way hoped to gain advantage in incessant tribal wars. Instead of slaughtering captives, as had been the custom, the chieftains took as many prisoners as possible. Thus, the slave trade was a joint venture between coastal chiefs and slave-ship captains.

In 1629, the West India Company changed its land policy to permit colonists to obtain estates. A document called a Charter of Freedom and Exemptions issued in that year permitted the creation of vast manorial estates, called patroonships. A responsible citizen of Holland who would promise to settle fifty adults in New Netherland could obtain a grant of land extending sixteen miles along one side of any navigable stream, or eight miles on both sides, as far "into the country as the situation of the occupiers shall permit. The grantee, known as a patroon, was required to compensate Indians for his land and had rights similar to those of an English lord of a manor. Within certain limits, he could impose regulations with the force of law, hold manorial courts from which defendants could appeal to the director and council of New Netherland, collect rents, and dispose of his grant by sale or bequest.

Since the West India Company reserved the entirety of the island of Manhattan for its use, land available to patroons lay elsewhere along rivers. Several prosperous investors at once laid claim to patroonships. Samuel Godyn and Samuel Blommaert chose land along the Delaware River; Michael Reyniersz Pauw picked out a vast estate across the Hudson from Manhattan, including Staten Island, and gave to this holding the name Pavonia, a Latinized form of his name.

None of these patroonships proved as successful, however, as one on both sides of the Hudson in the vicinity of Fort Orange called Rensselaerswyck in honor of its patroon, Kiliaen Van Rensselaer, a wealthy jeweler of Amsterdam who decided to become a landowner in the New World. Although Van Rensselaer did not emigrate, he sent over the largest group of colonists recruited by any individual landowner. To promote their spiritual welfare - and to convert the Indians - he enlisted a minister, Johannes Megapolensis, who contracted in 1642 to go to the New World for six years.

A description of the country and the Indians, published by Megapolensis in 1644 as *A Short Account of the Mohawk Indians,* gave a favorable picture of the land, if not of its native people. Megapolensis was impressed with the richness of the soil. Strawberries were so abundant, he said, that a man could lie down in a field and eat his fill. Grape-laden vines climbed to the tops of trees. The grapes were excellent for wine, as the parson discovered via his experiments, "and the color of the grape juice here is so high and red that with one wine-glass full you can color a whole pot of white wine." Game was so plentiful, he reported, that turkeys and deer came to feed around the houses, and during the spring and autumn a settler could stand at his door and shoot all the ducks and geese he needed.

When it came to the original inhabitants of this earthly paradise, Megapolensis was less enthusiastic. The Mohawks carried on fierce wars with the Indians allied with the French. He took pains to point out that "though they are so very cruel to their enemies, they are very friendly to us, and we have no dread of them." Mohawk women, the preacher asserted, "are exceedingly addicted to whoring; they will lie with a man for the value of one, two, or three schillings [twelve cents] and our Dutchmen run after them very much."

Although Kiliaen Van Rensselaer was eager for profits from trade, he was anxious to develop a farming economy in his American barony. The emigrants he sent over were for the most part farmers, who cleared land and planted grain and tobacco on farms they held as tenants of Van Rensselaer. Taught by the example set by farmers of Rensselaerswyck, other colonists found an agriculture prosperity greater than they had dreamed of when they first had faced the task of clearing the forests. Cattle thrived on the grass and wild forage, and hogs roamed the woods and fattened on acorns and other food they found. The rich soil produced large crops of wheat, rye, barley, Indian corn, and tobacco. Farmers hardly could have found a more favored place than the river valleys of New Netherland.

Two flaws, however, prevented the rapid development of the land. Unfriendly Indian tribes were a constant hazard every settler had to take into account, and the West India Company at first did not make it easy for small farmers to acquire land. Since most emigrants came to the New

World in search of land, the company had to make it possible for farmers to obtain property without becoming tenants of some great patroon.

The settlers around Fort Orange negotiated a treaty with the Mohawks that enabled farmers of Rensselaerswyck to live in relative peace, but further south the Dutch were not so farsighted. Although the Dutch bought land from the Indians, they habitually cheated the natives. During the regime of Wouter Van Twiller (a nephew of Kiliaen Van Rensselaer), who succeeded Sebastiaen Jansen Krol as director general of New Netherland, the Dutch established an uneasy peace with the Indians on upper Manhattan and along the lower Hudson, but it was not destined to last. Van Twiller, remembered in legends of New York as a drunken incompetent, won the friendship of the Indians, partly by honest dealing, partly by providing them with liquor. When at last, in 1637, complaints against Van Twiller forced the West India Company to recall him, they sent Willem Kieft, a more sober but harsher man, as director general. Kieft precipitated a war that brought ruin upon the colony and threatened to destroy most of the settlements below Fort Orange.

During the years before Kieft took over, colonists established many scattered settlements that could not be defended easily. English settlers had filtered into Dutch territory from Massachusetts Bay and other English colonies. Anne Hutchinson, who had stirred a religious controversy in Boston, ultimately moved with her family and a few friends from Rhode Island to Long Island, where the Dutch let her preach as she pleased. Other nationalities established farms in Dutch territory. A Dane named Jonas Bronck settled a spot that eventually took its name from him and became the Bronx. A Dutchman, who insisted on his title of *jonker*, had an estate north of the Harlem River that is today's Yonkers. Many isolated farms were being cultivated on upper Manhattan, on Long Island, and along the Hudson River. Their prosperity, indeed their very existence, depended on keeping peace with the Indians. If Kieft understood this fact, he showed no capacity to act on it, and the measures he took incited disaster.

Kieft accused Indians of many crimes that Dutchmen had committed, and his soldiers shot natives with little thought of the revenge their tribesmen might exact. When Indians killed a Dutch wheelwright on Manhattan, Kieft planned their extermination. In February 1643, he sent troops to Staten Island, where they slaughtered at least eighty Indian, men, women, and children, and in another assault, assassinated forty more, deeds that prompted a critic of Kieft's, David De Vries, to ask: "Did the Duke of Alva in the Netherlands ever do anything more cruel?" If Kieft's cruelty had brought the Indians into subjugation, he might have argued his actions were justified by dangers to his people. But on the contrary, his wanton slaughter merely enraged the tribesmen to a general attack on outlying farms. Anne Hutchinson, her family, and many other settlers on Long Island, Manhattan, and elsewhere in New Netherland were killed.

To protect lower Manhattan, Kieft built a palisade of heavy timbers (the line of his fortified barricade against raiding Indians became Wall Street). Had it not been for English volunteers, recruited by Isaac Allerton, one of the Mayflower passengers who had moved from Plymouth to New Netherland, the Dutch settlements around Manhattan might have been destroyed. But Allerton persuaded Captain John Underhill, a mercenary who had been banished from Massachusetts Bay for heresy, to organize a company of English settlers for war against the Indians of the lower Hudson Valley. In February 1644, Underhill joined the Dutch in an attack on an encampment of Indians in Westchester that left between 500 and 700 dead Indians on the field. The war dragged on until in August 1645, the Mohawks helped negotiate a peace treaty with the Indians to the south. Had the Dutch not maintained their alliance with the Mohawks, the French, with their Algonquin allies, might have occupied the Hudson Valley and created a wedge between the English colonies on the Atlantic seaboard. Thus in 1645, the Mohawks helped the Dutch end a war that threatened the life of the colony.

Isaac Allerton, Captain Underhill, and the English militia who aided the Dutch against the Indians had a stake in the welfare of New Netherland. Englishmen had infiltrated Dutch territory on Long Island and disputed territory in the Connecticut and Delaware valleys. Some had settled legally, but others had simply moved in as squatters. They were a potential danger to Dutch sovereignty in the event of a conflict with the English, who never had conceded Dutch rights to territory in North America.

Kieft's rule over New Netherland proved as unpopular as it was incompetent. To placate his people, he was forced to permit the election of a body of twelve counselors, called simply the Twelve, who later were replaced by a smaller body called the Eight. The complaints of these counselors to the West India Company resulted in Kieft's replacement by Petrus Stuyvesant.

Stuyvesant had experience as a soldier and administrator. He had served the West India Company in Brazil and in 1643 was governor of Curaçao. On a military expedition against a French fort on the island of St. Martin the next year, he lost a leg. But its replacement was no ordinary wooden leg; to call attention to his loss in the service of his country, Stuyvesant had the prosthesis decorated with silver bands, and he was sometimes referred to as Old Silver-Leg. In 1646, he received a commission as director general of New Netherland. When he reached New Amsterdam in May 1647, citizens of that town, eager to give him a royal welcome, were taken aback at his arrogance, which, one observer noted, was as great as if he had been the czar of Muscovy.

Stuyvesant, the son of an orthodox minister of the Dutch Reformed Church, had a Calvinistic assurance of his own right to prescribe law and justice for colonists, and he failed to encourage any religions other than the Reformed Church. Dissenters might worship in secret, but no other church would be approved openly. If the mother country had more liberal views, that did not bother Stuyvesant. In New Netherland, he was the law.

Despite his arbitrary and often tyrannical rule, Stuyvesant was New Netherland's most competent director general. He brought order out of administrative chaos, imposed discipline on an unruly citizenry, curbed the sale of liquor in New Amsterdam, and restricted the use of brandy and guns in trade with the Indians. He was determined to make a successful colony of New Netherland despite its citizens.

When Stuyvesant began his rule, New Amsterdam lacked schools. A church started earlier was unfinished. One- fourth of all buildings in the town were taphouses, and loafing and drunkenness in these taverns created a public scandal. Stuyvesant began to address these issues with Calvinistic zeal.

Though his motives were often well-intentioned, he was a dictator at heart and antagonized the populace. Realizing he must give the people some voice in government, he appointed a board called the Nine from a list of eighteen men elected by inhabitants. The Nine quickly exerted pressure to modify the dictatorial rule of the director by sending to the States-General a *Remonstrance of New Netherland,* drawn up by Adriaen Van der Donck. This document asked for a reduction in taxes and port duties, a reduction in the number of traders licensed for business in New Netherland, and an increase in the number of farmers sent to colonize. It requested schoolmasters for children, adequate public buildings including a schoolhouse, and rulers "not too covetous." The document appealed to the States-General to take the colony under its authority and thus end the monopoly of the West India Company. Just as a joint stock company in control at Jamestown had proved inadequate for the larger purposes of colonial development, so the West India Company, intent upon profits for shareholders, had proved inadequate in the New Netherland colony.

The West India Company, however, was not ready to surrender to the States-General. To prevent control by the government, the company made some concessions, including the establishment of a town government for New Amsterdam modeled on the type of town government in Holland. A municipal charter created two classes of citizens, greater burghers and lesser burghers. One could become a greater burgher by purchasing the right for fifty guilders; thus the rank was ensured to the wealthy, although military officers, preachers, and government officials enjoyed the rank without payment of a fee. Although this effort to establish class distinctions by law was abandoned after the English took over New Netherland, the notion of a mercantile aristocracy was prophetic of a social evolution that eventually occurred in America.

A development on the Delaware River threatened Dutch claims in that area and provided Stuyvesant with an opportunity for action that pleased the veteran of wars against the Portuguese. This time the enemy was Swedish. Stuyvesant disliked the Swedes on two counts - they were interlopers, and they were Lutherans - and he intended to exclude them from the territories of New Netherland.

Ironically, the Swedes had first entered the Delaware Valley under the leadership of the same Peter Minuit, who had purchased Manhattan Island for the Dutch. In the 1630s, Sweden, then leading a crusade against the Hapsburgs and the power of Catholic Spain, were determined to create a base for attacking Spanish possessions in the New World. At the same time, its rulers hoped to reap some of the profits of colonial trade. To that end, Sweden chartered in 1637 the New Sweden Company, modeled after the Dutch West India Company, and sent Minuit with a party of Swedes and Dutchmen to settle on the Delaware. Minuit selected a spot where the city of Wilmington now stands and called it Fort Christina after the Swedish princess and later queen.

Sweden, like Holland, had no surplus population or dissident groups who wished to emigrate, and enlisting settlers for New Sweden was difficult. Since the Finns, a minority in Sweden, were typically skilled woodworkers, the New Sweden Company induced a few to settle on the Delaware to help clear the forests. But try as it might, Sweden could not inspire any enthusiasm for emigration to America. The New Sweden Company found the fur trade sufficiently profitable to maintain its bases on the lower Delaware, but it could not develop the back country. So the Dutch retained a tenuous hold on the upper Delaware with a few soldiers at Fort Nassau and watched with misgivings as the Swedes established themselves on the lower portion of the river. Since the infiltration of English settlers from neighboring colonies threatened both, they joined forces against the English invaders and in 1642 burned one of their villages on the Schuylkill.

In the same year, the New Sweden Company sent Johan Printz to be director of the colony. Printz, like

Stuyvesant a veteran soldier, had fought for King Gustavus Adolphus and was a man of courage and competence (because of his huge girth, the Indians called him Big Guts). Between 1643 and 1653, Printz labored to make something of the Swedish colony. He dealt fairly with Indians, kept peace, and increased profits from the fur trade. His continued efforts induced the company to send more farmers and artisans. Some of the English who had become squatters in the valley were so impressed they swore allegiance to Sweden in order to live under Printz's rule. As the colony grew to something approaching 200, Printz moved a few settlers up the river and built two forts there.

As long as the Swedish colony remained a small trading post with little prospect of growing, Stuyvesant tolerated it, but when Printz established additional bases on the Delaware and began to recruit colonists, the Dutch director general acted. Moving 200 men to the Delaware, he attempted to limit Swedish expansion by establishing Fort Casimir between Printz's new fortresses and Fort Christina.

Although Printz strove to recruit settlers and to induce the New Sweden Company to send aid, his efforts had little effect. An insurrection among his people so discouraged him he left the colony to settle its own quarrels and went to New Amsterdam to await a ship bound for Europe. With Printz's departure, the best days of New Sweden ended. Though the Swedes in 1654 sent over another vigorous director, Johan Risingh, with additional settlers, he made the fatal mistake of taking Fort Casimir from the Dutch, an act Stuyvesant would not tolerate. Consequently, in the summer of 1655, Stuyvesant sent troops to the Delaware who forced the capitulation of the Swedes and ended any effective development of a rival colony.

Although the Swedish population never exceeded 200, the Swedes helped establish the Lutheran Church in America. They contributed a technique of building that became enormously useful on the frontier, the use of notched logs to make cabins. Only the Swedes - and later the Germans - used this type of construction, which other frontiersmen adopted.

Dutch rule in New Netherland was coming to an end. After the Restoration of Charles II as king of England, his courtiers began a systematic search for recouping losses they had suffered during the years of Puritan domination. One source of wealth lay in lands across the seas and in trade with the colonies. Charles was prepared to make grants of vaguely defined territory in America, grants that required merely a stroke of the king's pen, for neither he nor his counselors had much knowledge or concern about existing boundaries.

The king's brother, James, Duke of York, fancied the vast territory, claimed by the Dutch, between the Hudson and the Delaware rivers. The Duke of York was head of the Royal African Company, which was intent upon monopolizing the slave trade with the New World, and their chief rival was the Dutch West India Company. As it happened, the duke was also Lord High Admiral in command of Charles II's navy.

In 1664, James dispatched a fleet to American waters to protect English interests against violations of the Navigation Acts and to assert English authority over trespassers on English territory. The worst offender was the West India Company, and at the end of August, the English fleet anchored off New Amsterdam and summoned Peter Stuyvesant to surrender. This was not an act of war against a friendly nation, the duke made clear, but merely a police action to remove trespassers from land rightfully English.

Stuyvesant became enraged. He mounted the ramparts of the fort and threatened to open fire, but his chief gunner informed him the powder was so damp that no proper defense was possible. Stuyvesant then offered to lead his men in an assault upon the English. The parson pleaded with him to be calm, and a petition from the women and children of New Amsterdam begged him to surrender without exposing them to destruction. Though the old director declared he would rather be carried out dead, he agreed to surrender. The

English commander, Colonel Richard Nicolls, named deputy governor, promised to respect all property rights of the Dutch inhabitants and to give them a voice in government. Although Stuyvesant was bitter at having to surrender, he was not so heartbroken that he could not return to New York and live out his days there. He had a farm in the Bowery and a house near the site of St. Mark's Episcopal Church. He died there in 1672 and was buried in a chapel on his farm.

With the exception of a period from July 30, 1673, until November 10, 1674, when the Dutch temporarily regained control, the English henceforth occupied the former Dutch territory and consolidated their possession of the Atlantic seaboard from Maine to Florida. Thereafter, the city on the Hudson and the province would be called New York. The Dutch left their mark, however, on the architecture, customs, business practices, language, and history of New York. Perhaps the most pervasive commercial contribution they made was to introduce Santa Claus to the American people.

The greatest benefit to the English of the Dutch occupation of the Hudson Valley was a gift of time. The Dutch and their Indian allies served as a shield against the French until the English were strong enough to resist French attempts to seize this vital and strategic territory.

6
THE SETTLER S
PROSPER

In the seventy years between 1630 and 1700, English colonists succeeded in establishing an unbroken chain of settlements that spanned the Atlantic seaboard from northern Maine to the Savannah River. The French held Canada and would continue to penetrate the western lake country and the interior river systems to the south. The Spaniards clung to Florida and were a danger on the southern flank of the colonies, not yet protected by friendly settlements in Georgia. But during these seventy years, the English were masters of the intervening coastal regions, consolidated their gains, and gradually began to push inland. Spain and France might threaten, and the English would have to struggle to retain their land and settlements, but England in the seventeenth century gained the strategic bases that enabled it to hold its possessions.

In the North, New England, dominated by the Massachusetts Bay colony, made a phenomenal development, both economically and culturally. The Puritans who settled Massachusetts Bay were driven by purposefulness, energy, and a sense of destiny. Convinced they were chosen of God to create a commonwealth of his saints in America, they were determined to allow neither the forces of nature nor the hostility of the Indians to deter them from their manifest destiny. Equipped with muskets, Bibles, supported by the law, and reinforced with a theology congenial to their spirit, they moved into the wilderness intent on conquering it for themselves and the Lord.

Early in the development of Massachusetts Bay, colonists realized they would require an increasing number of ministers, and to that end in 1636 they established a college in Cambridge, named Harvard after its first benefactor, John Harvard. Many learned men had emigrated to Massachusetts in the period before the outbreak of the Puritan Revolution in 1640, and the colony had a nucleus of scholars and teachers. During the middle years of the seventeenth century, Harvard College earned such a reputation for the purity of its orthodox teaching that some of the stricter Puritans in England sent their sons to Harvard rather than risk their heresy at Oxford and Cambridge. Not all these youths from the mother country were models of behavior. Evidence indicates that some parents looked to Harvard and the rigors of the New World to work a reformation in their errant sons.

Three years after the founding of Harvard College, Stephen Day began operating a printing press in Cambridge, and in 1640, he released the first important work published in English in the New World, *The Whole Book of Psalms,* edited by Richard Mather. Known as the *Bay Psalm Book,* this work was the precursor of a flood of books published in Massachusetts Bay. Most of these publications were works of piety or of religious controversy, but they were indicative of the intellectual caliber of a literate citizenry. Massachusetts Bay was the first colony to have a printing press, and Boston eventually became an important publishing center. It was from Boston that printers went out to the other colonies to establish presses and newspapers.

The printing press in Massachusetts Bay in the seventeenth century was an important instrument for disseminating and propagating religious and secular ideas of the dominant Puritan group. The Mathers alone, Increase and his son Cotton, printed more than 400 titles. Cotton Mather, a zealous propagandist, supplied peddlers with tracts for distribution and even sent printed sermons to

Puritan settlers in South Carolina to keep them from falling into the heresy of Anglicanism.

The main concern of the ruling class in Massachusetts Bay was to maintain their commonwealth of God's saints uncorrupted by outside influences. They felt obliged to prevent schisms in the religious community and exclude heretics from their community. To accomplish this, they had to retain control of the government. But controlling orthodox leaders and maintaining strict conformity proved more difficult to achieve than Winthrop and his colleagues would have believed.

By a curious irony, the abundant resources of Massachusetts Bay helped to disrupt the neat patterns of orthodoxy. The Puritan emphasis upon diligence, thrift, sobriety, and prudential virtues, to the exclusion of every wasteful activity, made prosperity almost inevitable. Since it was sinful to waste God's precious time, and since extravagance and wasteful expenditure were forbidden, a strict Puritan hardly could do otherwise than prosper materially. So the citizens of Massachusetts Bay increased in wealth and praised God. They failed to realize that prosperity would bring with it corruption.

A thrifty population had developed a diversity of trades and industries. Hundreds of farmers combined agricultural pursuits with a variety of home industries: woodworking, barrel making, weaving, tanning, leatherworking, shoemaking, milling, and the manufacture of almost anything required by the demands of everyday life.

The forests of New England supported a thriving shipbuilding industry and also supplied material for the cooper's trade. During the long winters, farmers would make barrel staves and hoops for casks required for wine, oil, and fish - the waters of New England supplied a seemingly infinite quantity of cod, mackerel, and other seafood for the European market. Thousands of casks of salt mackerel were shipped to the West Indies to feed slaves working in sugar cane fields.

From the West Indies, New Englanders imported molasses and sugar and soon learned the art of distilling rum. The rum distilleries of Boston, Newport, and other New England towns provided an invaluable commodity in international trade.

Early in the history of Massachusetts Bay, shipbuilding became an important industry. In 1631, John Winthrop built the *Blessing of the Bay,* whose launching was prophetic of an industry poised for rapid growth. Eleven years later, a much larger vessel, the *Trial,* launched in Boston, and, with a sermon by John Cotton to give it an auspicious start, voyaged to the Canary Islands with a cargo of fish and barrel staves and returned via the West Indies with wine and sugar.

The enterprising captain of the *Trial*, aware that anchors and other hardware for ships were in great demand in Boston, acquired a cargo of these commodities in the West Indies by salvaging them from sunken ships. He obtained fifty guns, a supply of anchors, hardware, and a quantity of cable. He traded some of his wine for cotton and molasses and reached Boston with a mixed cargo of highly profitable wares. The maiden voyage of the *Trial* was an omen of future trade with the Wine Islands and of the development of one element of the famous triangular trading ventures that proved so profitable to New England skippers in years to come. On its second voyage, the *Trial* went to Spain with fish and barrel staves and returned with wine, oil, fruit, iron, and wool.

Other vessels soon followed the method of trade established by the *Trial*. Before the end of the century, ship captains from Massachusetts and Rhode Island discovered the profits to be made in taking rum, distilled from West Indian molasses, to the coast of Africa, where they used it to barter for slaves. The Royal African Company held a monopoly, at least in theory, of the slave trade, but in 1698 Parliament legalized slave trade for private individuals. A traffic in slaves that colonial shippers had conducted surreptitiously before 1698 now lured many New England captains to the African coast.

Slavery was seen at the time as a benefit to mankind - Puritan slave owners justified the practice from Scripture (as southern slave owners in the nineteenth century continued to do). Had not William Perkins, a prominent English preacher, shown that slavery was not against "the law of corrupted nature since the fall [of Adam]"? Were not Christian captains bringing these heathen souls to a land where they could exchange their labor for salvation? For generations to come, New Englanders engaged in the slave trade would thus salve their consciences. Before the development of trade in African slaves, they had trafficked in Indian slaves, whom they sold in the West Indies.

The Reverend Patrick Copland, a preacher in Bermuda, writing to John Winthrop in 1639, commented: "If you send us any more of your captive Indians, I will see them disposed of here to honest men; or if you send mee a couple, a boy and a girl for myselfe, I will pay for their passage, so they be hopefull.

Even so devout a Puritan as Cotton Mather owned both Indian and African slaves. In 1641, a pious citizen of Boston, Samuel Maverick, devised a scheme of making Noddle's Island, now East Boston, a breeding ground for African slaves. Wait Winthrop, writing from Boston on July 7, 1682, to Fitz-John Winthrop, said that a slave named Black Tom threatened to kill himself, and though he thought he was bluffing, it might be well to sell him in Virginia or the West Indies.

By 1676, more than 230 vessels called Boston their home port. Other towns, especially Newport, had vessels engaged in international trade. Sometimes these ships were loaded with cargo and taken to England, where both cargo and craft were sold. The export of ships built in New England was an important component of the developing industry of that region.

Not only were New England sailors exposed to outside influences in foreign ports, but many vessels from England, Holland, and other countries also brought to New England foreigners with alien customs. Some ships, particularly those from Holland, brought contraband that was delivered without the payment of duties, since New Englanders, despite their religion, were not immune to smuggling. Foreign sailors swaggering about Boston paid little attention to disapproving Puritans and disregarded conventions in a way that Boston youths were ready to imitate. In 1699, Ned Ward wrote that Lecture Days were "call'd by some amongst them Whore Fair," and that many young people after wanton pleasure "have recourse to the Ordinaries, where they plentifully wash away the remembrance of their Old Sins, and drink down the fear of a Fine or the dread of a Whipping-post."

Even Harvard College reflected the iniquity

of the times. On May 5, 1672, a group of irate citizens presented a petition to the magistrates of Massachusetts Bay against the ungodliness of Harvard in permitting students to wear their hair long. Petitioners desired "the removal of an evyl (as it appereth to us) in the educasion of youth at the Colledg and that is, that they are brought up in such pride as doth no waves become such as are brought up for the holy service of the lord, either in the Magistracy, or ministry especialy and in perticular in their long haire, which last first tooke head, and broke out at the Colledg so far as we understand and remember, and now it is got into our pulpits, to the great greife and feare of many godly hearts in the Country." Pious citizens recalled earlier days of the colony fondly. Although virtue, even in the first years, had not always prevailed, conditions toward the end of the century were more distressing to strict Puritans.

If worldliness and iniquity undermined the authority and effectiveness of the agents of the Lord in Massachusetts Bay, these Christian warriors battled long and earnestly against the hosts of Satan. They used every weapon in their arsenal to eliminate nonconformity and heresy and to punish sinners. Wickedness they made as unprofitable and unpopular as possible, and they struggled to maintain the authority of the church by means of civil law. For many years, only church members could vote, and only those who had experienced conversion were admitted to the church. But as Massachusetts Bay grew, the proportion of church members diminished until even the ruling oligarchy was forced to consider broadening the franchise. They brought this about by a compromise known as the Halfway Covenant, adopted by churches in 1662, which provided that children of church members, even though they could not avow they had experienced salvation, might be admitted to church membership and thus vote, though they could not take the sacrament of the Lord's Supper. This crack in the monolithic authority of the church signified a gradual weakening of theocratic influence.

As much as the rulers tried, they could not suppress all manifestations of independence. One institution that became famous as the epitome of democratic institutions, the town meeting, provided a platform to express opinions. Everyone, whether church member or otherwise, could attend a town meeting, to present petitions, to complain, either verbally or in writing, against any injustice or inequity, and to express any opinion that seemed pertinent. The town meeting became the means of shaping public opinion, and not even the most fanatical members of the oligarchy could flout public opinion indefinitely. By degrees, democratic institutions and procedures were introduced.

Under the charter John Winthrop and his

colleagues brought with them to Massachusetts Bay, the colony was virtually independent, but the freedom of the Puritan commonwealth from interference depended upon the continuance of that charter. Naturally, the Puritans regarded the charter as their Magna Charta. So long as they were an obscure and distant group of dissidents, better forgotten than remembered, the home government left them undisturbed. But when Massachusetts Bay grew wealthy and capable of launching satellite settlements in adjacent regions, authorities in London began to look closer at it, and what they saw did not always please them.

Under an economic theory described as mercantilism, the English government regarded colonies as the source of raw materials needed by the mother country and as a market for manufactured products produced in England. Raw materials had to be processed in England and shipped to England in English or colonial vessels. The idea was to create a self-sufficient empire. Beginning in 1650, Parliament passed a series of laws, known as the Navigation Acts, to implement the mercantilist doctrine and to prevent outsiders, particularly the Dutch with their enterprising merchant marine, from usurping trade the English claimed for themselves.

During the reign of Charles II, colonial affairs had become so important that in 1675, he appointed a special committee from the Privy Council, known as the Lords of Trade, to administer the business of the colonies. In 1696, to increase scrutiny of colonial matters, William III reorganized the administrative control of the colonies by placing responsibility for them in a Board of Trade and Plantations, usually referred to simply as the Board of Trade.

The English colonies had been doing business with the Dutch before the first of the Navigation Acts, and New England continued, more or less openly, to engage in trade against the law. The laxity of enforcement of the laws of trade, particularly in Massachusetts Bay, displeased London so much that in 1676, the Lords of Trade dispatched an inquisitive agent, Edward Randolph, to investigate and report on the state of affairs in New England. Randolph, loyal to Charles II and the Church of England, could find little good about the people of New England. He described the harshness of their laws, their persecution of those who did not conform to their religion, their evasion of the Navigation Acts, and their arrogant and independent ways. Since Randolph's charges confirmed views already held by the Lords of Trade, they persuaded the king on October 23, 1684, to nullify the charter of Massachusetts Bay.

For a time, the colony was without any legal government, for the governor, the magistrates, and the deputies chosen by the electorate under the charter no longer had any official status. After a few years of a provisional government dictated by London, the Lords of Trade appointed Sir Edmund Andros as governor general of New England. Rhode Island and Connecticut were required to surrender their charters and submit to Andros' rule. Connecticut made the rather futile gesture of hiding its charter in a tree instead of surrendering it, but that did not prevent Andros from extending his authority over that colony.

In 1688, two years after Andros' arrival in New England, London authorities commissioned him to extend his rule over New York and the Jerseys, but the overthrow of James II in the Glorious Revolution of 1688 gave colonists an opportunity to rebel. They resumed their former status, and Massachusetts sent Increase Mather to London to plead for renewal of its charter. In 1691, Mather managed to procure a compromise charter, under which William III appointed the governor, and the electorate chose a legislative assembly that in turn chose the governor's council. Under this charter, Massachusetts relinquished control over New Hampshire, which became an independent colony. Maine, however, remained under the jurisdiction of Massachusetts until the early years of the nineteenth century.

Another calamity that overtook the orthodox Puritans of the Bay colony, along with the loss of their charter, was the arrival in Boston in 1686 of the Reverend Robert Ratcliffe, an Anglican minister who organized the first congregation of the Church of England in Boston. To the dismay of Puritan conservatives, he obtained permission to hold service in Old South Meetinghouse before the regular Congregational service on Sunday.

If the Puritans had failed to keep Boston virtuous, it was not for lack of diligence in decrying heresy and in casting out nonconformists. Many settlers in Rhode Island, New Hampshire, and even Connecticut had left Massachusetts after being reminded of their obligation to conform. A few had not been lucky enough to escape and had suffered for their unorthodoxy.

The Puritans of Massachusetts Bay were particularly disturbed by Quakers, who came to Boston despite the threat of death. In 1658, two ministers of Boston, the Reverend John Norton and the Reverend Charles Chauncy, persuaded the General Court it was imperative to impose capital punishment on Quakers who insisted upon returning after banishment. Otherwise, they pointed out, these pests would plague Boston forever. Two years before, in 1656, Mary Fisher and Ann Austin, Quakers from Barbados, had suffered for five weeks in a cell without light after being stripped and searched for signs that might identify them as witches and provide a legal reason for hanging them. At the time, authorities had just convicted Ann Hibbens of witchcraft and hanged her.

The two parsons assured the General Court that the laws against Quakers were too lenient, for they permitted only torture, imprisonment, mutilation, and banishment. For example, they argued, authorities had to release an elderly man named William Brend with only torture: He had his heels and his neck locked together for sixteen hours and then was beaten into unconsciousness with 117 lashes applied with a tarred rope that cut flesh from his back. The populace of Boston had not seen the justice of this punishment and had rebelled, but Parson Norton delivered a sermon defending the sentence and the jailer who carried it out.

After 1658, the law was clear. Quakers could be hanged for returning after banishment, and in October 1659, John Endecott and fellow judges sent William Robinson and Marmaduke Stevenson to the gallows. A third member of the group, Mary Dyer, was sentenced to hang but was reprieved at the place of execution and banished. When she insisted upon returning the next year, she was hanged.

The Quakers, then more assertive than they later became, upset the religious Bostonians. For example, a Quaker had gone to Rome to convert the pope. Another had journeyed to Constantinople and had attempted to convert a sultan. Others had made disturbances in church and had interrupted sermons of the most respected ministers. They refused to pay certain taxes or to take oaths. The orthodox people of Massachusetts Bay saw no reason why they should tolerate them.

Traditionally, saints suffer many temptations to test their virtue and try their patience, and the founding fathers of New England felt they were in a similar situation. They were obsessed with the notion that Satan had singled them out for attack. For this reason, they felt they had to remain vigilant and stamp out satanic influences as quickly as they spotted them. One of Satan's most effective agencies for evil, the Puritans believed, was witchcraft. And although the belief in witchcraft was not confined to Puritans, they were the most vigorous witch hunters in the seventeenth century.

From 1647 until the end of the century, Massachusetts Bay and Connecticut were particularly concerned about witches and sought zealously to eradicate them. The largest campaign took place between 1688 and 1693. Increase and Cotton Mather endorsed witch hunting. In 1684, Increase Mather published *An Essay for the Recording of Illustrious Providences,* which a populace already in an uproar over supernatural appearances eagerly read. Mather quoted from the church fathers, classical writers, and theologians to prove the existence of black and white witches, and he called the wrath of God upon both. "They that do hurt to others by the devil's help are called black witches," he explained, "but there are a sort of persons in the world that will never hurt any; but only by the power of the infernal spirits will un-bewitch those that seek unto them for relief. I know that by Constantius his law, black witches were to be punished, and white ones indulged; but M. Perkins saith, that the good witch is a more horrible and detestable monster than the bad one."

Five years later, when children of a Boston brick-mason named Goodwin claimed they were bewitched, Cotton Mather undertook a careful examination of the case and wrote an analysis, *Memorable Providences Relating to Witchcrafts and Possessions*, which helped to confirm fears that were tormenting the community. Between 1689 and 1692 more than 200 in Massachusetts and Connecticut were accused of witchcraft, and more than twenty were hanged. One older man, Giles Corey, confused and perplexed by charges against him, refused to plead either guilty or not guilty. For this offense, he suffered the penalty prescribed by English common law: pressed to death under heavy weights.

Although the hysteria enveloped several communities, it was most intense in Salem, for there witches were believed to have congregated - and the imaginations of the residents of Salem were inflamed. Cotton Mather lent his help to judges and offered expert testimony. The hysteria reached its peak in 1692, and the next year Mather published *Wonders of the Invisible World*, which defended the decisions of the Salem judges. The clergy had staked its prestige on the trials.

The persecution ended when a few prominent men protested. Thomas Brattle, a merchant of Boston, castigated prosecutors of witches as ignoramuses. In 1700, another merchant, Robert Calef, published a satirical attack on the credulity of the Mathers in a pamphlet entitled *More Wonders of the Invisible World*. Yet the prestige of the Mathers was such that no Boston printer would publish Calef's pamphlet. It was produced in London. Many New Englanders, including Judge Samuel Sewall of Boston, expressed regret over the excesses of the witchcraft trials. The part the clergy played in the trials damaged its reputation and weakened its influence in Massachusetts Bay.

While the witchcraft fury was raging, a colorful figure arrived in Boston to serve as royal governor. Sir William Phips, erstwhile ship's carpenter and contractor of Boston, had done what thousands had dreamed of: He discovered a sunken Spanish treasure ship off Haiti and succeeded in recovering gold, silver, and jewels worth more than 300,000 pounds. For this exploit, King James II in 1687 dubbed him knight. One of Phips' first duties upon arriving in Boston in May 1692 was to appoint William Stoughton, a fervent believer in the evils of witchcraft, to serve as judge in the Salem witch trials. Later, when even Phips came to believe the prosecution of witches had gone too far, he blamed the excess on Stoughton.

Once a companion of dubious waterfront characters in the days before the discovery of the Spanish treasure, Phips as governor was not above allowing piracy and smuggling. Thrifty and arrogant, he once publicly caned the captain of an English man-of-war. On another occasion, he pushed a customs officer off a wharf. In 1694, Phips was summoned to England to account for his shortcomings as governor, but he died before his case was heard.

West of the coastal regions, settlers were developing the back country. Colonists moved into the Connecticut River Valley as far as Deerfield and beyond. Farms dotted other river valleys, and farmers on these frontiers frequently engaged in peaceful fur trade with the local Indians. For the most part, New England had been lucky when it came to Indian relations. The first settlers found the coastal tribes so decimated by an epidemic that they posed little threat to the white invaders. Occasional quarrels between European traders and Indians caused trouble to outlying settlements. A series of murders and punitive measures by the whites led in 1637 to an outbreak of war with the Pequot Indians in the lower Connecticut Valley in which that tribe was virtually annihilated. Captain John Mason led an expedition that surrounded more than 400 Pequots in a palisaded fort on the Mystic River. Setting fire to the fort in the night, Mason's men burned all but seven occupants to death. William Bradford, describing this episode, commented: "It was conceived they thus destroyed about 400 at this time. It was a fearfull sight to see them thus frying in the fyer, and the streams of blood quenching the same, and horrible was the stinck and sente ther of; but the victory seemed a sweete sacrifice, and they gave the prays thereof to God, who had wrought so wonderfuly for them, thus to inclose their enimise in their hands, and give them so speedy a victory over so proud and insulting an enimie."

Before the campaign against the Pequots was over, militiamen had killed or captured more than 700 Indians. Indian captives were highly prized, for they could be sold as slaves in the West Indies or traded for more tractable African slaves. The Reverend Hugh Peter wrote to Governor Winthrop requesting a few slaves for himself: "Sir, Mr. Endecot and myself salute you in the Lord Jesus. Wee have heard of a dividence of women and children in the bay and would bee glad of a share viz: a young woman or girle and a boy if you thinke good. I wrote to you for some boyes for Bermudas, which

I thinke is considerable." They received seventeen Indian slaves - fifteen boys and two women.

For nearly forty years after the subjugation of the Pequots, there were few clashes between the colonists and the Indians. White settlers pushed into the interior and acquired land Indians once used. Some of this land came via treaty and purchase; some came into official possession of the colonies of Plymouth, Connecticut, or Massachusetts Bay as compensation for alleged wrongs committed by Indians. It became an easy matter to find a reason for imposing fines on the Indians, who could pay only by surrendering tribal lands.

During this period of peace, missionaries worked to convert Indians to Christianity, especially among tribes too weak to retain independence from stronger tribes. The Reverend John Eliot of Roxbury, who labored to gather the heathen into the Christian fold, conceived the notion of settling the "praying Indians" into towns, and established fourteen such settlements by 1674. Daniel Gookin, a devout Puritan who formerly lived in Virginia and Maryland, moved to Roxbury in 1644 and collaborated with Eliot in proselytizing to the Indians. Eliot's most remarkable feat was the translation of the Bible into the Indian language. The New Testament was printed in 1661 and the Old Testament in 1663, the first complete Bible to be printed in British America.

In 1675, the colonies' demands for land and the efforts of the Puritans to force the Indians to obey their laws precipitated a rebellion that involved most of the coastal Indians of New England. The conflict is known as King Philip's War, for Metacomet, whom the English called King Philip, son of Massasoit, leader of the Wampanoag tribe. Metacomet and his tribe were bitter over their treatment by Plymouth colony. Particularly unjust, the Indians felt, was the colony's demand they surrender guns they had bought legally at great cost from Plymouth traders. Metacomet was ordered to pay fines for tribal misdemeanors, sign away land, and declare himself the subject of the governor of Plymouth and king of England.

Humiliated by continued indignities, he at last revolted. Other tribes followed Metacomet's example, and the outlying districts of New England rang with the war cry of marauding Indians who burned isolated farmhouses and villages and slaughtered men, women, and children. In September, a band of Metacomet's warriors attacked Deerfield and shortly thereafter came upon a troop of colonial soldiers and killed sixty-four at a stream that ever since has been called Bloody Brook.

The flames of war enveloped the frontier from Maine to New York. Before it was over, the Indians had killed one man out of every sixteen able to bear arms. In Massachusetts, the Indians destroyed sixteen towns. Eventually, the colonists gained the advantage. An Indian friendly to the Europeans killed Metacomet in a swamp in August 1676. After almost two more years of frontier conflict, a treaty brought an uneasy peace. Many Indian captives, including Metacomet's wife and son, were sold as slaves in the West Indies. Some whites captured by the Indians never returned. One who did, Mary Rowlandson, left a vivid account of her sufferings, first printed in 1682 as *A Narrative of the Captivity and Restauration of Mrs. Mary Rowlandson.* Rowlandson's descriptions of the cruelty displayed by the Indians helps explain the vindictiveness of the whites. It led to the persecution of Christian Indians, who had remained loyal to the settlers, and to threats of violence against John Eliot and Daniel Gookin, who befriended them. After King Philip's War, missionary activity on the frontier virtually ceased, despite Eliot's continued efforts. The savagery of King Philip's War was a prelude to the fierce conflicts of the eighteenth century, when French Canada and English America involved the Indians in the dynastic wars of Europe.

While enterprising New Englanders were exploring and settling river valleys, moving west, and displacing Indians, colonists in New York and New Jersey were extending the settled areas of those regions.

The Duke of York, who assumed the proprietorship of New York after the displacement of the Dutch West India Company, had as his administrator Colonel Richard Nicolls. In 1665, Nicolls put into effect a code known as the Duke's Laws, which proved useful in melding the Dutch and English elements. However, the Duke of York was opposed to popular government and for several years refused to authorize a legislative assembly, which he suspected of "dangerous consequence, nothing being more known than the aptness of such bodies to assume to themselves many privileges which prove destructive to, or very oft disturb, the peace of the government wherein they are allowed." In 1683, however, continued pressure from English settlements, particularly those on Long Island, forced the duke to call an assembly representing the landed property holders. They drew up a Charter of Liberties and Privileges, which the duke approved, but before it became the operating constitution for the colony, the duke had ascended the throne as James II and at once attempted to change the governments of New York and New England.

Shortly after the Duke of York had taken over New York, his brother, Charles II, with careless generosity and an indifference to precise geography, awarded him not only New York, but much of what is now New Jersey. In turn, the Duke of York transferred his right to the territory between the Hudson and the Delaware rivers to two courtiers,

John Berkeley and Sir George Carteret, who had defended the island of Jersey off the English coast against Puritan troops. As a compliment to Carteret, the territory was given the name of New Jersey. These proprietors divided the grant between them, Berkeley taking West Jersey and Carteret East Jersey. Berkeley soon sold his portion to two Quakers, John Fenwick and Edward Byllinge, who quarreled so bitterly over the division of the land they had to ask William Penn to mediate, a move that resulted in piquing Penn's interest in America.

Both Quakers eventually sold their proprietary rights to others. Thus, the problem of land tenure in West Jersey became complicated. When Carteret died, his widow sold his rights to East Jersey to a syndicate of twelve men, who later added twelve more. As they bequeathed their proprietary rights to numerous heirs, the problem of land tenure in East Jersey became as complicated as that in West Jersey. To this day, proprietary boards are necessary in New Jersey to untangle titles to landed property.

The two Jerseys attracted settlers of all kinds. Persecuted Quakers from England flocked to West Jersey and established prosperous communities at Burlington, Salem, and Greenwich. They combined trade, farming, and industry. Like New Englanders, they became shipbuilders. Some developed plantations, and if they had any distaste for slavery, it was overcome by the need for servants to work their farms. Since landowners in the two Jerseys and New York were eager for immigrants willing to rent or purchase land outright, they showed little concern about the religious or political beliefs of settlers. As a result, these colonies developed a more diverse population than existed in New England. Quakers, Catholics, French Huguenots, Germans from the Palatinate, Scots, Irish, Jews, and an occasional adventurer from other countries of Western Europe found a welcome and an opportunity to acquire land in the Jerseys and New York.

In the second half of the seventeenth century, the province of New York was developing social qualities that would be characteristic of its history. Merchants, who had gained wealth in trade through the growing port of New York, sought land in the interior, and many assembled vast estates. Toward the end of the century, royal governors designated some of these estates as manors and invested the owners with the privileges accorded lords of manors in England. These landowners constituted an aristocracy that monopolized power and privilege in the province. Their names comprise a significant place in the history of New York.

In 1693, for example, Frederick Philipse, a merchant-trader, shrewdly managed to stay in favor with the ruling power, whether it was Dutch or English. His ships traded with pirates off the Madagascar coast, and he consolidated large blocks of land into the manor of Philipsburgh and built Castle Philipse in Sleepy Hollow and the Manor Hall in Yonkers, landmarks of early New York. In 1686, Robert Livingston, a refugee Scot, received a patent for the manor of Livingston, which consisted of at least 160,000 acres in Dutchess and Columbia counties. In 1697, Stephanus Van Cortlandt obtained a patent for the manor of Van Cortlandt, comprising 85,000 acres in the Hudson highlands. He wielded great power over the lower Hudson Valley. Peter Schuyler, made mayor of Albany when that town was incorporated in 1686, owned enormous holdings of land on the upper Hudson. He gained the friendship of the Iroquois Indians with whom he traded and was one of several successive landowners in upper New York who maintained the alliance with the Iroquois against the Algonquins and the French. All these magnates exerted an enormous influence on provincial government. The power that the merchant-landowners gained in New York in the seventeenth century was challenged but never broken during the colonial period.

Since manorial estates had to be populated and worked, proprietors tried to attract tenants by offering land on easy terms. Some land they rented; other tracts they sold outright. Small traders also could buy land from the Indians, and in time many yeoman farmers secured their own in the province of New York, as they had in New

Jersey. As these small farmers grew, they became increasingly restive under the domination of the land barons, who continued to hold advantages in the assessment of taxes and to monopolize public offices and opportunities for adding more land to their holdings.

Discontent over the power and arrogance of the wealthy aristocracy reached its zenith in 1689, in a conflict known as the Leisler Rebellion, a movement so muddled by prejudice and personal animosities that a clear understanding of all the issues is difficult to ascertain.

When James II named Sir Edmund Andros governor general of New York, he appointed Francis Nicholson lieutenant governor. A few months later, James was deposed and succeeded by William of Orange and Mary (daughter of James II). Andros, who had ruled New England since 1686, incurred so much hostility that New Englanders rose against him in April 1689, immediately after they heard news of James II's deposition, and imprisoned him. That left Nicholson, his lieutenant, as acting governor of New York, but public opinion and a man named Jacob Leisler unseated him.

Leisler, a soldier who had come to the New World as an employee of the Dutch West India Company, married the rich widow of Pieter Van der Veen and grew wealthy himself in the fur, tobacco, and wine trade. A devout member of the Dutch Reformed

Church, he resented the appointment of an Anglican parson to serve as pastor of his church and became convinced Anglicans and Catholics were about to restore the authority of King James in the province. Nicholson was accused of being in the conspiracy. Wild rumors circulated that papists were plotting with the French to invade the colony from Canada and slaughter Protestants. At this juncture, Leisler, a militia officer, announced his intention of saving New York for William and Mary. He made himself commander of the militia, seized the fort, and assumed the title of lieutenant governor. Then, in 1690, a legislature called by Leisler enacted a law that abolished special privileges enjoyed by the merchants of New York City and declared all towns in the province should have equal rights to sell and distribute their goods and produce where they wished. Nicholson escaped to England.

Leisler, an obstinate man, was unpopular among the merchants of New York, and now the magnates looked upon him as a troublemaker. Yet tradesmen and yeoman farmers flocked to his support, and the disturbance took appearances of a class struggle.

At this point, William and Mary commissioned a royal governor, Colonel Henry Sloughter, and sent with him two companies of troops, commanded by Major Richard Ingoldesby, to resolve the conflict. When the troops arrived in January 1691, ahead of the governor, Leisler refused to surrender to Ingoldesby and on March 17 fired on the royal troops, killing two. This act sealed his fate. When Governor Sloughter arrived and received Leisler's surrender, the governor placed him, his son-in-law, Jacob Milborne, and eight others under arrest, charged with treason. Tried before judges already convinced of their subversiveness, Leisler and Milborne were condemned to death and hanged. (It was reported the executioners obtained Sloughter's signature to the death warrant while the governor was drunk, a frequent occurrence.) Thus ended Leisler's Rebellion - but not the underlying discontent against aristocratic monopolists in the province of New York. Class feeling and the bitterness engendered by Leisler's execution long plagued New York politics.

Despite Indian wars, the growing threat of French intervention, and occasional periods - typified by Leisler's Rebellion - when home rule was interrupted, the colonies in the North prospered. By the latter years of the seventeenth century, New England was a populous region with growing towns stretching from Maine to New York, and England had established its claim to a valuable portion of the New World.

7
YEARS OF EXPANSION

The rapid growth of Pennsylvania in the last two decades of the seventeenth century was the result to a large degree of William Penn's skill as a real-estate salesman and advertiser. Along with an altruistic vision of a domain where fellow Quakers and other oppressed peoples might find peace and prosperity, Penn dreamt of a land where his family would prosper. When Charles II confirmed to him the proprietary grant of the territory of Pennsylvania in 1681, he set out to achieve both goals.

To excite interest among prospective colonists, Penn published his first promotion piece in July 1681, titled *Some account of the province of Pennsilvania in America; Lately Granted under the Great Seal of England to William Penn, etc. Together with Priviledges and Powers necessary to the well-governing thereof. Made publick for the Information of such as are or may be disposed to Transport themselves or Servants into those Parts.* Penn attempted to accurately describe the land he wished to settle, but he also emphasized points that would appeal to persecuted and landless people of Europe. He noted that the "Rights and Freedoms of England (the best and largest in Europe) shall be in force there," and he stressed the ultimate freedom, economic as well as personal, that a colonist might expect. The conditions he outlined were clearly expressed, and he provided information any prospective emigrant would need: the cost of land, the cost of passage, the equipment needed, and the procedure that a settler might expect to follow on first arrival. Land either could be purchased or rented. Buyers might procure land at the cost of 100 pounds for 5,000 acres plus an annual rent of one English shilling per 100 acres. Renters could obtain land for an annual rental of a penny an acre. In addition, anyone who brought servants would be allowed fifty acres for each servant, and the servant, at the expiration of his contracted period of service, would be allowed fifty acres for himself.

To the land-hungry people of Great Britain and the continent, these terms must have read like a promise of prosperity. No one was so poor he could not look forward to being a landowner. Even though he came as a bond servant committed to serve from four to seven years, he could expect to own land when his contract expired.

In 1683, after a visit to his domain, Penn wrote another, more appealing tract bearing the title *A Letter from William Penn . . . to the Committee of the Free Society of Traders of that Province, residing in London,* which provided a matter-of-fact description that managed to convey the notion that the New World was an earthly paradise. It was a land where "the Air is sweet and clear, the Heavens serene, like the South-parts of France, rarely Overcast." The fertility of the varied soils, Penn pointed out, would simplify the growing of the crops, vegetables, fruits, herbs, and trees needed by man. "Of Fowl of the Land," he wrote, "there is Turkey (Forty and Fifty Pound weight) which is very great; Phesants, Heath-Birds, Pidgeons and Partridges in abundance." The duck and teal, Penn maintained, were better than anyone could "ever eat in other Countries."

Of the origin of the Indians, Penn observed: "I am ready to believe them of the Jewish Race, I mean, of the stock of the Ten Tribes" (a misconception that has produced considerable literature). Although he thought Indians were "under a dark Night in things relating to Religion," Penn wrote of them in a way to fascinate rather than frighten his readers, describing them as people in a golden age: "They care for little, because they want but little, and the Reason is, a little contents them. . . . if they are ignorant of our Pleasures, they are also free from our Pains. They are not disquieted with Bills of Lading and Exchange, nor perplexed with Chancery-Suits and Exchequer-Reckonings. We sweat and toil to live; their pleasure feeds them, I mean, their Hunting, Fishing, and Fowling."

Translated into Dutch, French, and German in 1684, this tract was circulated widely in areas where Penn believed he might recruit settlers. A year later, he published *A Further Account of the Province of Pennsylvania*, with a Dutch translation in the same year. This served as a sequel

to his *Letter to the Free Society of Traders* and pointed out improvements and developments occurring in the province. These tracts and other news of Pennsylvania that circulated in Great Britain and on the continent generated widespread interest in Pennsylvania. Ships loaded with immigrants were soon dropping anchor at Philadelphia, and a stream of hopeful settlers began making their way toward the interior of the new colony.

Most of the early colonists in Pennsylvania were English and Welsh Quakers, along with a small number of Welsh Baptists and Anglicans. The Welsh settled on what became known as the Welsh Tract west of the Schuylkill River. There, they prospered, built homes, and bequeathed to their descendants what was to become the most aristocratic section of the Philadelphia region - the Main Line of the late nineteenth century, where Welsh names such as Bryn Mawr, Merion, and Haverford, given by early settlers, survive.

Penn was fair in his dealings, and he compensated the Indians for land he acquired from them. Word of a pact he made with the natives prompted Voltaire to observe that "this is the only treaty between those people and the Christians that was not ratified by an oath and was never infringed." Not until those believers in the Old Testament, the Presbyterians from Scotland, began coveting Indian land did Pennsylvania have conflicts with Indians. The Scots, with ample texts from Scripture, equated the Indians with the Canaanites and found reasons to take their land.

Philadelphia, which Penn's surveyor general, Thomas Holme, had laid out in broad squares, grew rapidly. The more prosperous Quakers bought town lots and built large houses on tree-lined streets. Penn had a house there and another more imposing establishment at Pennsbury in Bucks County. Merchants built warehouses along the Delaware River, which was deep enough to allow ocean-going vessels to tie up at the wharves. Before the end of the century, Philadelphia was a busy port and trading center with the promise of further growth as immigrants arrived to push into the back country.

The promise of a peaceful land where they could worship as they pleased appealed to German Mennonites living in the Rhine Valley who had been harassed by warring armies through much of the seventeenth century. The Mennonites were pacifists, and they came to Pennsylvania in large numbers. In 1683, the first group, led by Francis Daniel Pastorius, a lawyer from Frankfurt, settled near Philadelphia and established a community that came to be known as Germantown. Pastorius' group included other oppressed people searching for freedom and opportunity. During the next forty years, several thousand German and Dutch sectarians (as the first wave of German immigrants were called) settled in Pennsylvania. A few found work in Germantown, but most moved into the country and became farmers. Early in the eighteenth century, thousands of other Germans followed, chiefly of Lutheran and Reformed faiths, many so poor they had to mortgage their freedom for years to pay for their passage. For this reason, they were called redemptioners. The length of time they had to serve before they could redeem themselves and go free ranged from four years to ten years.

Sectarians were varied, for in their strongly individualistic society, anyone with even a slight difference of belief could start another sect. But while their beliefs differed in many important aspects, they shared a common hatred of war and its associations (one sect refused to use buttons on their clothes because they associated brass buttons, and hence all buttons, with military uniforms). Though most were of German origin, they became known as Pennsylvania Dutch.

The Germans were industrious, hard-working, and skillful in a variety of trades. The province of Pennsylvania owed much of its early agricultural growth to their labor. They hauled produce to the Philadelphia market - corn, wheat, barley, butter, cheese, beef, pork, and fresh and dried fruit. Both coastal and ocean-going vessels loaded food in Philadelphia for sale in other colonies, the West Indies, and across the Atlantic. The days were long past when colonists such as those at Jamestown devoted their time to vain pursuits and later starved.

When Penn assumed the proprietorship of Pennsylvania and the Three Lower Counties, later known as Delaware, the land was not free of European settlers. Some Dutch and Swedes had settled in the territory, and a number of English farmers had established themselves. These early settlers either made satisfactory arrangements with Penn's agents or, in out-of-the-way places, remained as squatters. As pioneers, however, this initial wave of colonists served an important function in opening the wilderness and developing trade with the Indians. In part, they were responsible for the ease with which those that came later developed the colony.

While William Penn was populating Pennsylvania, an older proprietary colony to the south was developing a civilization quite different from Pennsylvania's and more like that of the royal colony of Virginia. In 1632, Charles I granted regal rights to George Calvert, Lord Baltimore, to rule the colony of Maryland, but Calvert died before the charter was issued, and his son, Cecilius, became proprietor. In November 1633, he sent two ships, the *Ark* and the *Dove,* with the first settlers. They landed at St. Clements Island, in the mouth of the Potomac. Father Andrew White, a member of the Society of Jesus, erected a cross and said mass, the first such service in Maryland, as Calvert called his domain in honor of Queen Henrietta Maria, the wife of Charles I.

King Charles I granted Cecilius more than 10 million acres. He was entitled to hold this land "in free and common socage" after the manner of the county of Durham, which enjoyed almost an independent status within the kingdom of England (during the Middle Ages, the Lord Bishop of Durham also had been a temporal prince with power virtually absolute over his subjects). The proprietor was required to establish a legislative assembly, but this body could not initiate legislation; it merely could approve or disapprove laws submitted by the proprietor. This arrangement gave Lord Baltimore the right to make laws for the colony, provided these laws did not run contrary to the laws of England. He was empowered to establish manors, determine rent, levy taxes and duties, and serve as a court of last appeal, for the king had yielded to the proprietor his right to pardon criminals in Maryland.

Yet with all these trappings of medieval absolutism, the Calverts - Cecilius' two sons served terms as governor of Maryland, and one later succeeded his father as proprietor - were not quite monarchs of all they surveyed, for they had to make concessions to attract settlers to their territory, and prospective tenants were not going to leave Great Britain or any other country merely to exchange one hardship for another. Consequently, the proprietors of Maryland had to offer attractive terms for land and had to make leasing land nearly as attractive as ownership. This they did, and Maryland developed an agricultural economy similar to Virginia's.

Since the Calverts were Catholics, they appealed to oppressed English Catholics, but they were too concerned with making a profit from their colony to restrict emigration to any religious group. Indeed, as a protective policy for themselves, they had guaranteed religious toleration in Maryland and had attracted several Puritans, who in the end quarreled with the proprietors and were instrumental in temporarily repealing some of the liberal policies instituted by the Calverts.

In 1654, during the period of Puritan domination in England, the Maryland assembly, then featuring a majority of Puritans, repealed an earlier Act Concerning Religion, which guaranteed religious freedom, and passed a law forbidding freedom of worship to adherents of "popery or prelacy," that is, both Catholics and Anglicans. Fortified with this law and aided by New England ship captain Roger Heamans, in command of the *Golden Lion,* Puritan zealots began a brief but systematic persecution of Catholics. They condemned ten to death and hanged four, drove out priests who had to flee to Virginia, and seized Catholic property.

Lord Baltimore appealed to Oliver Cromwell, who ordered his parliamentary commissioners in Maryland to curb the actions of fellow Puritans. Forces loyal to Lord Baltimore managed to quell the revolt against the proprietor and re-establish his authority. But malcontents continued to grumble and call for actions against Catholics. In 1688, when news reached Maryland of the deposition of James II and the accession of William and Mary, rebels again overthrew the proprietary government, which was not restored until 1715. In the interim, Maryland was a royal colony. In 1694, the capital was moved from Catholic St. Marys to Protestant Annapolis, and Francis Nicholson, who had served briefly and unhappily as lieutenant governor of New York prior to Leisler's revolt, and then as lieutenant governor of Virginia, was appointed governor of Maryland.

Despite occasional political upheavals, Maryland prospered. The Calverts had awarded to friends or sold to wealthy men large tracts of land along Maryland's rivers. With these property holders at its core, Maryland quickly developed a landed aristocracy of tobacco planters whose operations brought wealth to the colony. Until the end of the seventeenth century, these men worked plantations chiefly with white bond-servants, but by the last quarter of the century, they increasingly had begun to use African slaves. In the next century, in Maryland as in Virginia, slavery would be a dominant factor in the production of tobacco.

But the popular image of the landed gentry, surrounded by slaves, has obscured the fact that yeoman farmers far outnumbered aristocrats. Many farmers were immigrants who reached Maryland from Pennsylvania by way of Philadelphia. They found their way across the border and settled on what was then a frontier. This movement did not develop fully until after 1700, when Germans and Scots began to move into Maryland's mountain valleys, but before this time, Quakers and other immigrants had entered Maryland and settled in what became Cecil and Baltimore counties.

Many immigrants into Maryland and Virginia came as indentured servants. At the conclusion of their service, they expected to receive a suit of clothes, tools, and fifty acres. That an indentured servant in seventeenth-century Maryland and Virginia enjoyed a better life than the poor of London was attested by John Hammond, who in 1656 wrote a tract entitled *Leah and Rachel* (Virginia and Maryland) to defend the sister colonies against their detractors. "I affirme the Country to be wholesome, healthy and fruitfull; and a modell on which industry may as much improve it self in, as in any habitable part of the World," Hammond wrote, "yet not such a Lubberland as the Fiction of the land of Ease is reported to be, nor such a Utopian as Sr. Thomas Moore hath related to be found put." On a visit to London, Hammond saw the misery of the poor, some of whom were eking out a living selling "Matches, Smal-coal, Blacking, Pen and Ink, Thred-laces, and a hundred more such kinde of trifling merchandizes," and he commented that "their manner of living was degenerate and base; and their condition to be far below the meanest servant in Virginia." Hammond expressed sorrow over dissensions that malcontents had stirred up in Maryland, but he expressed assurance that after the settlement of its internal disputes, the province, like Virginia, would flourish. At any rate, he declared, "it is that Country in which I desire to spend the remnant of my dayes, in which I covet to make my grave."

Ten years later, another pamphleteer, George Alsop, a former indentured servant, published *A Character of the Province of Maryland* in London, in which he gave a sometimes ribald description of the colony but nevertheless declared the life of a servant in Maryland preferable to that of an apprentice in England. "And let this be spoke to the deserved praise of Mary-Land," he remarked, "That the four years I served there were not to me so slavish, as a two years Servitude of a Handicraft Apprenticeship was here in London . . . . Not that I write this to seduce or delude any, or to draw them from their native soyle, but out of a love to my Countrymen, whom in the general I wish well to. . . . I say they may for the debarment of a four years sordid liberty, go over into this Province and there live plentiously well."

Since the first unsuccessful attempts at colonization, the character of immigrants improved. Fewer adventurers enlisted in the colonial enterprises in the expectation of quick riches. Those who emigrated expected to work, and they came in the hope of bettering their lot by labor rather than luck. Some unsavory residents of the slums of London still found their way to America, sometimes kidnapped by unscrupulous captains who sold them into bondage. And authorities continued to ship convicts to plantations overseas. John Hammond admitted that in its early stages, Virginia was afflicted with "a nest of Rogues, whores, desolute and rooking persons," but that even then, Virginia had "divers honest and vertuous inhabitants."

Legend has it that Virginia and Maryland received a large increment of aristocratic refugees during the Puritan regime in England from 1640 to 1660. The notion that titled cavaliers and landed gentry fleeing the parliamentary forces of Oliver Cromwell found a haven in the tobacco colonies is largely untrue. A few royalist gentlemen did arrive, but the largest number of royalists were prisoners of war, mostly Scots, who were sent to be sold as indentured servants.

During the middle years of the seventeenth century, Virginia, like Maryland, saw an increase in the number of yeoman farmers who arrived in the colony with enough capital to procure land on the expanding frontier. Some even bought farms of 500 to 600 acres in the more settled areas adjacent to the holdings of the large planters who had established themselves as a ruling class. The yeoman farmers, however, had few social ambitions, owned few or no slaves, and frequently moved to more promising farm sites on the frontier.

The great day of the Virginia landed aristocracy came in the eighteenth century, but before 1700, many families who would be important in later generations were already established. The Lees, Carters, Corbins, Wormeleys, Fitzhughs, Byrds, and others had laid the foundations of dynasties that would grow in wealth and influence in the next century. Most of these families came from English middle-class stock, whatever the pretensions of later genealogists, but they successfully imitated the English gentry and created a social caste much like England.

Both small farmers and great planters in Virginia and Maryland depended upon tobacco as their primary crop. Tobacco became the medium of exchange, and prices within the colony were calculated in pounds of tobacco. It proved so profitable that in good years, one man could earn a comfortable livelihood, and even the smallest farmers tended to neglect growing food in favor of tobacco. But as overproduction glutted the market, and prices decreased, the wealthier planters who could afford slaves and indentured labor had a great advantage over farmers who had no servants. As tobacco became less profitable and the eastern land was barren as a result of overproduction, the necessity for subsistence farming and the search for fresh land drove many small farmers into the interior.

In 1642, William Berkeley, a colorful, courageous, impulsive, and sometimes despotic character, became royal governor of Virginia at a time when the Puritans in Parliament seriously challenged the king's authority in England. Berkeley was a royalist and had no intention of turning over Virginia to parliament. But before the efforts of the parliamentarians came to a head, he faced other problems.

The movement of farmers to the frontier had provoked the Indians, who had been quietly coexisting with the colonists since the uprising of 1622, when, led by Opechancanough, Powhatan's half brother, they had nearly wiped out the colony. Though Opechancanough was old and so frail he had to be carried in a litter with an attendant to prop open his eyelids, his mind was keen and his will resolute. As he saw the continued incursions of Europeans, he planned their extermination, and on April 18, 1644, his men attacked outlying farms and settlements and slaughtered 350 men, women, and children. Although the attack was a major setback, it did not threaten the colony's existence as the massacre of 1622 had done, and Governor Berkeley mustered enough militia to defeat the Indians. His troops captured Opechancanough, whom the governor planned to ship to England, but a vengeful militiaman shot him. In the treaty that Berkeley made with the Indians, he forced them to pay a tribute "of twenty beaver skins at the going away of geese yearly," to cede all tribal lands between the James and York rivers south of the falls, and to retire to hunting grounds north of the York River.

Berkeley's difficulties with men of his own race would linger. Members of the ruling class in Virginia were mainly royalist in politics and Anglican in religion. Although the English church was established by law and nonconformity was technically illegal, Virginia, like Maryland, had many dissenters within its borders. In 1642, the year Berkeley became governor, zealous Calvinist Richard Bennett, with a few others of his faith, wrote to Boston requesting ministers. Boston obliged by sending three Calvinist preachers who so enraged Berkeley that he put through the House of Burgesses an act requiring strict conformity of all ministers to the doctrine and procedures of the Church of England. With this law threatening them, two of the Boston preachers departed, but one, William Thompson, managed to preach and make converts. Puritans in the colony carried on an agitation against the governor and his aristocratic council.

After the execution of Charles I in 1649, the matter came to the fore. In 1650, parliament passed an act cutting off trade with Virginia because of its alleged treasons. Berkeley, in defiance of parliament, told his people that Dutch ships would come to buy their tobacco, as, indeed, happened. As a result, in 1652, parliament sent two armed vessels to the James River with parliamentary commissioners to force the royalist governor to surrender. Although Berkeley threatened war, wiser heads in his government prevailed. The parliamentary commissioners granted amnesty for all previous offenses and permitted the governor and any royalist who refused to take the oath of allegiance to parliament to sell their property and leave the province.

The House of Burgesses was called upon to act as a sort of convention to re-establish the government of the colony, and for the duration of the commonwealth period in England, the Burgesses ruled Virginia. In 1652, they chose Calvinist Richard Bennett as governor. He held office until 1655. Edward Digges succeeded him for a term, followed by Samuel Matthews, who died at the end of 1659, a few months before the restoration of Charles II. Now without a governor, and lacking any instructions from the leaderless regime in England, the House of Burgesses persuaded Berkeley to come out of retirement and once more assume the governorship.

Berkeley's second administration was less successful than his first, for hard times fell upon the colony, and the governor, older and more avaricious, used his office for his personal aggrandizement. Charles II's government enacted another Navigation Act in 1660, which had the effect of choking off a flourishing trade with the Dutch that had been developing during the Puritan regime. The production of tobacco had by this time increased to such a degree that the English market could not consume it all, and the price in the 1660s dropped from three pence a pound to a halfpenny or less. In an effort to bolster the price of tobacco, Virginia and Maryland tried to restrict planting, but no measures restored prosperity. The English wars with the Dutch in 1664 and 1672 further depressed the tobacco market as Dutch warships and privateers preyed on the tobacco fleet, even sailing into the James River, where they took vessels loaded with tobacco.

In an ill-considered decision, the king awarded the Northern Neck (the region between the Rappahannock and the Potomac rivers) to several of his favorites and then the whole of Virginia to Lord Culpeper and the Earl of Arlington as Lord Proprietors. This disposal of the entire colony created such a commotion that Charles had to rescind his action and issue letters patent renewing Virginia's status as a royal colony. However, in order to purchase the Northern Neck from the king's favorites, the House of Burgesses had to impose a poll tax of fifty pounds of tobacco. Natural disasters added to Virginia's troubles. On August 27, 1667, a hurricane, worse than any ever known in Virginia, destroyed more than 10,000 houses and all crops. In the winter of 1672–73, during a spell of intense cold, an epidemic killed more than half of the colony's cattle.

Political corruption and economic disaster brought such widespread discontent to England's oldest colony that it was ripe for rebellion when Nathaniel Bacon, whom romantic writers have described as a precursor of the patriots of 1776, arrived in the New World. Despite certain parallels between Bacon and some of the patriots, this interpretation doesn't align with the known facts, and it is difficult to construe the civil conflict of 1676, known as Bacon's Rebellion, as the beginning of the American Revolution.

Bacon, a hot-headed young planter related to the family of Sir Francis Bacon, owned a large farm at Curie's Neck on the upper James River, then a frontier region. In the spring of 1676, Indians in the backwoods of Virginia were on the attack. Senecas from the North had driven the Susquehannas from the upper Chesapeake Bay southward until they and their allies began raiding outlying plantations. Many marauding Virginia Indians were equipped with guns they had bought from traders sent out by William Byrd or by Governor Berkeley, and the governor was anxious to avoid another Indian war that would disrupt a profitable trade. Bacon, however, was in the path of the Indians, and when his overseer was killed, he took action without waiting for the slow-moving governor. Byrd, whose trade was being ruined by the invaders from the North, supported Bacon's action.

With many frontier farmers and some established planters in the back country supporting him, Bacon undertook a successful campaign against the Indians. He and his followers pressured Berkeley and his reactionary council to correct injustices that small farmers suffered. But when Bacon's men turned from fighting Indians to demanding social reforms, Byrd and other larger planters deserted Bacon's cause. The Bacon supporters tried first to accomplish their goal by electing their leader to the House of Burgesses. When Bacon reached Jamestown, however, Berkeley had him arrested as a traitor for raising an army without permission although he later pardoned him. In a rage, Bacon retired to his plantation on the upper James River, raised an army of 500 men, and marched back to Jamestown, where he coerced the House of Burgesses into enacting several bills demanded by the back-countrymen, including one to broaden the right to vote.

This action was more than Berkeley could tolerate. After proclaiming Bacon a traitor, he fled to the Eastern Shore. Bacon again had to lead his men against the Indians on the upper Potomac. Returning in September to find Berkeley's men entrenched in Jamestown, he drove them out and burned the town. Unfortunately for the rebels, Bacon became ill, and, on October 18, 1676, died. Though his lieutenants buried him secretly, they could not conceal the fact their leader was gone, and Bacon's force disbanded. Berkeley came back for vengeance against each of Bacon's colleagues whom he was able to apprehend.

The vengeful governor hanged so many of Bacon's followers that Charles II grumbled the "old fool has hanged more men in that naked Country, than I have done for the murder of my Father." The executions were profitable for Berkeley and his government, for he confiscated and appropriated the victims' property. The reforms that Bacon had forced through the legislative assembly were nullified, and Berkeley reigned unchallenged - for a time. At length, however, even King Charles had to notice so great a miscarriage of justice in a crown colony, and after sending a commission to make a report, he recalled Berkeley. In time, life in the colony returned to something approaching peace.

The Glorious Revolution of 1688, however, created another period of uncertainty and threatened civil strife in Virginia until 1689, when the new sovereigns, William and Mary, appointed that ubiquitous colonial official, Francis Nicholson, lieutenant governor of Virginia. (The previous governor, Lord Howard of Effingham, against whom petitioners from the colony had lodged complaints before the Lords of Trade, retained the title of governor but remained in England.)

The most notable contribution of Nicholson's administration was the establishment of the

College of William and Mary, the second college in the British colonies. For several years, Virginians had been campaigning for a college, and some wealthier planters and English merchants doing business in Virginia had contributed 2,500 pounds toward an institution of higher learning. James Blair, commissary of the Church of England (as the church's colonial agent was called), gained Nicholson's support for a petition sent to London requesting financial assistance. Blair went in person to plead for a college to train ministers and educate youths, but he found the task difficult. To the argument that a college for ministers would help save souls of the colonists, Sir Edward Seymour, one of the Lords of the Treasury, exploded, "Souls! Damn your souls! Make tobacco!" Yet in spite of official disinterest in education, Blair succeeded in persuading the government to appropriate 2,000 pounds from fees, to impose an export tax of a penny a pound on tobacco, and to allocate 20,000 acres for the support of the college.

Middle Plantation, soon to be renamed Williamsburg and to become the capital of the colony, was chosen as the site of the college. On August 8, 1695, the cornerstone was laid with considerable pomp, and by May Day of 1699, five students had advanced to deliver orations in praise of learning before Governor Nicholson and members of the council and the House of Burgesses. For some years, the College of William and Mary would remain little more than a high school, but Virginia had initiated higher education. By the end of the seventeenth century, the colony was on its way to the development of a sophisticated society.

Since the days of Richard Hakluyt, Englishmen had dreamed of dominating Spain in the Caribbean, of seizing its islands, and of gaining a portion of its tropical riches. A first step came with the colonization of Bermuda shortly after the wreck of the Gates-Somers expedition there in 1609. Of far more economic importance, however, was the island of Barbados, first occupied by Englishmen in 1625 and from 1629 a proprietary colony under the jurisdiction of the Earl of Carlisle and his successors. Englishmen also seized other islands in the Leeward Group in this period. Barbados became a major producer of sugar, and some of its planters made fortunes, but before the end of the seventeenth century, it had become overpopulated. Less productive but still useful as a base for English pirates was Jamaica, taken from Spain by forces dispatched by Oliver Cromwell in 1655 as part of his ill-conceived and poorly executed Western Design for taking Spain's Caribbean possessions. Despite these British outposts in the Caribbean, Spain remained a potential threat to the more southerly of the British colonies, for there was always the danger of encirclement by a combination of Spanish and French forces. Hence, northern colonies welcomed the settlement of Carolina by

Englishmen in the latter part of the seventeenth century, just as the occupation of Georgia in the eighteenth century gave South Carolina security against Spanish attack.

After Raleigh's abortive efforts to establish a colony on the coast of North Carolina, no successful colonizing activities had taken place in this region for more than three-quarters of a century. Charles I in 1629 had granted the territory, called in honor of himself "Carolina," to his attorney general, Sir Robert Heath, but Heath had failed to colonize it. In 1663, Charles II granted to eight proprietors land from Currituck Inlet to a line sixty-five miles south of St. Augustine, Florida, and extending from ocean to ocean. The eight who received this imperial domain were Edward Hyde, later Earl of Clarendon, George Monck, later Duke of Albemarle, William Lord Craven, John Lord Berkeley, Sir William Berkeley, Anthony Ashley Cooper, later Earl of Shaftesbury, Sir George Carteret, and Sir John Colleton. These men, backed by bankers and merchants of London, were the Lords Proprietors of Carolina, vested with the ownership of the land and the power to make laws and administer justice.

To provide a legal instrument of government, philosopher John Locke and politician Anthony Ashley Cooper drew up what is likely the strangest charter any British colony ever tried to practice.

Called the Fundamental Constitutions, it set forth a plan for an aristocratic hierarchy. The Lords Proprietors stood at the apex, and each proprietor had an individual right to 12,000 acres in each of Carolina's counties. Below the Lords Proprietors stood the landgraves, with a right to not less than 48,000 acres. The third and lowest rank of the nobility were the caciques, with 24,000 acres. After them came gentlemen commoners, who were required to have not less than 3,000 but not more than 12,000 acres. They were to be appointed as lords of manors, with manorial rights similar to those in medieval England. At the bottom of the hierarchy of landowners were the yeomen, who had to possess not less than fifty acres in order to vote. The hierarchy, of course, conceived a laboring class of landless workers composed of free laborers, indentured servants, and African slaves. This elaborate system never actually became a social reality, but proprietors did create twenty-six landgraves and thirteen caciques.

The Fundamental Constitutions not only sought to create an aristocratic social system, but the document also outlined an elaborate system of government that proved impracticable. Proprietors would appoint a governor, but if any proprietor emigrated to Carolina, he would take precedence over the governor. In the absence of proprietors, each would have a deputy resident in the colony. The government of the colony would be entrusted to a legislative assembly composed of the governor, the proprietary deputies, the nobility, and elected representatives from the landholding commons. After 1693, the assembly split into two branches, with an upper and a lower house. Because the Fundamental Constitutions proved so unworkable, the proprietors constantly revised the document, but by the end of the century, they abandoned it as a constitution of government because the assembly would never accept its complicated provisions.

The London courtiers of Charles II who concocted unworkable schemes for enriching themselves from estates in Carolina did realize it would take numerous settlers to make their dreams come true. To that end they began a campaign to encourage colonists to emigrate. One influential tract, written by a Barbadian ship captain, William Hilton, was published in London in 1664 as *A Relation of a Discovery Lately Made on the Coast of Florida*. Sugar planters in Barbados had employed Hilton to search for land where they would have more opportunity for expansion than existed on their overcrowded island.

After two voyages, Hilton reported so favorably about the Carolina coastal country that his Barbadian employers petitioned the Lords Proprietors for the privilege of settling in their domain, and an agreement was reached that ultimately led to the migration of many colonists from Barbados. The proprietors were so pleased with Hilton's report they had it published to stimulate further emigration. (Hilton had been careful to contradict criticism from a few New England cattle breeders, who for a time had settled in the Cape Fear region.) Other pamphleteers soon were extolling the Carolina country for its healthful climate, fertile soil, lush forests, and the prospects for getting rich. Thomas Ashe, for example, in a pamphlet published in 1682 called *Carolina, or a Description of the Present State of that Country, and the Natural Excellencies Thereof,* promised that a native herb, "the famous Cassiny," made into a tea, would "wonderfully enliven and envigorate the Heart . . . preserving the Mind free and serene, keeping the Body brisk, active, and lively." To anyone suffering from baldness, he promised that Carolina bear's grease had "great Vertue and Efficacy in causing the Hair to grow."

The publicity worked, both in England and Barbados. In the summer of 1665, a contingent of ninety Barbadian settlers, who had planned to land at Port Royal near the site of Jean Ribaut's ill-fated colony, were carried by adverse winds to the mouth of the Cape Fear River. There, they built houses and named their village Charles Town. But the colony dispersed after two years, and the name of their settlement was left to another town that was settled in 1670 at Albemarle Point on the Ashley River by a party of Englishmen led by Joseph West. Ten years later, the site was moved to the confluence of the Ashley and Cooper rivers, and much later the name of the settlement was altered to Charleston.

West brought his group of ninety-three English colonists to Carolina by way of Barbados. There, Sir John Yeamans, the governor, had been instructed to fill in a blank commission with his name for governor of Carolina, or with that of some other person if he chose. Yeamans decided on octogenarian former governor of Bermuda, William Sayle. After Sayle's death a year later, West became governor.

Although Carolina's growth was slow initially, the colony did not suffer hardships characteristic of some earlier settlements. West was intelligent and managed to supply, even before Sayle's death, the kind of leadership the colony needed. In February 1671, the first Barbadians arrived, and for many years the colony received a steady flow of settlers from that island.

The early colonists were convinced, probably from some of the enthusiastic pamphlets they had read, that they had reached a tropical paradise where oranges, lemons, dates, and other exotic fruits would grow. The first winter freeze discouraged them, but gradually they learned to grow corn, grains, and other food crops. Cattle, hogs, and horses flourished, and, as in other colonies, the forests provided naval stores. In 1685, ship captain John

Thurber brought some rice seed from Madagascar, and the colonists soon discovered rice grew well in the rich black soil of the swamplands. Within a few years, rice was one of the most important products in Carolina.

Early settlers brought a small number of African slaves, and slavery quickly became an important factor in the colony's economy. Manual labor in the forests and swamps required little skill, but much endurance, and the slaves suited the planters' needs. Like New Englanders, they felt no compunction about enslaving Africans, salving their consciences with the notion they were bringing heathen people to a land of Christian salvation. The Barbadians were accustomed to African and Indian slavery, and in conflicts with the Carolina Indians, they were quick to take prisoners whom they could sell into bondage. Since Indian slaves could easily escape into the forests, Carolina Indian slave-traders found it expedient to ship such captives to the West Indies.

Trade with the Indians of the interior helped to increase the prosperity of the merchants who settled in Charles Town. They bartered for deerskins, mink pelts, and other furs - and also bought captives whom the Indians had taken in their wars. The slave trade was a factor in the commercial development of Charles Town.

Before the end of the seventeenth century, many

settlers were moving to Carolina. Huguenots came from Virginia, England, and later France. A considerable number of people crossed the border of Virginia into northern Carolina, mostly runaway servants and others who wanted to escape Virginia authorities. The great period for the development of Carolina, however, was to come in the eighteenth century.

Contrary to a popular belief, most colonists did not seek religious freedom or refuge from political oppression. The majority had a basic human yearning for more of the good things of the earth. Labor was scarce, and the newcomer with a skill or talent had little trouble making a living. But the greatest lure was cheap or free land, and farmers dominated life in the colonies. Some 95 percent of colonists lived on farms, a term that encompassed everything from a frontier cabin with a corn patch to a Virginia tidewater plantation. The soil was deep and productive, but with supply seemingly inexhaustible, most colonists became irresponsible farmers. They wore out the soil, then moved to virgin land. Wasteful though it was, this agriculture nevertheless produced enormous crops. The natural bounty of the region provided other harvests: Lumbermen, fur traders, and fisherman all prospered. With seemingly unlimited natural resources, the colonies developed a prosperous and sophisticated economy that could support goldsmiths, wigmakers, and dancing masters.

8
THE LONG CONFLICT
BEGINS

The accession of William of Orange and Queen Mary to the English throne after the overthrow of James II in 1688 profoundly influenced the course of events both in England and in the most distant settlements of British America. As ruler of Holland as well as king of England, William III was committed to maintaining a balance of power in Europe, and to that end he had to curb the ambitions of Louis XIV. From 1689 until 1763, England was intermittently at war with France in an effort to prevent French domination of Europe, and the outcome was not settled until the defeat of Napoleon in 1815.

When William attacked France in 1689 in a conflict called in Europe the War of the League of Augsburg, he formalized a state of war in the colonies that already was regional. The conflict in America came to be known as King William's War. Fighting between the French in Canada and the English to the south was inevitable, for the two competed for the fur trade with the Indians. Each side had its own Indian allies. From the time of Champlain, the French had cemented their alliance with the Algonquin tribes. French Jesuits and other Catholic missionaries had won the friendship of tribes in the interior. At the same time, the French had incurred the hostility of the Iroquois, traditional enemies of the Algonquins. The Iroquois confederation, known as the Five Nations (and after the Tuscaroras joined them in 1711, the Six Nations), found it advantageous to maintain peace with the Dutch and the English. Their hunting grounds extended from Pennsylvania and New York to the Great Lakes and the upper reaches of the Ohio and Mississippi valleys. There, the Iroquois came into conflict with hostile tribes under the influence of the French.

French traders, the *coureurs de bois,* showed great ingenuity and enterprise in winning the friendship of the Indians. They went into the back country, often took Indian women as wives, and assimilated into tribes with whom they traded. The English were rarely able to adapt to Indian life in this fashion.

Although the Iroquois and allied tribes maintained a nominal peace with the English, they were unhappy over the continued advancement of white settlers. Their leaders realized Englishmen were exerting pressure from the east and south, just as the French and Algonquins were pressing them from Canada, and they were troubled about the future as they saw the boundaries of their hunting grounds contracting. However, the Indians acquired a taste for manufactured goods and had come to depend on traders to supply guns, ammunition, blankets, and rum. English blankets were more to their liking than those the French offered, and rum was cheaper than French brandy. (France had suppressed making rum in the West Indies in order to preserve the market for cognac, and this embargo on rum gave English traders an advantage in the Indian trade.) Despite the mutual interest of Indians and Europeans in maintaining trading relations, tension existed on the frontier, and localized violence sporadically occurred.

There was a vast difference between the French settlements in Canada and those of the English to the south. Imperial France regarded North American settlements as trading posts that would serve as outlets for French goods in exchange for furs. Some agriculture was necessary to supply traders, but only a few habitants considered Canada a place of permanent residence, and no Frenchman looked at Canada as a self-sustaining or self-governing province. Control of French Canada was entirely in the hands of officials sent from Paris. Furthermore, the French population of Canada was sparse. At the beginning of King William's War, Canada boasted only 13,000 French inhabitants, while the English colonies had 200,000 settlers. By 1715, the population of the English colonies had increased to 400,000 while the French in Canada numbered just 25,000.

In effect, Canada served France, not as an outlet for surplus population, as the English conceived of America, but as a place for garrisons to protect the fur trade. Regular troops from the king's armies came from France to protect French trading posts. They made maximum use of their Indian allies, but the fighting strength of Canada depended upon professional soldiers, not upon a militia raised from the *habitants.*

Conditions were different in the British colonies. Although the fur trade was critical there, English settlers planned to stay. They were ready to defend their lines of communication with the trading posts on the frontier, but they also were fighting for homes in a land they had seized for themselves. From time to time, the English sovereign had to send soldiers and ships, but colonial militia did much of the fighting in all wars. Ill-trained and ill-disciplined, the militia was not always effective, but these troops constituted a force of citizen-soldiers who saved the colonies from devastation. Without them, English expansion along the frontiers would have been held in check.

When King William led England into a coalition at war with Louis XIV to prevent French aggression upon the Rhenish Palatinate (a part of the Holy Roman Empire), hostilities had already begun on the American frontier. English fur traders based at Albany had pushed west in search of beaver pelts and were taking furs from areas on the Great Lakes that the French regarded as private preserves. In 1687, the governor of Canada, Marquis de Denonville, sent troops into western New York to attack the Seneca Indians who were fighting Algonquin tribes on the Great Lakes. Denonville destroyed the Senecas' cornfields, captured some Indians and English traders, and built a fort on the eastern projection of land between the Niagara River and Lake Ontario. This campaign temporarily relieved Iroquois pressure on Indian allies of the French, but Denonville had, as one Indian explained, knocked down a wasp's nest without killing the wasps. Furthermore, he stirred to action Governor Thomas Dongan of New York, who protested and called a council of the Iroquois at Albany. Dongan pointed out to the tribal representatives that they had invited trouble by attempting to trade with the French instead of bringing beaver pelts to English traders. He recommended the Five Nations unite with some of the western tribes and drive out the French. He warned them against French Jesuit missionaries.

Dongan wrote to Denonville demanding that English and Dutch captives be returned. "I hope, notwithstanding all your trained souldiers and greate Officers come from Europe, that our masters at home will suffer us to do ourselves justice on you for the injuries and spoyl you have committed on us . . . and I assure you, Sir, if my Master gives me leave, I will be as soon at Quebeck as you shall be att Albany. . . . I advise you to send home all the Christian and Indian prisoners, the King of England's subjects, you unjustly do detein." Although Denonville wanted peace - and the opportunity to trade with the Iroquois - he could not return all prisoners because some had been shipped to France. Moreover, Denonville's Indian allies, who disliked the notion of the French trading with the Iroquois, sabotaged peace negotiations.

On the night of August 4, 1689, the Iroquois struck back at the French. Fifteen hundred men fell on the settlement at Lachine, eight miles from Montreal, massacred inhabitants, and set fire to their houses. The French reported nearly 200 casualties and 120 taken prisoner. The Iroquois roamed the countryside for weeks, burning and killing where they could. Denonville called in his garrisons at Fort Niagara and Fort Frontenac in the west to protect Montreal.

Louis XIV chose an able veteran of New France, seventy-year-old Comte de Frontenac, to return to command French forces. Frontenac arrived in October 1689, with orders to capture New York, an assignment that proved impossible. But he did begin a campaign of revenge for the massacre at Lachine. Organizing three groups, he planned to attack Albany and the border outposts of Maine and New Hampshire. The first group to march was composed of Indians and French *coureurs de bois,* with a handful of professional soldiers to lead. In the dead of winter, they set out for Albany across an endless white waste, moving silently on snowshoes. When the Indian allies grew sullen over the unending journey, the war party chose an easier objective, the outpost of Schenectady on the border of Mohawk country. They approached the stockaded village during a blizzard on the night of February 8, 1690. Less than a dozen militiamen from Connecticut were stationed at Schenectady, and they were not on guard. Someone had built two snowmen that stood as silent and futile sentinels in front of the two open gates of the stockade. No one dreamed of danger. Most inhabitants were Dutch farmers who went to bed at nightfall. The French force waited until the villagers were asleep and quietly surrounded houses. At a signal, they gave a war whoop and attacked. A few Mohawks sleeping in the village were spared so they might carry a message of friendship to their tribesmen, whom the French hoped to keep neutral. Sixty were killed, between eighty and ninety were taken prisoner, and a handful escaped and fled toward Albany.

The French gesture of friendship for the Mohawks did them no good. As soon as word of the foray reached these tribesmen, they set out in pursuit. One band of Mohawks clung to the enemy's trail even to the outskirts of Montreal and killed or captured fifteen men.

Frontenac's Indians and *coureurs de bois* harassed other frontier settlements. On the night of March 27, 1690, they reached Salmon Falls on the border between Maine and New Hampshire and killed more than thirty inhabitants. Fifty-four others were captured.

Late in May, another of the three raiding groups organized by Frontenac attacked an English settlement at Casco Bay, now the site of Portland, Maine. Outnumbered and surrounded, the English surrendered after the French promised protection from the Indians. But no sooner had they laid down their arms than the French turned the captives over to their allies, who killed many of them. The French excuse for this treachery was that the English in New York had persuaded the Iroquois to attack and torture Frenchmen. The New England prisoners disclaimed responsibility for what New Yorkers had done, but it made little difference to the French what colony the British were from.

At this time, both New York and New England colonies were fighting under handicaps because of internal dissensions that followed the overthrow of James II. King James had organized the New England colonies, New York, and the two Jerseys into the Dominion of New England, with Edmund Andros as governor. But when news of the Glorious Revolution reached the colonies, they rebelled against Andros, the Dominion fractured, and the colonies reverted to something approaching their previous status. New York, meanwhile, was dealing with the revolt of Jacob Leisler. These quarrels and disruptions of orderly government at home made it difficult for northern colonies to unite in their common defense.

None of the colonies had forces capable of sustained military action. Local militia, whose only training was an occasional drill on the village green, were unprepared for war. Even on muster days, they usually spent more time in taverns than practicing with their weapons. Although all able-bodied men were accustomed to firearms, their muzzle-loading muskets were not effective except at close range. Their sidearms were sometimes homemade, and powder and shot were often in short supply. Supplies usually consisted of what the men could carry on their backs.

Mutual suspicion and jealousy helped prevent any joint action by the colonies. Although several colonies sent representatives to a conference called by Jacob Leisler in New York in April 1690 in an effort to plan collective action against the French, nothing came of it. New York, Connecticut, Massachusetts Bay, Plymouth, and Maryland promised small contingents for a campaign - less than 1,000 altogether, and not all of them reported for duty. An expedition of sorts, under the command of Major Fitz-John Winthrop, finally set out at the end of July toward Montreal. After waiting in vain on Lake Champlain for adequate supplies and for a force of Iroquois allies, they turned back to Albany. Governor Leisler of New York blamed Winthrop and threw him into jail, an action that antagonized Winthrop's fellow militiamen from Connecticut.

Except for intensifying intercolonial animosities, the expedition accomplished nothing. One small detachment led by Captain John Schuyler raided as far as La Prairie, on the St. Lawrence opposite Montreal. The party killed six men, burned outlying houses, captured nineteen prisoners, slaughtered a large number of cows, and returned.

Massachusetts Bay, which had furnished no men for Fitz-John Winthrop's expedition, decided on its own campaign. This would be a sea-borne expedition against Port Royal in Acadia, led by Sir William Phips, then a hero as the result of his success in recovering a treasure from a sunken Spanish hulk in the Bahamas. Phips was no great naval strategist, but in May 1690, with a flotilla of fourteen assorted vessels manned by 700 fishermen, sailors, and farmers, he managed to intimidate the French commander at Port Royal and persuade him to surrender. On the flimsy excuse that the French had violated terms of surrender, Phips and his men pillaged shops at Port Royal, stole the communion plate from the church (an act of piety in the opinion of some of Phips' Puritan followers), and sailed back to Boston. Shortly after Phips departed, Fort Royal suffered again when English pirates reached the town and burned a number of houses.

Encouraged by the success of Phips' expedition against Port Royal, the leaders of Massachusetts Bay decided to attack Quebec. In August 1690, the colony collected thirty-four ships and 2,000 men, placed them under Phips' command, and dispatched the expedition against Quebec. Phips' ships did not arrive at the scene until October 17, when the weather was turning cold. After a futile attack on the fortifications, led by Major John Walley, with the loss of thirty men, the survivors returned to the ships. After dallying in the St. Lawrence in an effort to repair two damaged ships, Phips sailed home. He had failed to coordinate the naval bombardment of the town with the attempted assault, and the operation impressed the French regulars as an amateur performance (fortunately for Phips' reputation, the Puritans blamed his failure on God rather than on incompetence). So hard-pressed was Massachusetts Bay to find money to pay the 50,000-pound expense of the expedition that it decided to issue paper scrip, an innovation the colonies found feasible in later times.

Frontenac, the French governor, made it his goal to detach the Iroquois from their alliance with the English, and he nearly succeeded. The Iroquois were disenchanted with the English because of their indecision, their lack of force, and their disorganized efforts to meet the French invasions. If Frontenac had known how to negotiate differences between the Algonquins and the Iroquois, he might have succeeded, but while the Iroquois were willing to make peace with the French, they would not agree to do so with the Algonquins. The hostility between some of the tribes, the Senecas and the Hurons, for example, spilled too much blood for them to sit down together. Frontenac had to forego his scheme of dividing the English and their Indian allies, for he would not make a unilateral treaty with the Iroquois.

For the next seven years, war dragged on. The conflict took on the characteristics of modern guerrilla warfare, and frontier settlements were never safe from hit-and-run attacks. The killing of settlers and the burning of cabins were common. Settlements in northern New York, western Massachusetts, New Hampshire, and particularly Maine suffered from frequent Indian raids, sometimes led by detachments of French. Frontenac, though he had to be carried in a chair because of his age, led one of the heaviest raids into New York in the summer of 1696, when he ravaged the country of the Onondagas.

Ferocity and cruelty were characteristic of both sides. When a raiding party of Indians from Maine reached the settlement at Haverhill, Massachusetts, they carried off Mrs. Hannah Dustin, her infant child, and its nurse. Annoyed by the baby's crying, an Indian killed it. During the long trek back through northern Maine, Mrs. Dustin, a boy prisoner, and the nurse planned an escape. In the night, they seized hatchets and dispatched their ten captors, each of whom Mrs. Dustin scalped. Hannah Dustin's ten scalps netted her a fifty-pound bounty from Massachusetts Bay when she returned.

News that the war between Louis XIV and William III had ended reached the warring colonials at the end of 1697. The Treaty of Ryswick, signed on September 30, 1697, left Europe and the colonies of England and France much as they had been before the outbreak of hostilities. About all the war did in America was to sharpen animosities between the English and French and their respective Indian allies. The patterns established in King William's War would be followed in successive conflicts.

The first of the colonial wars with the French revealed the weakness of the English colonies, caused by their inability to unite either for common defense or for punitive campaigns against enemies. Furthermore, the conflict showed that the colonies could expect little help from the mother country. Whereas Louis XIV, despite pressures of his European campaigns, sent regular troops to defend Canada, William III gave almost no aid to his beleaguered colonies. Not until much later would British regulars fight effectively against the French in North America.

The Treaty of Ryswick may have ended the official war between France and England, but no document signed in Europe could make Indians in the forests of North America peaceful. Sporadic raids on the frontier continued despite the withdrawal of French soldiers from the conflict. Even the relative calm would not last long because the European powers again were jockeying for position in Europe, in America, even in Asia.

Spain pressured the southern flank of the colonies. The little English settlement at Charles Town on the Carolina coast for years stood in danger from the Spanish in Florida. The Spaniards had missions and trading settlements in the Southwest, and they hoped to consolidate their possessions on both sides of the Mississippi.

France, meanwhile, continued efforts to surround the colonies. In 1699, Pierre le Moyne, Sieur d'Iberville, landed a party at Biloxi on the Gulf of Mexico and took possession of the land in the name of the king of France. A few years later, in 1702, the French occupied Mobile. The French had been pushing down the Mississippi and had made a settlement near the present site of St. Louis. Soon French forts would stretch from Detroit to the Gulf of Mexico, and the founding of New Orleans in 1718 by D'Iberville's brother, Jean Baptiste le Moyne, Sieur de Bienville, solidified French holdings in the interior of North America. An alliance between France and Spain after 1700 completed the encirclement of the British colonies by their enemies.

Nevertheless, English and Scottish traders from South Carolina began to compete with the Spaniards for Indian trade - and land - in the region that would one day become Georgia, Alabama, and Mississippi. This was the country of powerful Indian nations, the Creeks, Chickasaws, and Choctaws. In northern Georgia and South Carolina lay the territory of another powerful Indian nation, the Cherokees. On the coast were many small tribes usually at war with one another. The Westos in the vicinity of Charles Town were the most warlike Indians at the time of the first white settlements;

later the Yamasees, pushed north by the Spaniards, created a problem for English settlers.

At the end of King William's War, the South Carolinians were not in danger from Indian attack. Indeed, their traders were moving west and making alliances with Indians of the interior. Before 1700, traders from Charles Town had made treaties with the Creeks, the Chickasaws, and the Cherokees. In 1698, an enterprising trader, Thomas Welch, led an expedition from Charles Town through northern Georgia, Alabama, and Mississippi to the western bank of the Mississippi River below the mouth of the Arkansas River. In the course of time, Welch reached an understanding with the Chickasaws and managed to persuade them to make war on the Choctaws, whom French traders had already won over. Welch's contributions to English power politics on the frontier were not patriotic in nature, for Indian wars meant captives whom he could sell as slaves to sugar planters in the West Indies. The trade in Indian slaves through the port of Charles Town would continue to grow in importance during the wars that began afresh in 1702.

That year marked the beginning of a new outbreak in Europe, the War of the Spanish Succession, in which England, Holland, Austria, Portugal, Prussia, and various other German states sought to curb the growing power of France. (The death of the king of Spain, Charles II, without an heir had given Louis XIV an opportunity to advance the candidacy of his grandson Philip, with the probability that eventually the crowns of Spain and France would be united.) Shortly after the conflict began, it spread to North America, where it was known as Queen Anne's War.

The outlying settlements bore the brunt of Indian attacks, but the theater of operations was far more extensive than in King William's War, for military activity extended from the Caribbean to Canada. New York suffered less than in the previous war, however, for the French had persuaded the Iroquois to maintain neutrality by promising freedom from raids by France's Indian allies.

In 1702, James Moore, governor of South Carolina, organized an expedition against the Spanish base at St. Augustine, which he hoped to destroy before the French could come to its aid. Moore was an Indian trader trying to expand Charles Town's commerce with the tribes of the interior. He was concerned about the threat to English trade with the Creeks and the Chickasaws in the Southwest caused by French occupation of the Gulf Coast. Not all the English settlers in South Carolina were so farsighted, however, and Moore became leader of an unpopular war party. (His enemies claimed he wanted to invade Florida merely to catch hostile Indians to sell into slavery.) What popular support Moore commanded was further diminished when he failed to capture the Spanish fortress at St. Augustine and had to be content with burning houses outside the fort, stealing the church plate, and marching away. When two Spanish warships bottled up his small vessels in the harbor, he had to burn them and retire overland until he could construct enough dugout canoes to take his men to the Carolina coast. The reluctant South Carolinians found themselves saddled with a debt of over 8,000 pounds, which they sought to liquidate by issuing paper money.

But lack of success at St. Augustine did not deter Moore from planning another expedition to thwart the French and Spanish allies in the Southwest. A century before Thomas Jefferson urged the purchase of Louisiana, Moore used the same arguments to seize that territory. In a letter to the English admiral commanding in the Caribbean, Moore declared that if the English could capture Pensacola, Biloxi, and Mobile, it would "make Her Majestic Absolute and Soveraigne Lady of all the Maine as farr as the River Mischisipi, which if effected the Colony of Carolina will be of the Greatest vallue to the Crown of England of any of Her Majesties Plantations on the Maine except Virginia by ading a Great revenue to the Crown, for one halfe of all the Canadian Trade for furrs and Skinns must necessarily come this way, besides a vast Trade of Furrs and Skinns extended as far as the above mentioned River, Mischisipi, which is now interrupted by these Two little Towns [Biloxi and Mobile]."

When the colony of South Carolina would not finance a new expedition, Moore organized a private army of fifty Englishmen and 1,000 Indians. In 1704, he initiated a two-year campaign in which his forces annihilated the Spanish missions in southern Alabama and northern Florida and devastated the country of the Apalachees in the Tallahassee region. Moore captured hundreds of Indians for slaves and relocated more than 1,000 on the South Carolina border near modern Augusta, Georgia, to serve as a fortress against Spanish attacks on that frontier. The plunder of the Spanish missions and profit from the sale of Indian slaves were sufficient for Moore to boast that the expedition had not cost the colony a penny. He had virtually neutralized the Spanish Indians on the southern frontier.

The Spanish and the French attempted to avenge the Carolinians' invasion of territory they regarded as their own with an attack by sea upon Charles Town in the late summer of 1706. Five French privateers aided Spanish troops from Cuba, but they failed to take the town and lost 230 prisoners. The English, warned of this action, strengthened their defenses, improved their alliances with the Indians, and managed to withstand attacks from the south in the succeeding years of the war. In

1707, the English and their Indian allies again took the offensive, burning houses outside the fort at Pensacola and threatening Mobile. But Bienville, the French governor at Mobile, retained enough Indian support to prevent the English from wiping out the French establishments on the Gulf, and during the next few years, he made sure to secure alliances with a number of tribes bordering French possessions on the Gulf.

In the meantime, the French in Canada were continuing a guerrilla campaign against outlying English settlements in the North. All along the Maine border, the French incited the Abnakis to burn the cabins of English settlers and slaughter their occupants. Although Maine was a political dependency of Massachusetts Bay, that colony did little to save the borderers from devastation. Not even the offer of forty pounds for each Indian scalp induced the Puritans to rescue their brethren in Maine.

The French were determined to maintain an alliance with the Abnakis. They sent a large raiding party under Hertel de Rouville into northwestern Massachusetts in the winter of 1704. On February 29, the Indians arrived at the village of Deerfield.

Deerfield's forty-one houses stretched along a ridge overlooking the Deerfield River Valley to the west. Near the center of the settlement, on Meeting House Hill, a palisade surrounded the village church and adjacent houses where the villagers took refuge in time of danger. Although warnings from Mohawks had alarmed the settlers during the autumn, they felt secure on this snowy February night, and nearly 300 occupants of the village were sleeping when De Rouville and his Indians reached them two hours before dawn. The marauders climbed the palisades and splintered doors with their hatchets. Since they were eager for loot and captives, whom they hoped to ransom, the slaughter was not complete. The Indians burned several houses and took as many prisoners as they could capture (a total of 111). Among the captives was the village minister, the Reverend John Williams, who wrote an account of the attack and the hardships of the prisoners that has helped to focus unusual attention upon the Deerfield "massacre. The disaster at Deerfield, however, was typical of what other settlements suffered during the Indian wars.

Williams and fellow prisoners suffered intensely from the cold on the long road back to Canada. When the minister's wife, weak from recent childbirth, could not keep up, an Indian bludgeoned her to death. The Indians had killed two of Williams' children before leaving Deerfield, but five others made the long journey to Canada and survived. Other prisoners were not so fortunate. The Indians killed those too sick and feeble to keep up.

When the prisoners at last reached French territory, Jesuit priests attempted to convert them to the Catholic faith. For Williams and his Puritan brethren, this was as grim as the fear of death from the Indians, for they believed that converting to "popery" would mean their damnation. Williams exhorted his flock to stand firm in their faith, but a few, including two of his children, accepted the Jesuits' faith. After two years, Governor Dudley of Massachusetts procured Williams' release and return to Massachusetts; he immediately put his narrative together (with the help of Cotton Mather) and gave it the title *The Redeemed Captive Returning to Zion* (1707). Williams' account of life in Canada emphasized the double threat the French posed to the New Englander: physical death from marauders and spiritual death through conversion to Catholicism.

Massachusetts had done little to protect the frontiers before the raid on Deerfield, but that attack aroused the ire of Colonel Benjamin Church, an Indian fighter who served in the previous war. Church was so overweight he required a private soldier to march beside him to help him over logs, but he roared into Boston and demanded action from Dudley. Dudley allowed Church to raise a force of some 700 men, English and Indians, who in May of 1704 began an expedition along the Canadian coast. Church hoped to capture Port Royal in Acadia, but Governor Dudley forbade an attack without permission from London. (Rumor had it Dudley and certain Boston merchants were trading with the enemy and wanted to keep the peace.) Church's force, a quarrelsome lot, made a few raids on coast villages, including Grand Pré, which they burned, and at length anchored their vessels off Port Royal. When the garrison declined to surrender, the invaders burned a few outlying houses and sailed home with 100 prisoners to ransom or exchange for English captives held by the French and Indians.

Although a few merchants in Boston profited from trading with the French in Acadia, the Port Royal garrison was a menace that most New Englanders wanted to see destroyed. Consequently, in 1707, Governor Dudley authorized another expedition to the North, and on May 13, two regiments embarked for Acadia under the command of Colonel John March. New Hampshire and Rhode Island contributed 140 men, but the remainder of the 1,076 militia and 450 sailors came from Massachusetts. None of the force had any military training worth mentioning. Unaccustomed to discipline, they showed little respect for officers, who were hardly more competent than their men. On reaching Acadia, they went ashore, marched about Port Royal, had a few skirmishes with the French, argued among themselves, and eventually left for the coast of Maine, where they sent word of their failure to Dudley. One Bostonian wrote that if the officers had permitted, the men might have captured the town, but "at the end we broke up with the confusion of Babel, and went about our business like fools." The British commander of a frigate, complaining to Governor Dudley about the behavior of some officers, added: "I don't see what good I can do by lying here, where I am almost murdered by mosquitoes."

Incensed over the failure, Dudley sent three members of the provincial council (including John Leverett, soon to be president of Harvard College) to advise the commander. The commissioners, in a frigate with 100 additional recruits, arrived off Casco Bay in August and ordered the militia and sailors to return to Port Royal. Once again they landed, skirmished a bit with the enemy, killed a few Frenchmen in an orchard, and sailed away for Boston. Thus ended the effort to take the French bastion in the North.

Frustration and disappointment at the conduct of the war were general throughout New England at the end of 1707. All efforts to avenge frontier raids had failed, and attempts to ensure unity of action by the several colonies had been unsuccessful. Many settlers were bitter because they believed (with some justification) that merchants in Albany and Boston, finding trade with Montreal and Quebec profitable, hoped to maintain peace with the French. It was a time of dread and uneasiness all along the border, and no effective relief appeared to be forthcoming.

The fears of the frontiersmen were justified in the summer of 1708, when Hertel de Rouville led a war party of Indians and Frenchmen into English territory. This time he struck into northeastern Massachusetts, at Haverhill. As at Deerfield four years before, the marauders surprised the village at night and concentrated their attack upon the church. They killed forty-eight villagers, including the minister, his wife, and one child (his slave girl saved two other children by hiding them under tubs in the cellar while the Indians plundered the house). During the summer and autumn, raiding French and Indians continued to slaughter isolated settlers in eastern Massachusetts and New Hampshire.

One of the traders who had profited from illegal trade hatched a plan to expel the French from North America. His motives were less than altruistic, for the expulsion of the French would give the British a monopoly of the rich fur trade with Canada and the back country, which the French had developed. This would-be savior was Samuel Vetch, a Scot who had combined soldiering with commerce and had been a member of a short-lived Scottish colony on the Isthmus of Panama.

Vetch had come to New York in 1699 after the failure of that venture and had married the daughter of Robert Livingston, secretary of Indian affairs. Soon Vetch was involved in illicit trade with Canada. In

1702, he moved to Boston, where he expanded his trade with Acadia. At one point British authorities seized and condemned Vetch's ship *Mary*, but this only temporarily halted Vetch's trade.

Because of Vetch's connections with the French, Governor Dudley, believed to have an interest in the French trade, sent Vetch to Quebec in 1705 to negotiate a truce with the French and to arrange for an exchange of prisoners. Improving his opportunity, Vetch made deals of his own with the French. Finally, his open disregard of the law could not be overlooked, and in 1706, he and five others were tried and fined by the General Court of Massachusetts. Appealing the case to the Privy Council, Vetch and his companions had their sentences annulled on the ground the General Court was not competent to try them.

This did nothing to curb Vetch's interest in Canada or his influence with Dudley, who sent him to London with a request to the queen from the General Court begging for military aid against the French. Vetch proved such a persuasive emissary that early in 1709, authorities in London sent him back with a promise of help - five regiments with naval support - and a commission to raise troops in the colonies north of Maryland. Colonel Francis Nicholson, the colonial expert, came along as a volunteer.

Vetch was to raise all the troops he could muster.

The combined English-colonial force was to attack Montreal by way of Lake Champlain and Quebec by sea. This movement would force the French to surrender Canada. The plan was excellent; the execution was faulty.

By summer, Vetch had raised three regiments, though Pennsylvania and New Jersey refused to send troops. Colonel Nicholson was placed in command of the troops to attack Montreal. All through the summer, the colonials waited for British ships and the promised five regiments. Nothing happened, and the morale of the volunteers deteriorated. Finally, on October 11, Governor Dudley received a letter from the British ministry that the promised aid had been diverted to Portugal for an emergency. Vetch and others proposed they attack Canada, but British captains refused to cooperate.

Colonial leaders once more appealed to London. The General Court of Massachusetts sent Nicholson with a petition to the queen, requesting help in launching an attack on Port Royal. Peter Schuyler took five Mohawk chiefs to London (one died before reaching England) to plead the cause. The Mohawks proved to be a sensation. Dressed in exotic apparel supplied by a theatrical costumer, the Indians were presented to Queen Anne, one as an emperor and the others as kings. Schuyler's showmanship probably did more than Nicholson's petition to focus the government on North America. In 1710, the government authorized an attack on Port Royal, commissioned Nicholson as commander, and promised 500 marines with supporting naval vessels.

Although colonial authorities had requested shipping by March, the British vessels did not arrive until July, and the expedition was not ready to sail until September. In the meantime, volunteers had been slow to leave their labors for military ventures; they remembered the long and fruitless wait the previous year. But Massachusetts encouraged enlistment by promising a month's pay in advance, a coat worth thirty shillings, and the right to keep the queen's musket after the return from Port Royal.

On September 24, the expedition arrived off Port Royal, and the attack began the next day. The garrison was too weak to withstand a long siege, and the French gave up on October 2. The surrender was conducted with much ceremony. The French troops, marching out with drums beating and colors flying, passed between the ranks of the British and colonials and saluted. Nicholson, now a brigadier general, Vetch, commissioned as military governor, and Sir Charles Hobby, naval commander, marched into the fort after accepting the keys from Daniel d'Auger de Subercase, governor of Acadia. As a mark of their respect for French ladies, conquering officers provided a breakfast for them.

In honor of Queen Anne, Nicholson changed the name of the settlement to Annapolis Royal. Its capture gave the British command of all Acadia. But the French remained entrenched in the St. Lawrence Valley, and Samuel Vetch's plan for the complete elimination of the French in Canada awaited fulfillment. Nicholson appealed to London for sufficient troops and ships to conquer Quebec and, surprisingly, gained the promise of adequate military and financial support.

The new expedition began in June 1711 with the arrival in Boston harbor of nearly seventy naval vessels under the command of Admiral Sir Hovenden Walker, with more than 5,000 troops commanded by General John Hill. This imposing expeditionary force was enough to satisfy the wildest dreams of colonial governors, but they knew little about the character of the expedition's leaders. Hill, known about the court as "Jolly Jack Hill," had no qualifications as an officer. He had received his appointment because he was a brother of Mrs. Masham, Queen Anne's favorite of the moment. Walker, equally incompetent, was timid and vacillating.

Although Bostonians did their best to entertain the British officers with proper ceremony, they made no favorable impression upon the arrogant visitors. The British regarded colonials as ill-trained buffoons and made no effort to hide their feelings. One artillery officer wrote in his journal he found the New Englanders intolerable because of their "ill Nature, and sowerness," their "Government, Doctrine, and Manners," their "hypocracy and canting." And he added that until the government canceled their charters, they would "grow more stiff and disobedient every Day." Many colonials were just as critical of the English troops. The stricter Puritans disliked soldiers and sailors carousing and swaggering in the streets on the Sabbath.

On July 30, augmented by New England militia, the expeditionary force sailed for Canada. Counting soldiers, sailors, marines, and provincial militia, the force numbered 12,000. Never before had such a large force been assembled in North America.

Lacking pilots for the St. Lawrence, they captured a French vessel and bribed the pilot to guide them. On the night of August 22, the fleet was near Anticosti Island, in fog with a stiff east wind blowing. Walker, confused and unfamiliar with his course, led his ships onto reefs off the Isle aux Oeufs, where eight transports, a store ship, and a sloop were wrecked, with the loss of 740 lives.

In the face of this disaster, Admiral Walker and General Hill held a council of war and decided that without pilots, they never could find Quebec. They sailed to Spanish River (now Sydney Harbour),

Cape Breton Island, where they held another council of war over whether to attack the little town of Placentia on Newfoundland. When they convinced themselves this also was too risky an undertaking, Walker sailed for England, New England transports took the militia home, and the vast show of might vanished into the mists.

In the meanwhile, Francis Nicholson was holding an army in camp on Lake Champlain ready to march on Montreal. When news reached him of Walker's failure, his rage intensified. Stamping on his wig and crying "Roguery! Treachery!" he damned Walker, Hill, and all their works. Nicholson then destroyed his own fortifications and disbanded his volunteers except for a small detachment to guard the frontier.

The war in Europe was about to end. After a truce in August 1712, Louis XIV sent his envoys to Utrecht to negotiate a peace, which was signed the next year. By the terms of the Treaty of Utrecht, Louis agreed that the thrones of France and Spain never would be united under one head. Acadia, Newfoundland, Hudson Bay, and St. Christopher and Nevis Islands in the Caribbean were to be surrendered to the English, and Louis had to acknowledge that the Iroquois were subjects of Great Britain. France retained Cape Breton Island, the St. Lawrence Valley, and territories beyond. No borders were established clearly, and no one knew where French possessions ended and British began. This failure to establish definite boundaries would lead to further conflict.

Spain, the almost forgotten ally of France, ceded Gibraltar and the island of Minorca to Great Britain and transferred from France the Asiento, a monopoly for thirty-three years of the African slave trade. Under this monopoly, the South Sea Company had the right to sell annually to the Spanish colonies in America 4,800 African slaves, obtained first from the Royal African Company and later from Jamaica. The Asiento provided that British merchants could send one ship each year to trade with the Spanish possessions.

The end of Queen Anne's War brought security to settlers on the frontiers of British North America, but the French did not suddenly disappear. In fact, they remained an obstacle to British expansion. They also continued to conspire with the Indians against the British. France hoped to regain Acadia and the rest of its lost territories in Canada. To that end, it began building a great fortification at Louisbourg on Cape Breton Island, a fortress that would enable it to command approaches to the St. Lawrence, the gateway to Canada. The next thirty years would be relatively peaceful for the colonies, but French power in the New World was by no means ending.

9
PEACE AND WAR

The Treaty of Utrecht in 1713, followed by the death of Louis XIV in 1715, brought a promise of peace to Europe and the colonies. A king obsessed with notions of military grandeur no longer governed France. Louis XIV had outlived his son and grandson, and the new king, Louis XV, the Sun King's great-grandson, was five years old.

England also had a new ruler. Queen Anne had died on August 1, 1714, without an heir. Her nearest of kin was a Stuart and a Catholic and therefore unacceptable, but she had a distant relative who was a Protestant. He was a German princeling, George, elector of Hanover, the great-grandson of James I of England through the union of James' daughter Elizabeth with Frederick, the elector of the Palatinate. Although George could speak no English, he was invited to take the throne. His accession introduced a system of rule by prime minister and cabinet that has persevered. The English people allowed the accession of a German king, but they showed little enthusiasm for the new monarch. At length, however, King George made amends by taking an English mistress too.

The formal treaty of peace in 1713 did not end all warfare on the American frontiers. Although delegates to the peace conference in Utrecht might sign an infinite number of papers, they could not control forces that had been unleashed in the North American wilderness. The English, French, and Spaniards living in the colonies continued to eye each other warily, and they often incited Indian allies in order to infringe on the others' territory. High stakes were involved, not only in the great territorial gamble of empire, but for merchants and traders in America. By 1713, trading centers existed in all the colonies, and in some an urban life had developed, with rich merchants eager to expand their commercial interests in the back country and overseas.

The eighteenth century is often described as the Age of Enlightenment because of its achievements in science, letters, and philosophy, but it might also be called the Age of Trade. The explorations of the sixteenth and seventeenth centuries were now bearing fruit. All the great maritime powers - England, France, Spain, Portugal, and Holland - had established overseas bases and were exploiting territories in Asia, Africa, and America. Although the wars that ravaged Europe - and the colonies overseas - through much of the eighteenth century frequently involved dynasties, the struggle to control commercial development and exploitation lay behind political rivalries. Commerce was to the eighteenth century what the Crusades were to the Middle Ages, an enterprise that absorbed the energies and aspirations of ambitious members of society.

In the British colonies of North America, the greatest urban development occurred in New England, which by the first quarter of the eighteenth century had a large number of towns depending upon commerce with the outer world. New York and Pennsylvania were becoming trading areas with a profitable back country that was a source of agricultural products for export. In the far South, Charles Town became an important center for the export of furs and deerskins, rice, indigo, and timber.

Provisions of the English Navigation Acts were designed to give the mother country a monopoly on colonial trade. Nevertheless, colonies profited from many of the restrictions, particularly one requiring commodities to be shipped in English or colonial vessels. Shipbuilding and shipping became an important source of profit for New Englanders.

Colonial affairs and the overseas trade had become so important by the end of the seventeenth century that in 1696, King William III created a Board of Trade and Plantations. This group replaced the Privy Council committee known as the Lords of Trade with an enlarged committee composed of councilors and eight paid members presumed to be specialists in various phases of activity such as fisheries and commerce, colonial legislation, and the appointment of personnel to serve in colonial administrations. The Board of Trade was an advisory body that made recommendations to the Privy Council and the sovereign. Until the end of the colonial period, it exerted varying degrees of influence. At times, it virtually controlled colonial affairs; at other times, the Privy Council or the secretary of state took direct action with little regard for the Board of Trade's recommendations, particularly in the appointment of colonial officials. The Board of Trade rarely could be held responsible for the poor quality of many colonial governors.

The English colonial structure, unlike that of Spain or France, was disastrous, with wide variations in the several colonies in the forms of government, the nature of land tenure, quality of inhabitants, religion, and the economic bases of development. Some colonies were virtually self-governing; others were under the jurisdiction of proprietors; still others were crown colonies with governors appointed from London. No two colonies were alike. For example, Pennsylvania and Maryland were both proprietary colonies, but they differed widely in economic and political characteristics. Communication between the colonies through much of the early period was slow and difficult. South Carolina had more direct and quicker communications with England than with Massachusetts Bay, and the same was true of other widely separated colonies. The disparate nature of the colonies and lack of an effective communications system prevented unity of action - even for the purpose of common defense - until late in the eighteenth century.

Colonials recognized the need for union as did government officials in London, and from time to time someone proposed bringing the colonies together. In 1697, for example, William Penn submitted a plan to the Board of Trade calling for a congress that would meet in New York with equal representation from all colonies. Four years later, an anonymous Virginian published a pamphlet in London entitled *An Essay upon the Government of the English Plantations on the Continent of America*. It advocated, among other things, a union of colonies with a scheme of representation nearly proportionate to the population. The author asserted it would be fairer to apportion the delegates so as to allow "Virginia four, Mary-Land three, New-York two, Boston three, Connecticut two, Rhode Island two, Pennsylvania one, the two Carolina's one, each of the two Jersey's one." His intention was to give the crown colonies the dominant voice in the congress, which would meet in rotation in each of five districts into which the colonies would be divided.

This *Essay* is revealing, for in addition to calling attention to the need for a union of the British colonies, it maintained that colonials were as much British subjects as if they lived in England itself, and they should have all the rights and liberties that other British subjects enjoyed. It called upon the authorities in London to send honest officials overseas, to provide colonies with competent administrators, and to reform the laws so all colonies could enjoy the same justice. Significantly, the *Essay* did not object to the Navigation Acts nor plead for a relaxation of the control of trade by the mother country. But it did ask for equity of treatment in several colonies. Although Virginia and Maryland were the most profitable colonies to England, the author maintained, they suffered from a heavy and unfair tax on their tobacco. He objected to the way New York and Philadelphia overlooked the actions of pirates and privateers.

Similar ideas were being expressed on both sides of the Atlantic, but the practical problems of union were too much for the ineffectual government in London and the rebellious colonies in America to overcome. The New England colonies, for example, always had been independent, and it was for this reason the government of James II had canceled their charters and placed them under the crown. Although the Dominion of New England under its royal governor, Edmund Andros, collapsed after the Glorious Revolution of 1688, and although New England colonies under William and Mary regained modified versions of their charters, they never recovered the freedom from interference they previously had enjoyed.

It had been the policy of William and Mary to bring the colonies under the authority of the crown. Massachusetts Bay, for all the efforts Increase Mather made to regain its charter, became a royal colony, as did New Hampshire. Henceforth, Whitehall appointed royal governors, who constantly squabbled with the legislative assemblies over royal prerogatives. Connecticut and Rhode Island retained the right to elect their governors and thus escaped some of the controversy that kept the colonies of Massachusetts and New Hampshire in turmoil throughout most of the eighteenth century.

Incompetent or corrupt governors, sent from London to improve their fortunes, plagued many colonies. "The chief End of many Governours coming to the Plantations, having been to get Estates for themselves," the author of the *Essay* complained, "very unwarrantable Methods have sometimes been made use of to compass those Ends, as by engrossing several Offices into their own Hands, selling them or letting them out at a yearly Rent of such part of the Profits, and also by Extortion and Presents, (or Bribery) these things have been [done] heretofore, and in ill Times may be done again."

Few colonies were more unfortunate in their royal governors than New York. The last decade of the seventeenth century had brought the administrations of a drunken profligate in Henry Sloughter, a friend of pirates and rogues in Benjamin Fletcher, and an ornamental but incompetent dandy in Richard Coote, Earl of Bellomont. The eighteenth century began even less auspiciously with the appointment in 1702 of Edward Hyde, Lord Cornbury, as governor of New York and New Jersey. Avaricious, arrogant, and dissolute, Cornbury loved to dress in women's clothes and visit the seamiest taverns in New York. He squandered money stolen from the public treasury and borrowed from anyone foolish enough to offer him credit. He was at last arrested for debt but managed to return to England to inherit the title of the Earl of Clarendon. Not until 1710 did New York receive a royal governor who combined honesty and competence. In that year

Queen Anne appointed Robert Hunter, a Scot, who labored to bring order into the administrative chaos of New York's royal government, as well as that of New Jersey. Nevertheless, New York remained split between factions: Rich merchants and great landowners monopolized power while farmers, craftsmen, tradesmen, and lesser merchants complained about taxes and inequities in government.

Pennsylvania proved a difficult problem for London authorities, who had frequent cause to regret its virtual independence. Penn's charter made the proprietor and his heirs owners of the land in Pennsylvania; the proprietor was supreme head and governor, though he could appoint a deputy to serve in his place. Penn had set forth his plan for ruling the colony in a document he called his first Frame of Government, under which a popular assembly was called on December 4, 1682. Under Penn's Frame of Government, the colony had a council (ultimately composed of eighteen members), elected by the freeholders. Together with the governor, the council initiated laws and submitted them for approval to the popular assembly. The Privy Council in London had to approve laws from the Pennsylvania assembly, and appeals could be taken from decisions of the Pennsylvania courts to the English courts. Both the people and the proprietor were unwilling to see the colony come under the rule of the crown, but for a brief time after 1688, William III converted Pennsylvania into a royal colony with Benjamin Fletcher as governor. This experiment did not work well, and in 1694, the king restored Pennsylvania to the proprietor. At the beginning of the eighteenth century, in 1701, the proprietor granted a new charter of privileges that made a single-chamber assembly the supreme law-making authority. The Quakers who controlled the assembly were unwilling to cooperate with other colonies and were opposed to participation in various wars that swept North America during the eighteenth century. Furthermore, the Quaker merchants of Philadelphia showed a persistent distaste for the acts of trade, and many smugglers made their home port on the Delaware River. Orders from Whitehall were often ignored in Philadelphia, and London found Pennsylvania more often obstinant than obedient.

The religious tolerance guaranteed settlers in Pennsylvania, the ease with which land could be had, the fertility of the soil, and the opportunities for trade combined to increase the flow of immigrants into Pennsylvania in the early years of the eighteenth century. Germans - Mennonites and related sectarians, as well as Lutherans - secured farmland in what is now Lancaster County. French Huguenots, including many skilled craftsmen, settled in Philadelphia. Scottish immigrants from Ulster in Ireland, unhappy over their treatment at the hands of the English, streamed through the port of Philadelphia into the back country, beyond the German settlements. They shared none of the pacifist notions of the Quakers and the sectarians. Although the Pennsylvania government officially might follow a pacifist line, the Scottish frontiersmen were ready to shoulder a musket in defense of hearth and home.

Maryland, like Pennsylvania, a proprietary colony, underwent a political upheaval after the revolution of 1688 and the flight of James II. Because the proprietary family, the Calverts, the Lords Baltimore, were Catholics, and Maryland had many Catholic settlers, William III's new government reasoned they would support the deposed king. Protestant dissidents in Maryland spread rumors of a Catholic uprising and petitioned William to take over the proprietary government, which he did in August 1691, with the appointment of Sir Lionel Copley as the first royal governor. Lord Baltimore was permitted to retain his rights in Maryland and to collect rent, but he no longer had any say in the government.

During the early years of the eighteenth century, Benedict Calvert, son and heir of Charles Calvert, third Lord Baltimore, publicly renounced the Catholic faith and became a communicant of the Church of England. Benedict was careful to bring this fact to the notice of the new sovereign, George

I, in a petition to have the proprietary government restored. King George looked with favor upon the petition and in 1715 reinstated the proprietary government. Benedict Calvert did not live to enjoy it, but his minor son, Charles, fifth Lord Baltimore, became the fourth proprietor. (Although the colony was again a proprietary government, the influence of the royal authority remained an important factor, and the proprietors were careful not to risk another suspension of their charter.) Before handing Maryland over to the proprietor, the royal government began to revise the laws of Maryland to conform to the common law of England, and in 1715, the legislative assembly adopted a code of laws that remained in effect with little alteration throughout the colonial period.

The two Carolinas, which had started as a single colony under eight proprietors, from the beginning found the rule of a conglomerate body of absentee landlords unsatisfactory. The unwieldy Fundamental Constitutions, spun from the fertile brains of John Locke and Anthony Ashley Cooper, proved an impractical instrument of government. Proprietary governors were incompetent or corrupt, and sometimes both. During the late seventeenth and early eighteenth centuries, friction was constant between settlers and the governing body of the aristocratic establishment, which had to be modified and eventually abandoned. In 1710, proprietors sent Edward Hyde, a cousin of Queen

Anne's, to be governor of North Carolina and to be independent of the governor of South Carolina, a date that marks the division of the two Carolinas into separate jurisdictions. The Board of Trade was eager to cancel the charters of the proprietors, but they were both numerous and influential, and it was not until 1719 that an opportunity arose. In November of that year, inhabitants of South Carolina rebelled against the proprietors, called a convention, and asked to be taken over by the crown. On May 29, 1721, Francis Nicholson, by now a sort of professional colonial governor, arrived in Charles Town as the first royal governor of the province.

In 1729, the king canceled the proprietary charters and made North Carolina a crown colony. George Burrington, appointed royal governor in 1731, was the first in a line of governors who sought to strengthen the crown's authority in North Carolina and to bring order out of the chaos that had existed under the proprietary government. North Carolina already had a diverse population, many seeking freedom from persecution. Quakers from colonies to the north, French Huguenots from Virginia and from overseas, Palatine Germans and Swiss brought to New Bern by two promoters, Christopher de Graffenried and Franz Louis Michel, native English of various religious beliefs, malcontents and refugees from Virginia justice found their way into North Carolina. The population of North Carolina in 1715 has been estimated at 11,200, of whom 3,700 were slaves, held for the most part by landowners on the coast. A few years after the establishment of the royal government, Scots in large numbers began coming to North Carolina. The older settlements on the coast developed an aristocratic plantation society, but in the back country, small farmers were a large part of the population.

Religious controversies rocked both the Carolinas. The wealthier settlers who had come early to the coastal regions had been English and predominantly Anglican in religion. But in North Carolina, where Quakers and dissenters were numerous, the Anglicans had difficulty maintaining an established church, and it was not until 1715 that they managed to enact a law that supported an established church by taxation. Even so, rebellious Quakers, Presbyterians, and other nonconformists worked to evade the provisions of the law. Anglican partisans regarded the state of the church in North Carolina as deplorable. William Byrd of Virginia, a biased and critical commentator on North Carolina society, remarked in his 1728 *History of the Dividing Line* that "this [Edenton] is the only Metropolis in the Christian or Mahometan World, where there is neither Church, Chappel, Mosque, Synagogue, or any other Place of Publick Worship of any Sect or Religion whatsoever. What little Devotion there may happen to be is much more private than their vices. The People seem easy without a Minister, as long as they are exempted from paying Him. Sometimes the Society for propagating the Gospel has had the Charity to send over Missionaries to this Country; but unfortunately the Priest has been too Lewd for the people, or, which oftener happens, they too lewd for the Priest. For these Reasons these Reverend Gentlemen have always left their Flocks as arrant Heathen as they found them."

In 1706, South Carolina, where Anglicans made up approximately half of the population, enacted a law making the Church of England the official church of the colony. The Huguenots, who might have been expected to question this, saw the wisdom of joining the tax-supported church. But, as in North Carolina, many nonconformists objected to paying taxes to support a state church and broke the law. The established church, here as elsewhere in the colonies, did not offer qualified ministers for the pulpit. In some instances, clergymen disgraced their congregation and brought scandal to the church by keeping concubines or being drunk in public.

Despite political bickering and religious controversy, both of the Carolina colonies made rapid progress in the first two decades of the eighteenth century. By 1720, settlers in South Carolina numbered 9,000, and the population of slaves was estimated at 12,000. The influx of slaves from Africa was the result of the Asiento, the monopoly of the slave trade granted to Great Britain by the Treaty of Utrecht. Because of the profits from this shameful traffic, English slave traders pushed their human cargoes upon the West Indies and the southern colonies. In the Carolinas, slaves from Africa could be used in the pine forests to produce naval stores. After the turn of the century, rice, first grown in South Carolina about 1685, became a profitable crop for export, and the labor of slaves was crucial to maintaining that profit. Customs records for 1718 show that South Carolina shipped to England in that year 6,773 barrels of rice, 18,414 barrels of pitch, and 27,660 barrels of tar, besides lumber, spars, and deerskins. Large quantities of these products were also shipped to other colonies.

During the first third of the eighteenth century, the Carolinas were outpost colonies standing as a barrier against Spanish penetration from the south and French infiltration from the lower Mississippi Valley. On their frontiers were powerful Indian nations. Populous and powerful, the Cherokees, Creeks, Chickasaws, and Choctaws prevented indefinite expansion west. These Indian nations had conflicting interests, and it was not always easy to keep peace with one tribe without antagonizing another. Furthermore, as in the case of the Choctaws, the Indians were shrewd enough to play off the French or Spaniards against English colonists.

In 1711, North Carolina suffered a devastating attack from an Iroquoian tribe, the Tuscaroras. These tribesmen, who had established themselves along coastal rivers, were concerned with European settlers occupying their territories. The settlement of De Graffenried's colonists at New Bern in 1710 posed a threat to the Tuscaroras' occupancy of land along the Neuse River, and they had other grievances. Traders, they claimed, had cheated them of their goods, abused their wives, stolen their children to be sold into slavery, and committed other egregious crimes. On September 22, 1711, the Tuscaroras made a concerted attack on settlements on the peninsula between the Neuse River and Pamlico Sound, slaughtering a large proportion of settlers in this area.

At this juncture, Governor Hyde called upon South Carolina and Virginia for help. Governor Alexander Spotswood of Virginia used the emergency to try to force North Carolina to cede disputed territory on the border as the price of assistance; when North Carolina refused, he ordered his militia not to go beyond the Virginia boundary. South Carolina, on the other hand, sent a force of thirty Europeans and 500 Indians under Colonel John Barnwell (who earned the moniker of "Tuscarora Jack") to aid the beleaguered North Carolinians. They were short of ammunition and other supplies, and the Quakers, a substantial part of the population, refused to fight or furnish food or horses. Nevertheless,

Barnwell and North Carolina militia won two battles with the Tuscaroras in January 1712 and made a hasty peace. Before the end of the ensuing summer, however, the truce was broken, and war resumed. This time South Carolina sent Colonel James Moore. On March 20, 1713, he killed several hundred Indians and captured 400 more to be sold into slavery at ten pounds each, a way of paying part of the cost of the expedition. After this defeat, the surviving Tuscaroras began retreating slowly to the North, where they eventually joined their Iroquoian brethren as one of the Six Nations.

Two years after the defeat of the Tuscaroras, South Carolina saw the beginning of a disastrous war with the Yamasees, a Muskhogean tribe that had moved from Georgia into territory north of the Savannah River. Like the Tuscaroras, they bore grudges against white traders who cheated them and against settlers who were moving into their hunting grounds. Early in the spring of 1715, rumors of an Indian conspiracy reached Charles Town, and on April 15, the Yamasees slaughtered members of a mission sent from Charles Town to negotiate their grievances. The Indians hoped to drive the settlers from their lands forever. The Yamasees had planned shrewdly and had won the promise of aid from Indians in South Carolina and adjacent territories, except for the Cherokees and the Chickasaws. The settlers in South Carolina, on the other hand, were ill-prepared for war. Such militiamen as the colony could muster were poorly trained, undisciplined, and badly equipped. In the emergency, the legislative assembly authorized an army of 600 South Carolinians, 100 Virginians sent by Governor Spotswood, 400 slaves, who, with great misgivings, were armed during the crisis, and 100 Indians.

Governor Charles Craven led a small force against the Yamasees on the Combahee River, and by early June 1715, he had stemmed the first onslaught upon the colony. Other Indian tribes, however, were already on the warpath. In midsummer, while Craven, reinforced by a small body of North Carolinians, was advancing against Cheraws north of the Santee, the Creeks and other tribes reached the settlements south of Charles Town. Beset on all sides, Craven sought aid from other colonies. Governor Robert Hunter of New York responded by trying to persuade Indians in his jurisdiction to help colonists in the south. At this juncture, the Cherokees, who had been neutral, attacked the Creeks. Their support was decisive, and by the summer of 1717, the Yamasees and their allies, the Creeks, were ready to make peace.

The Cherokees knew South Carolina owed its survival to their intervention, and they made the most of their position. The Cherokees had no love for the colonists and used the opportunity to drive a hard bargain in their own interest. In January

1717, they demanded and received privileges that traders considered insulting. Some South Carolinians asserted that the Cherokees treated them as a tributary nation.

But the Cherokees were as influenced by self-interest as the Virginians. Although Governor Spotswood had sent only a few militiamen to aid the South Carolinians, he attempted to use the emergency to increase the prestige of Virginia with the Indians. Other Virginians were actually glad to see their rivals in the Indian trade demoralized and, the South Carolinians charged, sold guns and ammunition to the warring Indians. These Virginians were angry with South Carolinians, who had tried to keep them out of the trading areas in their territory and even had appealed to the Board of Trade in London to forbid other colonials into the Carolina back country. Intercolonial rivalry for the lucrative Indian trade helps to explain why the colonies found it difficult to unite in a common cause.

During the early years of the eighteenth century, the South Carolina coast was prey to pirates who had bases in the Bahamas or on islands farther south in the Caribbean. The coves and inlets on the North Carolina coast were convenient hideouts for these marauders, who attacked ships of all nations. Many of the pirates had been legitimate privateers during Queen Anne's War, but after the Treaty of

Utrecht, they refused to give up an occupation so profitable. Henceforth, a ship's flag made little difference if the vessel carried a rich cargo. The Carolinians did not regard English pirates as pests. Some argued they served a purpose in fending off Spanish and French ships. Other Carolinians saw a chance to enrich themselves with pirate gold as New Yorkers were accused of doing. The pirate Edward Teach (or Thatch), known as Blackbeard, found a haven at Bath, North Carolina, and befriended Governor Charles Eden's secretary, Tobias Knight, who allowed him to use his barn as a warehouse. Governor Eden was accused of being friendly to pirates. Steele Stede Bonnet, a pirate more notorious in his day than Blackbeard, would raid shipping headed for Charles Town from a base on the lower Cape Fear River. These and other pirates became such a hazard to commerce that in 1718, Governor Robert Johnson of South Carolina ordered Colonel William Rhett on a mission to rid the coast of pirates. Rhett cornered Bonnet in Cape Fear River and, after a six-hour battle, captured him and his crew. Bonnet, a gentleman of wealth with a fine house on Barbados, had friends in Charles Town, and there is evidence of an attempt to set him free. But on December 10, 1718, he and twenty-nine members of his crew were hanged.

In May 1717, Blackbeard captured nine ships off Charles Town, then was brash enough to sail into the harbor and demand a chest of medicine. Unless the town supplied the medicine, he threatened to burn shipping in the harbor, kill his prisoners, and devastate the town. He got his chest of drugs. But Blackbeard's days were numbered. In the autumn of 1718, Governor Spotswood of Virginia heard the pirate was cruising off the North Carolina coast. He recruited sailors from the tobacco fleet and sent two armed sloops commanded by an officer of the Royal Navy, Lieutenant Robert Maynard, to pursue Blackbeard. Maynard encountered Blackbeard off Oeracoke Island. The pirates boarded Maynard's sloop, but the British lieutenant rallied his men and defeated the pirates. Maynard killed Blackbeard, cut off his head, lashed it to his bowsprit, and sailed for Virginia, taking along the surviving members of the pirate's crew, who were tried, convicted, and hanged.

Before the end of 1718, South Carolina listed forty-nine pirates hanged in Charles Town, and the combined efforts of the Virginians and Carolinians forced most pirates who survived to move to less hostile waters. Pirates continued to be a menace off the coasts of the northern colonies, but they developed a healthy respect for colonial justice in the South.

The end of the Yamasee War and the suppression of pirates increased opportunities for trade and commerce in the southern colonies, but the region was still a frontier in danger of attack, not only from the unpredictable Indians, but also from the Spaniards and French. The founding of New Orleans in 1718 gave France a bastion in the lower Mississippi Valley that increased the danger of encirclement from the rear. The Spaniards strengthened their base at St. Augustine and were ready to infiltrate disputed territory in present-day Georgia and Alabama. All three competed vigorously for Indian trade and sought to lure the border tribes into their respective orbits. English settlers on the southern frontier were aware of the three-cornered contest for imperial domination of disputed territories, and colonial officials constantly were writing to the Board of Trade about the problem.

All British colonies realized France was a threat to their existence. Spain was an established enemy, who from their base at St. Augustine could thwart any British expansion to the south, although Spanish strength, with less than 2,000 settlers in Florida, was limited. Nevertheless, Spain had troops and ships in Cuba and elsewhere in its American empire that were a potential menace. Furthermore, Spanish Indian traders were competing actively with the English and French in the lower Mississippi Valley.

The competition for Indian trade caused bitterness between all three countries. In 1717, the French granted a monopoly of the Indian trade in Louisiana to the Compagnie des Indes, and Bienville, now governor, began to strengthen French bases in the South. In addition to the base at New Orleans, which he made the capital of Louisiana, he moved east into what was clearly Spanish territory. By 1719, the French and the Spaniards were fighting for the possession of the Spanish fort at Pensacola. On their part, the Spaniards moved into Louisiana from New Mexico and attempted to establish themselves at the forks of the Platte River, in what is now Nebraska. A combined force of Indians and French traders drove them back to New Mexico. The conflict between the erstwhile allies ended in 1721, and the French and Spanish returned to the territories they previously had claimed or occupied.

To British colonists, the contention between Spanish and French colonials brought little comfort, for it meant each would try to strengthen its position in the disputed territory. It also meant continued confusion and disturbance among the Indians. From Maine to South Carolina, British colonists braced for further trouble. In London, the Board of Trade listened more attentively to reports from overseas and urged action upon the Privy Council and the king.

Authorities in London were beginning to realize the need to develop a policy to stop France and Spain. Acting on pleas from South Carolina, the royal government in 1721 dispatched a company of regular soldiers to occupy a fort at the mouth of the Altamaha River, south of Savannah, in territory claimed by Spain. Although these troops suffered disease and proved ineffective, they symbolized Whitehall's awareness of the colonial problem of defense against common enemies. The fort on the Altamaha was christened Fort King George.

South Carolinians had taken measures to guard their commerce with the Indians by establishing fortified trading posts along the Savannah River. One of the most important of these posts was Fort Moore, near Augusta, Georgia. Other fortified posts were established along the Savannah and on the Congaree River, near the site of Columbia, South Carolina. To protect the South Coast, a base was maintained at Port Royal with two scouting craft - the total navy South Carolina could support. From interior bases, rangers, recruited from the militia, patrolled the back country to keep Indians at bay and intercept French and Spanish emissaries and traders. In the eyes of these rangers - and of the merchants of Charles Town - traders from Virginia were almost as unwelcome as those from foreign countries.

Governor Spotswood of Virginia was eager to demonstrate to London and to other colonies that he was a leader in efforts to curb their common enemies on the frontiers. (His reports and recommendations to the Board of Trade, however, echo those sent by Governor Nicholson of South Carolina.) So concerned was Spotswood over the danger from French infiltration of the back country that, disregarding logistics and distance, he proposed to the Board of Trade that Virginia use funds from customs and other fees to build a fortress on Lake Erie to serve as an outpost of English power and help stop the French advance into the Ohio and Mississippi valleys. Spotswood's intentions were sounder than his knowledge of geography, but his concern about the French in the upper Mississippi basin and their increasing expansion from New Orleans helped alert authorities in London to the importance of devising a consistent western policy designed to contain both the French and Spaniards.

By the beginning of the second quarter of the eighteenth century, English colonies along the North American seaboard were pushing trade with the Indians of the interior and working to counter French efforts to restrict their presence to the coastal region. A map of Louisiana, made by royal cartographer, Guillaume Delisle, and issued in Paris in 1718, had indicated the French intention to deny all the interior of the continent to the English. Throughout the colonies, fear persisted that, unless the English took measures, the French ultimately might push them into the sea. By erecting forts on the Altamaha in 1721, and at Oswego in 1727, London showed its realization that the defense of the colonies required a chain of fortifications on the frontier and imperial troops to man them.

The southern frontier remained a problem for England. South Carolina traders, expanding business with the Cherokee and Creek Indians, competed directly with French *coureurs de bois* pushing east, and the Carolinians were aware of the seriousness of the French threat. The Carolinians welcomed the establishment of a buffer colony to the south in 1732, to relieve pressure on that frontier.

The settlement of Georgia was not the first attempt by British promoters to found a colony between Florida and South Carolina. Sir Robert Montgomery of Skemorlie, Scotland, devised the most unique plan - a feudal dominion in the New World that he would rule from a great palace in the center of his possessions. From the proprietors of South Carolina, who laid claim to the territory, Montgomery and two partners, Aaron Hill, a dramatic poet, and Amos Kettleby, a merchant of London, obtained a grant of all land between the Altamaha and Savannah rivers, extending west to the Pacific Ocean. This land the partners named Azilia, and in 1717, they published one of the most extravagant pieces of promotion to appear in the colonial period, a tract entitled *Discourse concerning the Design'd Establishment of a New Colony to the South of Carolina in the most delightful Country of the Universe*. The tract described the land as "our future Eden" and asserted that English writers "universally agree that Carolina, and especially its Southern Bounds, is the most amiable Country in the Universe: that Nature has not bless'd the World with any Tract, which can be preferable to it, that Paradise, with all her Virgin Beauties, may be modestly suppos'd at most but equal to its Native Excellencies." The pamphlet further pointed out that Azilia "lies in the same Latitude with Palestine Herself, That promis'd Canaan, which was pointed out by God's own Choice, to bless the Labours of a favourite People. It abounds with Rivers, Woods, and Meadows. Its gentle Hills are full of Mines, Lead, Copper, Iron, and even some of Silver. . . . Vines, naturally flourishing upon the Hills, bear Grapes in most luxuriant Plenty. They have every Growth which we possess in England, and almost every Thing that England wants besides. The Orange and the Limon thrive in the same common Orchard with the Apple, and the Pear-Tree, Plumbs, Peaches, Apricots, and Nectarins bear from Stones in three years growing. The Planters raise large Orchards . . . to feed their Hogs with."

Azilia, its promoters maintained, would supply England with all those commodities it lacked: silk, cochineal, coffee, tea, raisins, olives, currants, almonds, and wine. Unhappily, the schemes of Montgomery, Hill, and Kettleby were for naught. The crash of the South Sea Company in 1720 swept Azilia into oblivion.

Several years later, another Scottish baronet, Sir Alexander Cuming of Coulter, proposed a project more fantastic than Azilia, creating a refuge for 300,000 Jews on the tribal lands of the Cherokees. This colony would serve as a barrier against Indian or French aggression from the west. The Cherokees' opinion of the proposed Zion on their lands is not recorded, but Sir Alexander's visit created a lasting impression on the Indians. Looking like a counterpart of Don Quixote, the Scottish baronet appeared among the Cherokees in the spring of 1730. Well-armed and boasting of the power of King George II, he convinced them that he represented a king whose power reached even to their hill towns. At a tribal council, he urged the chiefs to kneel and swear allegiance to King George and had himself acclaimed the king's viceroy. With some persuasion, he induced six Cherokees, one a minor chief, to visit London and the court of King George. Near Charles Town, another Indian joined their party. When they finally reached England, the chief was a king, and the other Indians were dubbed chiefs or generals. On June 18, 1730, King George received the delegation, and during the next three months the Cherokee "king" and his fellows captivated London. They were entertained, feted, and introduced to English vices. At length, the Cherokees returned to their people with tales of the power of the English sovereign and the wonders of his court and country. Their report of the strength of the English undoubtedly helped persuade the Cherokees to remain loyal to England during the French wars.

The public excitement created by Montgomery and Cuming's schemes focused attention on the southern frontier. In the summer of 1730, General James Oglethorpe and a group of associates developed another plan for a colony, more practical than the others - the notion of a refuge in the New World for indigent debtors. Oglethorpe, a distinguished soldier and Parliament member, had served as chairman of a committee to investigate the condition of debtors' prisons. What he discovered stirred a philanthropic impulse, and he persuaded twenty like-minded men, prominent in government, to join him in petitioning for a grant of land to the south of Carolina (the area Montgomery had called Azilia) for debtors who would rehabilitate themselves by honest labor. Two years after the project was started, the government, on June 9, 1732, granted a charter to the twenty-one trustees for twenty-one years, authorizing the colony of Georgia. At the expiration of the charter, the colony would revert to the crown. Any rights that the Lords Proprietors of Carolina had to the land ended when seven of the eight proprietors sold out to the king.

The British government was eager to establish this colony, for it recognized its strategic values.

Oglethorpe, a military man, had pointed this out in his petition. The trustees, however, were determined not to let the colony become a military outpost. They were concerned about its philanthropic aims and formulated elaborate regulations to promote the cause. Because of the social prominence of the trustees, all England soon heard about Georgia, and pamphleteers outdid themselves in commending it. Money, commodities, and advice immediately arrived from sympathetic contributors, and the trustees began to process applicants for settlement. By the autumn 1732, more than 100 colonists had won the approval of the trustees, and they set sail in the ship *Anne*, accompanied by Oglethorpe. Arriving at Charles Town on January 13, 1733, they took additional supplies and sailed for Georgia. Oglethorpe got his people ashore on February 12, eighteen miles from the mouth of the Savannah River, and there he laid out a town that he named Savannah. Like William Penn in Philadelphia, Oglethorpe planned a town of orderly squares.

Again like Penn, Oglethorpe sought to make Georgia a refuge for oppressed people everywhere. The propaganda of the trustees induced 1,200 Lutherans from Salzburg to settle in Georgia. Another group of Germans, a body of Moravians who came under the sponsorship of Count Nikolaus von Zinzendorf, received land on the border, where they were subject to attack from both Indians and Spaniards. Since they were pacifists and refused to serve in the militia, they decided to move to Pennsylvania and other safer places in the North. During the period of the trustees' jurisdiction, Georgia acquired a diverse group of settlers from Switzerland, Germany, Italy, and Scotland.

Oglethorpe had the imagination and vision of an empire builder. In the spring of 1734, he returned to England to further his plans. With him he took a group of Creek Indians, including a chief, Tomo-Chi-Chi, from whom he had bought the site of Savannah and other land. The Creeks created a greater sensation in London than the Cherokees who had accompanied Sir Alexander Cuming of Coulter. The king and the Archbishop of Canterbury received the Indians in formal ceremonies. One Indian won acclaim by reciting the Lord's Prayer in both Creek and English. Crowds followed them wherever they went and at times rioted in an effort to see them. At last, after collecting many gifts, the Indians returned to Georgia and spread the word of the might and glory of England to such effect that both the Creeks and Cherokees made pacts of friendship with the new colony of Georgia. Tomo-Chi-Chi remained a friend of the colony, and when he died at the age of 100, he was buried, at his request, in Savannah.

Parliament was so impressed with the importance of Georgia that it appropriated 26,000 pounds to the settlement, and from 1735 onward, colonists sought land in the colony. In 1736, Oglethorpe returned, accompanied by John and Charles Wesley, founders of Methodism, and other zealous souls. Oglethorpe, a military man who realized the importance of fortifications and communications, began building forts and roads. He made his headquarters on St. Simons Island, in the town of Frederica. A fortified outpost far up the Savannah River at Augusta proved a useful center for frontier defense and served as a gateway to the Indian country, where Georgia traders competed with the Carolinians. On the Florida border, Oglethorpe persuaded Scottish Highlanders to establish outposts. To connect the various fortified areas, he laid out connecting roads, and the road from Savannah to Augusta became an important trade route.

The development of Georgia turned out to be more expensive than either the promoters or parliament had anticipated, but trouble with Spain prompted the government to continue its support of the colony's defenses and send troops to supplement the militia. The soldiers arrived just in time for, in 1739, England declared war on Spain, a conflict known as the War of Jenkins' Ear, and the border between Florida and Georgia was immediately involved. The smuggling activities of ship captain Robert Jenkins precipitated the war. Jenkins appeared in the House of Commons and reported that Spanish sailors had searched and pillaged his ship, cut off his ears, and told him to take them to his masters. To prove his contention, he took out his handkerchief and unwrapped a dried ear. In fact, Jenkins had been caught smuggling goods to the Spanish islands in violation of the provisions of the Asiento, but British shipping interests were so angry over the Spaniards assertion of the right of search and seizure at sea that they forced the government to declare war. Most of the fighting took place at sea and merged into the War of the Austrian Succession, known in the colonies as King George's War.

The Spanish, believing they could drive the English from Georgia and South Carolina, collected in Cuba an expedition of fifty ships, 1,800 troops, and 1,000 seamen. In July 1742, this force sailed for the coast of Georgia, but by bravery, stratagem, and the luck of the weather, Oglethorpe thwarted the attack and sent them back to the Caribbean. The next year he turned the tables on the Spaniards and attacked St. Augustine. However, lacking artillery to breach the walls and unable to lure the Spaniards to a fight in the open, he marched back to Georgia. Thus ended the War of Jenkins' Ear on the southern frontier.

In March 1744, after thirty-one years of peace, France and England again found themselves at war. Though the nations had not been hostile during this period, their subjects in the American forests occasionally had skirmished, and the declaration of war in the spring of 1744 made the whole frontier a war zone.

The French initiated war on the colonials by sending an expedition from their fortified base of Louisbourg on Cape Breton Island to prey on the New England fishing fleet and to capture the fishing town of Canso, Nova Scotia. The French commander promised to send prisoners taken at Canso to Boston, but kept them temporarily at Louisbourg while he made an unsuccessful attempt to take Annapolis Royal. When at length the prisoners were shipped to Boston, they took with them detailed plans of the French fortress of Louisbourg and a firm conviction they could take it. The capture of Louisbourg henceforth was the objective of Bostonians, who regarded it as a menace to the peace and commerce of all New England.

The French believed Louisbourg, anchor of their defenses in North America, to be impregnable. Built on plans made by the great engineer, Sébastien Le Prestre de Vauban, its massive stone walls held 250 guns. But, as the English prisoners reported in Boston, the garrison was weak. Convinced that Louisbourg could and should be taken, Governor William Shirley of Massachusetts launched a crusade that for once enlisted the support of all New England and New York. He collected ships, troops, and supplies in Boston and received from London the promise of naval support.

The expedition embarked on March 24, 1745, with William Pepperrell, a fish merchant from Kittery, Maine, in command. On April 23, his ships rendezvoused off Canso with Commodore Peter Warren, in command of three ships of the Royal Navy. During the last two days of April, soldiers began landing in preparation for an assault, but, to their surprise, on May 2, they found the Grand Battery abandoned and thirty of the guns disabled - the garrison had decided this outwork could not be held and had moved to the fortress. In a short time, the guns were repaired and turned against the fortress. Pepperrell decided to attack the fort from the land, where fortifications were weakest, and he dragged some of the captured guns around to bear on the walls. In the meantime, Warren was attacking the fort from the sea and preventing French supply ships from reaching the garrison.

The siege continued through the month of May. Pepperrell had trouble with undisciplined militia. A planned assault on May 23 had to be abandoned because most of the attacking force was drunk. Three days later, with enough sober troops to launch an attack, Pepperrell and his men landed at night at a point he believed vulnerable, only to have a drunken soldier cheer and give away their position. The ensuing fire killed at least sixty, and a French sortie captured 119.

Despite the gloom caused by this miscarriage of plans, the English forces continued to pound the fortress with shot and shell. On June 15, they planned to make a joint land and sea assault, but a flag of truce sent by the French opened the way for negotiations that on June 17 ended in the surrender of the Louisbourg fortification. A motley army of militia and fishermen, aided by three ships of the Royal Navy, had captured the strongest citadel in North America, and with it control of the St. Lawrence and the northern waters. No longer would French troops based at Louisbourg threaten New England fishermen.

To honor Pepperrell for his services, the British government created him a baronet. Governor Shirley was made colonel of a regiment that was presently disbanded. Commodore Warren was promoted to admiral and later knighted. He obtained large grants of land in the back country of New York, and his nephew, William Johnson, came from Ireland to look after his uncle's property.

In 1746, Governor Shirley, mindful of the great victory over the French at Louisbourg, proposed an expedition to capture Quebec. Acting on a promise of eight battalions of regular troops from England and British pay for the militia, he began to raise troops in New England. But the ministry in London decided to send troops to France and failed to notify Shirley of the change in plans.

Although reports of the expedition against Quebec alarmed the French in Canada, nothing came of it. Some of Shirley's men marched to join the New York militia in an attack on Crown Point, but they were recalled to resist a rumored attack by a French fleet on Boston.

In the meantime, the French had organized a fleet to recapture Louisbourg. Rarely, however, has an expedition encountered worse misfortune. Hurricanes battered it; two commanding officers died in succession, one by suicide; illness carried off hundreds of seamen and left the fleet barely enough men to work the ships. At last, the fleet returned to France without having damaged a single hostile ship or fortress in America. Although Louis XV ordered another fleet to retake Louisbourg, it, too, met disaster, this time at the hands of a flotilla commanded by Admirals Warren and Anson.

The war at last dragged to a close in Europe and dwindled to a few scattered forays on the borders in America. Politicians sat down to work out terms for peace, and by October 18, 1748, they completed the Treaty of Aix-la-Chapelle, which restored colonial America to its status before the war. The greatest blow to colonials was the return of Louisbourg to the French. With disdain for New England, the British ministry relinquished Louisbourg to gain Madras in India. The leaders and militia men of New England would not forget that London had let them down. The colonies had gained some military experience; they were beginning to perceive they must stand together.

10
DUEL FOR EMPIRE

In 1748, the Treaty of Aix-la-Chapelle ended the War of the Austrian Succession in Europe, but on the North American continent, it brought only temporary peace. The English and the French continued to try to outwit each other in competition for lands in the West and for profits of the Indian trade. Each side had its traditional Indian allies, and each side did its best to lure away the other's. In the mid-eighteenth century, through initiative and enterprise, English traders competed vigorously with the French on the frontiers across the Alleghenies - territory the French claimed as their own. Since English colonies also claimed lands stretching across the American continent to the Pacific, no one could foresee any prospect of reconciling these conflicting interests. The nations were on a collision course, and no treaties signed in Europe would influence French *coureurs de bois* or English traders.

Traders from Pennsylvania and Virginia were finding their way across the mountains into the country beyond. Since they were eager to protect their discoveries from competitors, they did not boast of their exploits. But English traders, hard-bitten frontiersmen, made their way along creeks and rivers across the mountains to reach the Ohio and the Mississippi. Before 1750, traders from Pennsylvania had made a base as far west as Pickawillany on the Miami River, near the present site of Piqua, Ohio. As many as fifty or more of these men were accustomed to bartering there with the western Indians for beaver pelts and other furs. A famous Miami Indian chief, called "Old Briton" by the English because of his friendship, and "La Demoiselle" by the French, for what reason is unclear, was the dominant power at Pickawillany. The English set up a blacksmith shop where they sharpened iron tools for Old Briton's Indians; they brought in guns, powder, and lead for barter; they maintained stores of blankets, rum, and other commodities the Indians desired. In short, the Pennsylvania traders had a thriving market at Pickawillany that pleased them and the Indians who flocked to it under the watchful eye of Old Briton.

Elsewhere in the western country, other traders were active. An important center for commerce with the Indians in the Ohio country was Logstown, on the north bank of the Ohio River, east of Beaver Creek and twenty miles northwest of the present site of Pittsburgh. There, Pennsylvanians and Virginians were accustomed to meeting with the western Indians. Pennsylvanians usually made their way into the back country by following the Susquehanna to its headwaters, while Virginians proceeded up the Potomac and its tributaries. At Wills Creek, now Cumberland, Maryland, they had an important supply depot for their traders.

Officially, Pennsylvania and Virginia were amicable and united in their efforts to counter the French and move to the West. Actually, their traders were often hostile to each other and were not above instigating dissension among Indians who favored their competitors. Furthermore, since Virginia claimed all land to the west of its border as far as the Pacific Ocean, Virginians regarded all outsiders who entered the lower Ohio Valley as trespassers.

While Virginians and Pennsylvanians were competing for trading posts in the West, the French were working with the Indians to circumvent their English rivals. Based on La Salle's discoveries, they claimed all the Ohio and Mississippi basin and the central area of the country south of the Great Lakes and west of the Alleghenies. In the summer of 1749, to reinforce their claim to the country, French governor general Marquis de la Galissonière ordered Captain Pierre-Joseph Céloron de Blainville (frequently called Bienville) to move down the Ohio River and repossess the country. On June 15, Céloron set out from Lachine with a party comprised of 156 to 246 men, counting French regulars, Canadians, and Indians, and including Lieutenant Philippe-Thomas de Joncaire, a Seneca by adoption and a shrewd diplomat with the Indians.

The expedition made its way from Lake Erie, down Lake Chautauqua, and overland to the Allegheny River, when Céloron proceeded downstream to its confluence with the Ohio. At various places, he buried lead plates engraved with the date, location, and the statement that this action was "a token of renewal of possession heretofore taken of the aforesaid River Ohio, of all streams that fall into it, and all lands on both sides to the source of the aforesaid streams, as the preceding Kings of France have enjoyed, or ought to have enjoyed it, and which they have upheld by force of arms and by treaties, notably by those of Ryswiek, Utrecht, and Aix-la-Chapelle."

Everywhere the French found evidence of English traders, but they had to be content with warning the Englishmen they encountered. They continued to bury lead plates claiming the country for France.

On August 31, having made a circuitous journey along various Ohio rivers, Céloron buried his last plate at the mouth of the Miami River and made his way back to Canada via Lake Erie. He had shown to the Indians and English traders that France was determined to hold the disputed territory. He had learned France must act quickly, or the land would be lost to invaders from the English colonies.

If the French needed any more evidence of the danger they faced of losing the West, an event at Pickawillany in the winter of 1751 provided it. George Croghan, Indian agent for Pennsylvania and a shrewd trader, came to Pickawillany with gifts from the government of Pennsylvania for the Miami Indians. Christopher Gist, an explorer and agent for the colony of Virginia, invited the Indians of the Ohio region to come to Virginia to receive gifts sent by the king of England. While Croghan and Gist were talking with the Indians, four Frenchmen arrived on a similar mission. They brought gifts and urged the Indians to engage in trade. The Indians received these gifts and listened intently to the speeches of the emissaries. During the council, English and French flags were flown. But when all had been heard, the Indians told the French to remove their colors.

What was more indicative, a delegation representing Indians in French territory on the Wabash came asking for an alliance with the English. For the time being, the English had won the day. Their secret lay in the abundance of their gifts and the strength they displayed.

The French, however, planned the destruction of the English in the Ohio Valley. The first blow came on June 21, 1752, when 240 Chippewa and Ottawa warriors from Canada, led by two Frenchmen, attacked Pickawillany. There were only eight Englishmen at the trading post; most were out hunting. After a futile battle defending the fort, the English surrendered. Old Briton was killed, and in a twisted celebration, the victors had a great feast at which he was boiled and eaten. The other Englishmen were taken to Canada. The conflict at Pickawillany signaled the beginning of a renewed French effort to drive the English from the West.

Meanwhile, a wave of land speculation was sweeping the colonies, and in Virginia particularly, the fever was rising. Dozens of land companies were being organized to capitalize upon Virginia's claims to the territory across the mountains. The most famous was the Ohio Company, organized in 1747 by Thomas Lee and a group of associates. Unlike some other syndicates bent upon exploiting western land, the Ohio Company applied to the Privy Council through the Board of Trade for a grant of 200,000 acres on the Ohio River. This was given in 1749, with the proviso the company should build a fort at the forks of the Ohio and settle 100 families on the grant within the next seven years.

While the Ohio Company was attempting to stabilize its possessions by invoking the authority of the Privy Council in London, another syndicate, the Loyal Company, headed by John Robinson, obtained from the provincial government 800,000 acres west of the border between Virginia and North Carolina. Still other grants were made to promoters who promised to fortify and colonize territories to the west.

Most Virginians with property were swept into the vortex of land speculation. All the great planters were dreaming of new estates in the West. Many already had taken land in the Shenandoah Valley, which by the mid-century was attracting German and Scottish settlers from Pennsylvania and the Carolinas. Tobacco culture in the tidewater had exhausted the soil of the older farming areas, and planters were eager for fresh land for their sons and heirs. Both the drive for land and the zest for speculation in a society in which gambling was common explain the personal concern Virginians felt about the French threat to the Ohio Valley.

Governor Robert Dinwiddie of Virginia was determined to checkmate the French by diplomacy, if possible, or by force, if necessary. Like all other prominent men of the colony, he was deeply involved in land speculations and did not intend to let the French ruin his investments. More than that, he realized that French domination of the Ohio and Mississippi river systems would mean disaster to all the English colonies, which forever would be confined to a narrow strip of the continent, east of the mountains. Both a personal and an imperial destiny were at stake, and Dinwiddie, along with other colonial administrators, tried to awake London from its lethargy.

But stirring London in the middle years of the reign of George II was not easy. The North American continent was a long way from Whitehall and the clubs in St. James Street. The War of the Austrian Succession in 1740-48, the Jacobite Rebellion of 1745-46, and the pacification of the Scots had sapped the energies of politicians and left them indifferent to new problems. Let judges send Scottish rebels to settle in America where they could do no harm, and let colonists fend for themselves. A few loyal soldiers might get lucrative appointments to colonial posts from the king as a reward for their services, but in general, the less Whitehall heard about North America, the better politicians liked it. They had difficulties closer to home, principally the struggle for place and preferment. Not much could be expected of men such as Thomas Pelham-Holles, first Duke of Newcastle, the real head of the government, one of the most powerful politicians of the day - and one of the most ignorant. The cabinet officer charged with responsibility for the colonies was Sir Thomas Robinson, of whom a contemporary said Newcastle had achieved the remarkable feat of finding a man for the post more incompetent than himself. Petitions to London from the colonies were disregarded. If the colonies were concerned about the French, they must act themselves.

That is what Governor Dinwiddie proposed. News filtered into Virginia that the French were planning to strengthen their outposts on Lake Erie and build forts in the Ohio country. In 1752, the Marquis Duquesne became governor general of Canada and submitted a plan to the ministry in Paris for garrisoning the country south of the Great Lakes. In February 1753, Governor Dinwiddie heard reports that the French were building houses at Logstown and expressed the hope these were only traders. The English realized they ought to have forts in the region, but neither the Pennsylvania assembly nor the Virginia House of Burgesses would appropriate the necessary funds. Ohio Indians friendly with the English realized the threat posed by the French and asked for guns and ammunition to defend themselves, which Dinwiddie promised and eventually sent. But while the English continued to discuss the need for a fort on the Ohio, the French erected and garrisoned forts: Fort Presqu'Isle on the present site of Erie, Pennsylvania; Fort Le Boeuf at the head of French Creek (the present site of Waterford, Pennsylvania); and Fort Venango, at the mouth of French Creek where it joins the Allegheny (Franklin, Pennsylvania is the site today).

At this juncture, Dinwiddie decided to send a mission to the French in Ohio to warn them they were trespassing on Virginia's territory. To convey this message, he chose twenty-one-year-old George Washington. Setting out from Williamsburg on October 31, 1753, Washington went to Fredericksburg to hire a French interpreter, and then to Wills Creek, where he enlisted frontiersman Christopher Gist. They recruited a small group of soldiers and set forth into the wilderness to order the French out of land claimed by Virginia. It was not an imposing force for such a difficult mission, but Washington did not complain.

Through snowy woods and across icy streams, Washington's little party pushed on to the forks of the Allegheny and the Monongahela, a spot that Washington decided was more suitable for a fort than one selected by the Ohio Company a few miles down the river. In his *Journal*, he explains his reasons, and the French later affirmed his judgment when they, too, decided the site where the city of Pittsburgh now stands was the strategic place to fortify.

Twenty-five days after leaving Williamsburg, Washington arrived at Logstown, where he held a council with Indians presumed to be friendly to the English and informed them of his mission. While there, four French deserters gave him information about the disposition of French garrisons on the Mississippi. Washington counseled with Seneca Indian chief Tanacharisson, called the Half-King by the English, who controlled a miscellaneous group of Indians near Logstown. The Half-King, who professed an abiding friendship for the English, gave Washington a report of his own speech to the French. He urged that both the French and English withdraw from the Ohio and leave it to the Half-King's followers to maintain a buffer

As Washington reported the speech in his *Journal,* the Half-King told the French: "Fathers, Both you and the *English* are white, we live in a Country between; therefore the Land belongs to neither one nor t'other: But the Great Being above allow'd it to be a Place of Residence for us; so Fathers, I desire you to withdraw, as I have done our Brothers the *English;* for I will keep you at Arms length: I lay this down as a Trial for both, to see which will have the greatest Regard to it, and that Side we will stand by. . . ." According to Washington, the French commander replied sternly to this speech that he would go down the river, even if it were blocked, and would "tread under my Feet all that stand in Opposition, together with their Alliances; for my force is as the Sand upon the Sea Shore."

The Indians were worried about the future, but for the time being, the Half-King, irritated by French arrogance, favored the English. He promised to go with Washington on the remainder of his journey and to supply bodyguards, which amounted to no more than three chiefs (including the Half-King himself) and a hunter.

By December 4, the party reached Venango, an Indian town and a former rendezvous of English traders at the mouth of French Creek. To Washington's surprise, he found that French soldiers commanded by Captain Philippe-Thomas de Joncaire were ensconced in a house seized from English trader John Frazier. They welcomed Washington, warmed their visitors and themselves with wine, and, Washington wrote, advised them "it was their absolute Design to take Possession of the Ohio, and by G - they would do it." Joncaire plied Washington's Indians with liquor and tried to win them away from the English, but the Half-King remained sober enough to deliver a speech to Joncaire renouncing any friendship for invading French.

At last Washington reached Fort Le Boeuf. This was his destination, and there he found French commandant Captain Jacques Legardeur de St. Pierre, "an elderly Gentleman" with "much the Air of a Soldier." Washington delivered Governor Dinwiddie's message to him. While St. Pierre and his officers translated the governor's letter, Washington noted the fort's construction and armament and instructed his men to count the canoes available for transport.

To Washington's verbal protests about the French seizing English traders, St. Pierre replied that the country belonged to the French, and that "no *Englishman* had a Right to trade upon those Waters; and that he had Orders to make every Person Prisoner that attempted it on the *Ohio,* or the Waters of it." To Governor Dinwiddie, St. Pierre wrote he should have sent his protest to the governor general in Canada, but "as to the . . . Summons you send me to retire, I do not think myself obliged to obey it."

St. Pierre treated Washington courteously and provided him with a plentiful supply of provisions and liquor for his return journey. On December 16, already having sent his horses to Venango, Washington and his group launched a canoe and set out down the creek, which they found blocked in places with ice. Several times "we had like to have been staved against the Rocks, and many Times were obliged all Hands to get out and remain in the Water Half an Hour or more, getting over Shoals," Washington noted in his *Journal.* From Venango onward, the going was rougher. Their horses were too weak to ride or even to carry all the luggage. Washington, Gist, and others in the party had to walk and carry part of their supplies in packs on their backs. To get across the Allegheny River, they had to cut down trees "with but one poor hatchet" to make a raft. The river was so choked with ice that their raft nearly floundered, and Washington was jerked into the water and almost drowned. Gist "had all his Fingers, and some of his Toes frozen."

Despite these hardships, they returned to Wills Creek on January 7, 1754. On the day before, they had met "17 Horses loaded with Materials and Stores for a Fort at the Forks of Ohio, and the Day after some Families going out to settle." The Virginians were moving at long last to fortify the Ohio, but they were too late with too little. Washington arrived at Williamsburg on January 16 and reported the failure of his mission to the governor. He had made an arduous journey, and his observations would be useful in the future, but if the English were to occupy Ohio, they would have to drive out the French by force.

This fact was apparent to Governor Dinwiddie, who did his best to rally support among other colonies and prompt the government in London to act in order to protect His Majesty's dominions. But some colonies could not see why they should spend their treasure and risk their militia to secure land for Virginia land syndicates. Dinwiddie's own legislative assembly balked at appropriating money for the defense of the Ohio. In February 1754, however, it agreed to grant 10,000 pounds in Virginia currency for the purpose. Although

Pennsylvania was as deeply involved in the fate of the West as Virginia, Governor James Hamilton was unable to induce action from the Quaker pacifists who controlled the assembly. Only North Carolina showed any urgency in responding to Dinwiddie's request - the assembly voted to pay 300 or 400 men.

The government in London was also miserly. On June 15, the Duke of Newcastle wrote to Horace Walpole, auditor general for the British Plantations, asking how to raise money for the defense of the colonies. Six weeks earlier the Earl of Halifax had proposed building a string of frontier forts from Nova Scotia to Florida, and Newcastle was concerned over the expense involved. Walpole could think of nothing better than a lottery to raise money because the mother country already was loaded with debts "contracted for the good of all His Majesty's Dominions." He feared that "the Landed Gentlemen of this Country will be terribly alarmed with a notion that might prevayl that they are to be taxed on all occasions to defend our American Borders . . . as this Nation is at present at so great a charge in the settlement of Nova Scotia for the security of these very Colonys." The London government finally authorized the governor of New York to send to Virginia two companies of regulars stationed in his jurisdiction and ordered a company stationed in South Carolina to march to Virginia.

With scant supplies and an inadequate number of soldiers, Dinwiddie prepared for action. He appointed a surveyor and professor of mathematics at the College of William and Mary, Colonel Joshua Fry, to command the troops along with Washington, now a lieutenant colonel, as second in command. Washington was at Alexandria attempting to recruit a company. His success was less than he desired, for he described his troops, almost in Falstaff's words, as a parcel of "loose, idle Persons . . . quite destitute of House, and Home, and . . . many of them without Shoes, others want Stockings, some are without Shirts." He characterized seventy-five men he recruited as "self willed and ungovernable." Finally, on April 2, 1754, with a total of 120 men formed into two companies, he departed from Alexandria for the wilderness. When he reached Wills Creek, he sent word ahead to the Indians that he was coming with an advance guard and that a large army with great guns would follow. He hoped Indian allies would support his forces.

Washington's party was to provide protection for the building of an English fort at the forks where the Allegheny and Monongahela rivers join to form the Ohio, the site Washington had selected as the best place for defense. A small detachment of forty men under the command of William Trent was already at work there. While Washington was making his way west from Alexandria, Trent put ensign Edward Ward in charge of the work and returned to Wills Creek. Ward urged his men to hurry. On April 17, he had hung the gate to the stockade when his workmen were terrified to see a great flotilla of canoes and rowboats loaded with Frenchmen and Indians coming down the river. Forced to surrender, Ward and his men were allowed to leave with their tools and guns. Captain Pierre Claude de Contrecoeur, the officer in command, offered to buy their tools, which his men could use in completing the fort, but Ward refused. With food supplied by the French, Ward and his men made their way to Wills Creek, where he reported to Washington.

The seizure of the forks of the Ohio posed a new problem for the English. They were not strong enough to drive out the French, and yet if they remained inactive, they would lose their Indian allies in the West. Since the Ohio Company already had built a storehouse at the mouth of Redstone Creek on the Monongahela, it was decided to fortify this place and make it a staging area for a future attack on the forks. Washington was to continue west toward the Redstone.

He was about halfway between Wills Creek and the Redstone, at Great Meadows, when he got word that a French force was nearby watching his movements. In a heavy rain on the night of May 27, Washington and about forty men set out to find the French scouting party, but it was not until the early morning of the next day that they surprised a patrol of Frenchmen in a rocky ravine. Both sides fired, and in the ensuing engagement, ten of the French soldiers were killed, including their commanding officer, Ensign Joseph Coulon de Jumonvilie. Twenty-one men surrendered, and one escaped to carry the news to Contrecoeur at the new fort, named Duquesne after the French governor general. Washington lost one man and had two or three wounded.

The French immediately claimed Jumonville had been on a mission to warn the English, as Washington had warned the French a year earlier, and that he had been "assassinated" by Virginians. The French made it appear that the English killed Jumonville while he was trying to read a communication to Washington. Although no credible evidence substantiates this, the French told the story as propaganda. England and France were nominally at peace, and France wanted to establish that the English had been the aggressors. As it turned out, Washington had fired the first shots in a new war.

The attack on Jumonville's scouting force would produce retaliation, and Washington was in a quandary as to the best method of meeting it. One thing was certain: He needed men and supplies, and he sent a message to his commanding officer,

Colonel Fry, asking for reinforcements. Fry had died at Wills Creek as the result of a fall from his horse. To succeed him, Governor Dinwiddie named an old friend, Colonel James Innes, and promoted Washington to full colonel. On June 9, 200 additional troops arrived at Great Meadows, followed three days later by a company of regulars from South Carolina under Captain James MacKay, who held his commission from the king and refused to take orders from, or even to recognize the rank of, a provincial officer. Washington wrote that MacKay's recall "would tend to the public advantage . . ." his soldiers would not dig trenches, cut trees, nor do any of the work expected of frontier troops.

At Great Meadows, Washington's men had made a small palisaded fortification, later christened Fort Necessity, but Washington did not intend that to be his main defense. He hoped to push across the mountains and establish a base at the Redstone. His men worked to cut a road across the mountains to a point now called Mount Braddock. Then, on June 28, Washington received a report that the French were advancing in strength, and after a council of war he decided to fall back, not merely to Great Meadows, but to Wills Creek. The expedition across the mountains had exhausted Washington's troops and their horses, and the retreat took a heavier toll. By July 1, when the troops regained Great Meadows, they were too worn and tired to go any farther. Washington, after consulting with Captain MacKay - by this time sufficiently knowledgeable in frontier conditions to communicate with a provincial - decided to make a stand.

The French, uncertain about the strength of the English, proceeded cautiously. Governor General Duquesne, having heard in Montreal that the English were sending 5,000 troops to occupy Ohio, dispatched Captain Louis Coulon de Villiers, Jumonville's half-brother, to Fort Duquesne with orders to rally Indian allies. He instructed Contrecoeur to organize a force to march against Washington. Because De Villiers wished to avenge the death of his half-brother, he received command of the expedition. Since France and England were not officially at war, Duquesne was instructed to retaliate for Jumonville's death. They were intent on chastening the English, even if it meant pursuing them to their settlements. After driving the English from the Ohio territory, the French planned to proclaim their desire for peace. When he left Fort Duquesne on June 28, De Villiers had 600 French soldiers and 100 Indians under his command. He expected to recruit other Indians on the way and receive further reinforcements of French troops.

Washington's force, reduced by desertion, amounted to approximately 400 men, of whom at least 100 were ill and unfit for duty. Nevertheless, he made such preparations as he could. Even

MacKay's soldiers, contemplating the fire of the French from all sides, agreed to dig trenches. On July 3, with fortifications dug in front of the stockade and platforms erected for six small swivel guns, Washington's men waited in the rain for the attack to begin.

That morning, during a rainstorm, the French opened fire and kept up a fusillade until dusk. Both the English and French had difficulty keeping their powder dry and guns in working order. By 8:00 that night, the French, who were nearly out of ammunition, offered to break off the fight. With his powder wet, thirty men killed, seventy wounded, and no hope of rescue, Washington had no choice except to surrender. He sent over a French-speaking Dutchman, Captain Jacob Van Braam, with his wounded adjutant, William Peyronie, to negotiate. By the light of a lantern, with rain dripping on the already damp paper, Van Braam and the French worked out articles of surrender, which Washington and MacKay signed. Washington unwittingly allowed the French to include the word "assassinated" in the agreement, referring to the death of Jumonville. The French used that apparent admission of guilt as proof of their former charges, and Washington's oversight was later criticized in Williamsburg and London.

Washington and his men were permitted to depart with the honors of war, taking with them their belongings, except artillery and munitions. They were allowed to cache such stores as they could not carry and return for them later with wagons. The next morning, with drums beating, the English marched out, leaving Fort Necessity to the French and Indians, who paid no attention to the articles of surrender.

While Virginia was carrying on its private war with the French in an effort to save its western lands, other colonies and the government in London were growing concerned with the deterioration of English relations with the Indians. The Iroquois confederation of the Six Nations, traditionally friendly to the English, showed signs of wavering. The French had sent missionaries among them and had lured away some groups. Now, with evidence of English weakness on the frontiers, many Iroquois might defect to France.

In New York, William Johnson, who had settled on the Mohawk River and acquired vast holdings of land, promoted the English cause. At Johnson's stone house on the Mohawk - "Fort Johnson" as it was called - Indians came and went in a feverish round of diplomacy as relations between the various parties deteriorated in the 1750s. Johnson's popularity with the Iroquois was secure. He was a chief of the Mohawks; his wife was a niece of Chief Hendrick, a powerful Mohawk leader, and he had several Indian mistresses, a situation that helped cement his relations with the clan. His trading ventures were carried on with fairness, in contrast with those of other traders, and the Mohawks and other Iroquoian tribes respected him.

Nevertheless, Johnson could not keep the Iroquois from listening to French agents, and in 1753, there was danger that the powerful Six Nations might defect to France. If these peoples allied with France, all of New York and New England would be endangered. The British colonial establishment from Maine to Georgia would be threatened.

Conditions had come to this state for several reasons. The most deep-seated was the rivalry between the separate English colonies in dealing with the Indians and an inability to agree on a common policy with regard to the native peoples. The French had a consistent policy they pursued with remarkable persistence, regardless of changes in administrations at Quebec. Moreover, missionary priests who served as political agents also helped them. Finally, since a government-controlled monopoly administered French trade, commercial activities and prices were regulated for all outposts. It was the opposite with the English. English traders, responsible to no one and coming from various political jurisdictions that could enforce no effective laws in the frontier zone, were free to drive hard bargains and cheat the Indians when they could.

The threat of losing support of the Iroquois confederation was so acute in 1753 that the Board of Trade in London wrote an urgent letter to the governor of New York instructing him to call a council of Iroquois leaders and of representatives from the colonies of New York, New Jersey, Massachusetts, New Hampshire, Pennsylvania, Maryland, and Virginia. Commissioners from various colonies should work out a plan for "one general treaty" with the Six Nations instead of separate treaties as previously negotiated. Acting on these instructions, a congress was called at Albany for June 14, 1754. From this congress, designed to settle problems with the Indians, grew the famous Albany Plan of Union.

Neither New Jersey nor Virginia sent representatives to the meeting. But other colonies mentioned by the Board of Trade, plus Connecticut and Rhode Island, sent commissioners. The Indians made long speeches in which they aired their grievances. The English were taking over their land. Moreover, Chief Hendrick declared, "You have . . . thrown us behind your back, and disregarded us, whereas the French are a subtle and vigilant people, ever using their utmost endeavours to seduce and bring our people over to them." For several days, the debate went on, the Indians stressing their grievances, and the English defending their actions. During the conference, some commissioners took advantage of the opportunity to purchase land from the

Indians on terms that pleased the sellers. By July 9, the commissioners and the Indians had come to reasonably satisfactory agreements and the Iroquois left with thirty wagons, lent by the governor of New York, to carry home presents from the colonial governments and from the king of England.

After much discussion, the commissioners in Albany wrote a "Plan of Union," which, if provincial governments approved, would be established by an act of Parliament. The plan provided for the king to appoint a governor general. The legislative assemblies of the provincial governments would choose a grand council that would govern for a term of three years. At the start, apportionment would be as follows: Massachusetts, seven; Virginia, seven; Pennsylvania, six; Connecticut, five; New York, Maryland, North Carolina, and South Carolina, four each; New Jersey, three; New Hampshire, two; Rhode Island, two. The frontier provinces of Nova Scotia and Georgia initially would not be represented. After the first three years, representation would depend in some measure upon the amount paid into the union's treasury by each provincial government. Annual meetings of the grand council would be required, but the governor general could call emergency meetings with the consent of seven members.

The governor general and grand council would be empowered to negotiate all treaties with the Indians, to purchase and administer all lands not within the boundaries of any provincial government, to defend the British possessions in America by erecting forts, raising armies, building ships, and levying taxes. Under the proposed regulations, the Privy Council had to be informed of these actions, and it might disapprove within three years.

Provincial governments were too concerned with their affairs, and too jealous of their prerogatives, even in the face of danger, to approve a plan that curtailed their powers. Without exception, they either disapproved of the Albany Plan of Union or ignored it. The Board of Trade countered with a tentative plan, but the Privy Council disallowed it.

If the colonies could not agree upon a confederation, at least they knew that Benjamin Franklin's cartoon, "Join or Die," which accompanied an article he had written for the *Pennsylvania Gazette* urging union, contained some truth. As the French threat to English security became more apparent in 1755, their governors showed a greater inclination to consult about defense - and offense. Governor William Shirley of Massachusetts, who had distinguished himself in 1745 in the War of Jenkins' Ear by engineering the capture of Louisbourg, was deeply concerned about French plans to encircle the colonies. Although France and England were nominally at peace, early in 1755, Shirley attempted to alert the heads of other colonies to the realities of the impending conflict.

The government in London, aware it must act in defense of the colonies, ordered two regiments of regular troops, adequately equipped with artillery and supplies, to Virginia. The commanding officer was Major General Edward Braddock, an orthodox, unimaginative, stern disciplinarian, just the sort of officer Whitehall believed could command untrained and unruly provincial militia. Braddock arrived at Williamsburg on February 23, 1755, and in March, after frequent conferences with Governor Dinwiddie, he proceeded to Alexandria, where his troops disembarked. There, Braddock called a conference of colonial governors on April 14 to plan for a broad attack on the French. Governor Shirley of Massachusetts proposed to the conference that he and Governor Charles Lawrence of Nova Scotia should attack the enemy at Fort Beauséjour at the tip of the Bay of Fundy. With help from all New England colonies, Shirley hoped to take Crown Point on Lake Champlain. With these two French bases secured, Shirley believed the northern colonies might be safe from invasion. The next objective after Beauséjour and Crown Point recommended by Shirley was Niagara, the capture of which would cut off the French from their bases in Ohio.

Braddock's instructions called for him to proceed against Fort Duquesne. After driving the French from the forks of the Ohio, he was to fortify the site. His orders called for him to engage both northern and southern Indians in his operations against the French if he deemed it expedient. Governor James Glen of South Carolina had influence with the Cherokees and other Indians in the South, but because Dinwiddie disliked Glen, he was not invited to the conference at Alexandria. Despite this slight, Glen persuaded the South Carolina assembly to appropriate 6,000 pounds for the campaign. Braddock's assistant commented that this "was the only money raised by the provinces which ever passed through the General's hands." Braddock induced Shirley to take a commission as a colonel and proceed against Niagara. To William Johnson he assigned the task of taking Crown Point. The reduction of Acadia to English authority was entrusted to Lieutenant Colonel Robert Monckton. Because all this action against the French was to take place during a period of nominal peace, the English were to claim they were merely driving marauders off land that rightfully belonged to the king of England.

Braddock's regulars consisted of two regiments, one commanded by Sir Peter Halkett and the other by Colonel Thomas Dunbar. He had sent Lieutenant Colonel Sir John St. Clair, quartermaster general, ahead to arrange for supplies. The regiments were not up to full strength, but Braddock intended to recruit provincials to fill out their ranks. He hoped to obtain grants from provincial governments to pay for maintaining his troops, but he had secret instructions authorizing him to proceed at the expense of the British government if the colonial governments proved uncooperative. Indian allies that Braddock had been assured would come to his aid never appeared, and in the end he had only eight Indians to serve as scouts. But by June 7, some 2,500 men were ready to march from Wills Creek, now christened Fort Cumberland in honor of the Duke of Cumberland. Their progress was slow, sometimes only two miles per day, for the road in places had to be hewed out of the wilderness, and Braddock insisted upon dragging along heavy artillery with which he planned to assault Fort Duquesne.

George Washington accompanied Braddock as a civilian assistant. The British general had offered him a captaincy, but since Washington had resigned recently as a lieutenant colonel of the Virginia militia, he thought it beneath his dignity to accept a lower rank.

The march toward Fort Duquesne was slow and frustrating. Braddock and St. Clair were both aware that the route chosen from Fort Cumberland by way of Great Meadows was the wrong approach, and they ought to have set out from Philadelphia across Pennsylvania. Furthermore, supplies, horses, and wagons that Virginia and Maryland had promised did not arrive in sufficient quantity. Beef sent by Maryland contractors spoiled before it reached camp and had to be buried. Contractors proved to be rogues and thieves. Because of improper food, men got sick and were hardly able to march. Washington was stricken with dysentery. The road was so rough that wagons shook to pieces and horses died in their traces from straining at the loads. Sailors assigned to the expedition hauled on the great guns with rope and tackle trying to get them over mountains. After the army had passed Great Meadows, Indians hiding in the woods occasionally shot a soldier and vanished into the dark forest. British officers were disdainful of the provincial troops, and the provincials had little respect for these arrogant martinets, whom they regarded as incompetent.

The army reached the Monongahela River and, because of the rough terrain, decided to cross to the left bank, march two miles down that side, and cross back to the right bank near the mouth of Turtle Creek. This the army accomplished safely by the early afternoon of July 9. They were nearing Fort Duquesne. Braddock ordered Lieutenant Colonel Thomas Gage to move forward with 450 men to inspect and lead the way to open ground where he proposed to make his last camp before attacking Fort Duquesne. A hill on the right commanded the route, but Gage failed to secure it. The twelve-foot road passed between wooded ravines.

Gage's scouts failed to secure wooded areas on his flanks.

A French officer, Captain Daniel Liénard de Beaujeu, was advancing to meet Gage with a troop of soldiers, French provincials, and Indians. When Gage's scouts observed the attacking force advancing down the trail, they fell back, and British grenadiers in the vanguard opened fire. Beaujeu was killed instantly and some of his provincials fled, but Captain Jean Dumas, second in command, ordered his troops to divide and take to the woods on each side of the British and to occupy the commanding hill. From these vantage points, they fired at Gage's troops. If Gage had pushed forward, he could have gained open ground. Instead, he ordered a retreat while the opposing force poured fire into the milling redcoats.

At this juncture, Braddock ordered a force of 800 men under Lieutenant Colonel Ralph Burton to reinforce Gage. Burton's soldiers met Gage's men, fleeing in panic, and blocked their retreat. The baggage train began to move up the narrow road, adding to the confusion. Officers were unable to organize their men for an attack, and the enemy in the woods, on their flanks, and occupying the hilltop continued to fire into closely packed troops. As the firing continued, Braddock rode forward and tried to rally the troops. Five horses were shot from under him before he was finally wounded so severely he had to be carried from the field. After nearly three hours, British troops fled in panic. Of 1,373 privates and noncommissioned officers in the regular troops, all but 459 had been killed or wounded. Of eighty-six officers, all except twenty-three were killed or wounded.

Losses among the provincial forces were heavy. Washington commented: "Our poor Virginians behaved like men, and died like soldiers; for I believe that out of three companies that were there that day, scarce thirty were left alive." He attributed much of the slaughter to the panic of the regular troops: "In short the dastardly behavior of the English soldiers exposed all those who were inclined to do their duty to almost certain death. It is imagined (I believe with great justice, too) that two-thirds of both killed and wounded received their shots from our own cowardly dogs of soldiers, who gathered themselves in a body, contrary to orders, ten and twelve deep, would then level, fire, and shoot down the men before them."

Controversy over the causes of the defeat soon raged - and has continued to rage ever since - but there can be little question that the incompetence and ignorance of British officers, including Braddock, must account in a large measure for the tactical predicament the army got itself into and the panic that followed. It was a black day for the colonial and British cause. The French celebrated their victory, for British fire had done them little harm.

Braddock was mortally wounded. Washington managed to procure a cart in which he conveyed the dying general for fifty miles to a base camp not far from present-day Uniontown, where Colonel Thomas Dunbar was stalled with the supply train. There, the refugee soldiers met, and Braddock died. Washington buried him in the roadway, which was churned into mud by the wagons, so that the Indians would not find his grave and mutilate the body.

The death of Braddock left Dunbar temporarily in command of the defeated army and Governor Shirley of Massachusetts the acknowledged commander in chief of all British forces in North America, a position to which he formally was appointed in August. Unless quick action could be taken to reverse the losses incurred by Braddock's defeat, the entire frontier of Virginia and Pennsylvania would be left at the mercy of the French and the Indians. Alert to the danger, Governor Dinwiddie of Virginia sent an urgent message to Shirley offering 400 or 500 men to reinforce Dunbar's decimated regiments if the British officer would renew the attack on Fort Duquesne. Shirley sent word to Dunbar to prepare for a second assault on Fort Duquesne unless he believed his force was not ready for the task, in which case he should march his soldiers to Albany to help in the northern campaigns against the French. After consulting with British officers, Dunbar decided he did not want to see any more fighting in the wilderness of Pennsylvania. He wanted to go into winter quarters in Philadelphia, though it was late July, but reluctantly he set out for Albany, leaving the frontier open to attack.

The Indian allies of the French were already attacking settlers and burning cabins in outlying districts. To give some measure of protection, Dinwiddie procured a colonel's commission for George Washington from Shirley and ordered him to use such troops as he could raise for the protection of border areas. It was a difficult assignment, but Washington accepted. Dunbar's refusal to use his forces to make a second attempt on Fort Duquesne further embittered Virginians against British officers sent to save them from the French and the Indians.

During this time, Governor Shirley was attempting to pressure the French in the North. The plan to attack Fort Niagara, the French outlying fort on Lake Ontario, and Fort St-Frédéric, at Crown Point at the southern tip of Lake Champlain, consumed Shirley during the summer of 1755. If the two attacks proved successful, Shirley planned to invade Canada and thus cut off the French from the Ohio Valley and relieve the pressure on the Virginia and

Pennsylvania frontiers. Shirley intended to lead an expedition against Fort Niagara, and he appointed William Johnson a temporary major general and ordered him to move against Crown Point. The strategy was sound, but the French were taking the offensive.

Late in May, Shirley sent Captain John Bradstreet with 200 regulars and a crew of shipwrights to Oswego, the English trading center on Lake Ontario, to build four ships to transport troops down the lake to Fort Niagara. Shirley commandeered all the rowboats in the region. Near the end of July, he began to transport additional troops up the Mohawk River and then into Lake Oneida and to Oswego. By mid-September, he had assembled more than 2,000 men at Oswego. With Indian support, he was preparing for a descent by water upon Fort Niagara, when storms accompanied by torrential rains forced postponement of the expedition. News came of French reinforcements at Fort Frontenac on the other side of Lake Ontario and of additional strength at Fort Niagara. In the face of bad news and worse weather, Shirley decided the onslaught on Fort Niagara would have to wait until spring. He had built a stockaded fort on a height outside Oswego to protect it, and he left two regiments there as a garrison. The militia left.

William Johnson used the summer months to organize his attack on Crown Point. In June and early July he had called a ten-day council of Iroquois and three other nations - more than 1,000 Indians - to gain their support for the campaign. He planned to advance up the Hudson and travel to Lake George, where his men would go by flat-bottomed boats and canoe to Lake Champlain. To secure his route, he planned to build forts at three strategic points.

With 3,500 men recruited from New England and New York, Johnson left in mid-July. Some 400 Indians were recruited along the way, especially during the building of the first fort, named Fort Edward, which Johnson erected on high ground overlooking the Hudson at a location called the Great Carrying Place - a portage between the Hudson and Lake George. Leaving a small garrison at Fort Edward, he pushed on to Lake George, where he began work on another fort. Reports reached them of a large contingent of French troops advancing south. Johnson sent 1,000 men under Colonel Ephraim Williams, with a contingent of Indians under Chief Hendrick. The leader of the French was a German professional soldier, Baron de Dieskau, who had been given command of French troops in North America.

On September 8, Dieskau's force of 1,500 French and Indians set out to attack Fort Edward, which would have cut Johnson's line of communication, but Indian allies of the French, hearing that Johnson was encamped on Lake George without a completed fort, urged Dieskau to attack that position first. When Dieskau was two miles from Fort Edward, he held a council of war and decided to turn toward Johnson's camp. Shortly after the change in the route, Dieskau suddenly met Williams' force and opened fire. Williams' men turned and fled back to the main camp on Lake George. Both Williams and Chief Hendrick were killed.

Fortunately for the English, Johnson had taken pains to fortify his camp with felled trees, and refugees streamed behind the barricade. But in pausing to regroup for the assault on the fortifications, the pursuers gave Johnson time to man his cannon and prepare for the attack. In the ensuing battle, Johnson's troops captured wounded French commander Baron de Dieskau.

The French then withdrew to the point where they had defeated Williams in the first encounter. There, a force of 200 n from Fort Edward struck them about 8:00 p.m. and routed them. Thus, the three battles of Lake George ended with an American victory, although Johnson was wounded, and the Americans did not pursue the French, who retreated to Crown Point. Although Shirley might later urge Johnson to get on with the campaign to take Crown Point, he had to be content with Johnson's building a fort on Lake George, which he named William Henry. It was too late to fortify the outlet of Lake George at Ticonderoga, as Johnson had planned, for the French were building their own stronghold, Fort Carillon, there. But the British government, grateful for one victory, made Johnson a baronet.

When Shirley kept insisting Johnson attack Crown Point, Johnson, who had been named superintendent of the Six Nations, resigned his commission with the excuse his other duties required all his time. Johnson disliked Shirley, and Lieutenant Governor James De Lancey of New York, and others encouraged his attitude toward the New Englander. De Lancey did not support Shirley's ambitious plans to invade Canada, for De Lancey, and other New Yorkers were interested in contraband trade with Montreal and did not want it stopped. Furthermore, Massachusetts and New York were engaged in a boundary dispute that did not improve the atmosphere for cooperation. Intercolonial rivalries once again prevented effective unity in pursuit of a common goal.

The year 1755 saw small gains in Nova Scotia that lightened the general gloom for the English. Governor Shirley recruited 2,000 volunteers in New England, who, with 250 regulars, all commanded by Lieutenant Colonel Robert Monckton, undertook in June to capture Fort Beauséjour. The French Acadians of that part of Nova Scotia, led by the Abbe Jean-Louis le Loutre, preferred to burn their houses and their church rather than let them fall into the hands of the English. Many took refuge in the fort, which held out against Monckton until his bombardment forced its surrender. Later, Monckton captured the remaining French point of defense in Acadia, Fort Gaspereau on Green Bay, opposite Prince Edward Island.

These two victories did not mean that French influence in the maritime regions of Canada was nullified, however, as the great fortress at Louisbourg, situated on the Atlantic side of Cape Breton Island, still stood.

France was determined to hold Louisbourg and reinforce the French armies in Canada. In the summer of 1755, it sent sixty-eight companies of regular troops to Canada in transports that managed to evade the watch that Vice Admiral Edward Boscawen maintained off Louisbourg. Although England and France were not yet formally at war, Boscawen had orders to capture or destroy French warships and transports found in American waters, and he managed to capture or sink three French ships. England maintained the fiction that these troops were going to invade its territory; it was on that pretext that Braddock had marched against Fort Duquesne and that Shirley and Johnson had clashed in New York. Still, both countries hoped to maintain peace in Europe and fight only a limited war in America.

The hostility that Acadians had displayed at the time of the attack on Fort Beauséjour convinced the English that they were a threat requiring drastic action. Though they were technically British subjects, many would not take the required oath of allegiance. Consequently, the Provincial Council of Nova Scotia, with the concurrence of Governor Charles Lawrence and Vice Admiral Boscawen, decided that those who refused to take the oath must be removed from the land and scattered through the English colonies. To allow them to flee to French Canada would have strengthened the hostile French.

The recalcitrant Acadians on the Isthmus of Chignecto, who had rallied to Abbé le Loutre's call when the forts at Beauséjour and Gaspereau were under attack, were the first to suffer. On August 11, the heads of families were ordered to report to Fort Cumberland to hear orders of the governor and the council. When some 400 men had gathered, they were informed that their lands and cattle were forfeited to the crown, and they and their families were to be deported. Nine transports arrived on August 21. Some Acadians escaped to the woods and joined the Indians, who attacked sailors and soldiers trying to remove the settlers. The ships, filled with 1,100 exiles leaving burned villages, sailed on October 13.

New England troops under Lieutenant Colonel John Winslow went to Grand Pré in the Minas

Basin to supervise the removal of Acadians in that region. By September 5, just as the Acadians were completing their harvest, Winslow summoned all the men and boys to Grand Pré and read them orders for their deportation. Their property was confiscated, except for personal belongings and such household goods as they could take with them aboard ship. Through the early days of October, Winslow was busy trying to get the Minas Basin Acadians aboard ships. On October 8, he wrote in his *Journal:* "Began to Embark the Inhabitants who went of [off] Very. . .unwillingly, the Women in Great destress Carrying off Their Children in their arms. Others Carrying Their decript [decrepit] Parents in their Carts and all their Goods. . . ."

The deportation of the Acadians was the theme of Henry Wadsworth Longfellow's "Evangeline":

> Waste are those pleasant farms, and the farmers forever departed!

> Scattered like dust and leaves, when the mighty blasts of October

> Seize them, and whirl them aloft, and sprinkle them far o'er the ocean.

> Naught but tradition remains of the beautiful village of Grand-Pré.

By October 13, Winslow had nine transports ready to sail, filled with deportees destined for Pennsylvania, Maryland, and Virginia. Additional habitants in the Minas Basin and other regions of Nova Scotia remained to be loaded on transports for the Carolinas, Georgia, Massachusetts, and Connecticut.

By the time the removal of the Acadians was completed, 6,000 had been scattered throughout the English colonies. Besides those removed by the English, many more fled to French Canada, making a total dispersal of between 12,000 and 15,000. Their reception in various colonies was anything but cordial. South Carolina, for example, which had a large group of Calvinist Huguenots, regarded the incoming Catholic French as potential enemies and took steps to prevent their departure to the interior, where they might stir up the Indians. The Huguenots were hostile to the newcomers and did all they could to prevent the ships from landing. The Acadians suffered hardships, and many wandered like Ishmael with every man's hand against them. Some drifted back north to Canada. Many found refuge in Louisiana, where their descendants to this day are called "Cajuns."

Despite Johnson's victory on Lake George and the English success in eliminating the Acadians, France threatened the destruction of English trade in the Ohio Valley and the future safety of the colonies on the Atlantic coast. England decided to check the French advance.

Although Governor Shirley of Massachusetts had shown considerable ingenuity and fortitude, he had enemies and could not unite the colonies behind him for effective military action. The authorities in Whitehall decided he must be replaced as commander in chief of the armed forces in North America. Accordingly, in January 1756, the Duke of Cumberland persuaded the Cabinet to appoint John Campbell, Earl of Loudoun, as commander in chief in America. His commission was issued on March 17, and on July 22, Loudoun, with staff and mistress, landed in New York. Shirley, in the meantime, had been relieved and had turned over his command, pending Loudoun's arrival, first to Major General Daniel Webb and then to Major General James Abercromby. Shirley was recalled to England in the autumn of 1756, after Loudoun complained that he had stirred up factions against him. Shirley, a competent official, was the victim of envious and hostile colleagues.

France also had appointed a new commander in chief for North America, Marquis Louis-Joseph de Montcalm de St.-Véran, an officer who was to show an ability no British general in America displayed. Montcalm's first official duty was to inspect French forts on Lake Ontario, Lake Champlain, and Lake George. Learning that sickness and death had weakened the English garrison at Oswego during the winter, Montcalm sent a force from Fort Frontenac in August 1756 and forced the English to surrender. The Earl of Loudoun did little other than blame Shirley for failing to reinforce the garrison at Oswego. The loss of this trading post meant that henceforth, the western Indians would side with the French.

Until 1755, England and France clung to the belief they could fight an undeclared war in America and still keep peace in Europe. But in the spring of 1756, the French invaded Minorca, then held by England, and on May 18, England declared war on France. The Seven Years' War was underway. In America, this conflict would be known as the French and Indian War. A crisis was impending, and much would depend upon the wisdom that authorities in Whitehall would muster. In November, the incompetent Duke of Newcastle resigned as prime minister. William Pitt succeeded to the power, if not the title, and his authority would have vast implications for the American colonies.

11
BRITANNIA RULES

When Englishmen sat down on New Year's Day in 1757 to take stock of the situation of the American colonies, they must have come to gloomy conclusions. Throughout the colonies, private interests, greed, envy, suspicion, and intercolonial rivalries prevented any effective action against the common enemy, France. When colonial troops were mustered, they were frequently undisciplined, untrained, and ineffective. British regulars had hardly proved any better, and the British officers sent to the colonies failed because of lack of understanding, lack of energy, or incompetence.

To the French, the beginning of the year held promise of success in America. Their earlier victories had won over most of the western Indians and had raised the morale of French provincials. The king of France had sent adequate reinforcements of regular troops and ample munitions. Further supplies were promised. Moreover, France had a new commander in chief of ability, courage, and energy, the Marquis de Montcalm.

During the early days of 1757, Montreal and Quebec rang with revelry as French officials and military officers vied with each other in the magnificence of their social affairs. Montcalm kept open house three days each week until Lent and entertained at sumptuous dinner parties. The French had reason to be relaxed, for they could count 6,600 seasoned troops in New France, and the French Navy provided considerable reinforcements to Louisbourg. The squadrons there were sufficient to threaten the English east coast. The French planned to block the English from the interior and deny them access to the Great Lakes. The English might continue to hold a narrow territory on the coast, but their hope of an empire in North America was dashed. No Frenchman and few Englishmen could have foreseen that in three years, their countries' fortunes would change.

Although the crisis facing the English colonies at the beginning of 1757 was acute - perhaps the most serious of the eighteenth century - many colonials were unaware of the danger. Indeed, complacency had settled over many areas as merchants, tradesmen, craftsmen, and farmers enjoyed the prosperity that military spending had brought. New York and Newport took advantage of the war with France to send an increasing number of pirates who brought in quantities of money and goods captured on the high seas. The ships' owners, their captains, and crews all profited, and privateering became so popular that deserters from English vessels in the harbors of New York and Newport hid until they could sign on with a pirate and sail away on a voyage that promised quick and easy money. The sheriff of Newport County asserted that men who enlisted in the army took their first pay and then ran off to sea "almost as fast as they can be recruited," he added. He estimated that 10,000 men, who might have been engaged in defending the frontiers, had been lured into privateering and related activities. So many deserted in New York that the governor of the province ordered three battalions to surround the city and to search houses. The rewards of privateering were widespread, for the money was quickly spent and served to stimulate business. In New York in 1757, pirates brought in 200,000 pounds.

But merchants were not above trading with the enemy. Ship captains loaded sugar and molasses in the French West Indies or traded with French vessels off Nova Scotia for silk, wine, and other luxury products. Winning the war in the North American frontier was of little concern to merchants and captains whose interests kept their attention focused upon more immediate benefits.

Although most colonials in settled areas were unconcerned about warfare in the interior, every colony had a few people who realized the danger. As in all the earlier wars with the Indians and the French, however, concerted action was lacking. Each colony tried to act in accordance with its special interest. Virginians under Washington were continuing to police as best they could the western frontier of their colony, but in 1757, Washington was despondent over the outlook. In the previous year, his men had suffered more than 100 casualties in some twenty encounters with the enemy. By the summer of 1757, Washington was attempting to guard 350 miles of frontier with 400 men, whom he described as "abandoned miscreants," clad in rags, for they had received no issue of clothing since 1754. Raids by French and Indians west of Winchester and Fort Cumberland were frequent, and a move on Fort Cumberland failed only because an illness of the French commander stopped the advance. To provide Washington with additional troops, the House of Burgesses passed an act drafting men from each county, but out of 400 draftees, 114 deserted, and Washington wrote his superior, Colonel John Stanwix, that he had "a Gallows near 40 feet high erected (which has terrified the *rest* exceedingly), and I am determined if I can be justified in the proceeding, to hang two or three on it, as an Example to others." Although Washington actually hanged two deserters on his gallows, defections continued, and he informed Governor Dinwiddie that without reinforcements, he did not expect to see left "one soul living on this side the Blue Ridge the ensuing autumn."

Maryland was less effective than Virginia in protecting its frontier. Although Fort Cumberland was within Maryland's borders, the assembly of that colony in 1757 objected to Lord Loudoun's efforts to have Maryland man the fort. Many of the people of Maryland argued that since Fort Cumberland was a protection for Virginia territory, Virginia should provide its troops. Indians, to be sure, were attacking and killing settlers on the Maryland frontier, but merchants and planters in the tidewater region showed little concern. Since Virginia and Pennsylvania had more exposed frontier than Maryland, they reasoned, let them protect the borders. In early 1757, Maryland had only 150 men under arms.

Some of the most critical points of danger, such as Fort Duquesne, were in Pennsylvania territory, and its long border tempted the French and their Indian allies. In November 1755, Indians attacked Moravian settlers at Gnadenhütten in the upper Lehigh Valley. Despite the danger, Quakers, pacifists who controlled the Pennsylvania assembly, refused to take action. German colonists on farms out of danger of Indian attack were likewise pacifists and opposed to any military action. As petition after petition for arms, ammunition, and troops came from border settlers, non-Quakers in the assembly, led by Benjamin Franklin, tried to move the Quakers, who declared they would investigate causes of discontent among the Indians. Fearful that the assembly might vote funds for military purposes, Quaker preachers, male and female, lectured crowds on the streets of Philadelphia on the iniquity of war; it was better to suffer, they insisted, than to take a life.

Some of those who had suffered in fact, rather than in theory, brought a wagonload of scalped and mutilated corpses to the doors of the assembly to let the Quakers see what really happened on the frontier. Faced with the threat of riot, the assembly voted to assemble a militia, exempted Quakers, and affirmed it would be lawful for others to volunteer, form companies, and elect officers by ballot. Articles of war would be drawn up with the approval of the governor, but unless an officer or enlisted man, after three days' consideration, agreed in the presence of a justice of the peace, he need not be bound by them.

If George Washington complained about the ease with which the Virginia militia evaded their duties, at least he was spared the frustration of trying to raise troops under the Pennsylvania assembly. Finally, the Quaker-dominated assembly appropriated 55,000 pounds "for the King's use," without mentioning war; the Proprietary office contributed 5,000 pounds more on the same vague basis; and frontiersmen were left to fend off the Indians with the hope that some of the money for the king's use might be spent for guns and ammunition. Eventually, Pennsylvanians built a chain of forts from the Delaware to the Potomac while Quakers salved their consciences by calling these strongpoints "posts."

The situation on the New York frontier was critical during the winter and summer of 1757. The Earl of Loudoun had placed the command of regular troops in the area under Daniel Webb and his second-in-command, James Abercromby. The two focused on a plan that obsessed Loudoun: an assault on the heart of New France. Loudoun frequently discussed an attack on Quebec during the early months of 1757, but on orders from London he changed his objective to Louisbourg. Meanwhile, the disposition of troops in New York was left to Webb's discretion. The two key fortresses in the north were Fort William Henry on Lake George and Fort Edward to the south, near the upper Hudson. From these bases, Webb might have advanced against the French at Fort Ticonderoga. In fact, the French thought he had such an attack in mind when Captain Robert Rogers led a group of rangers on a reconnaissance of Ticonderoga in January 1757. Rogers' men captured prisoners and gained information about the strength of the French strongholds at Ticonderoga and Crown Point, but Webb failed to take any action based on this intelligence.

Instead, the French took the initiative. An expedition of 1,500 French and Indians advanced across Lake George and Lake Champlain and on March 19 appeared before Fort William Henry and began an attack. The fort, defended by 500 soldiers and a small detachment of Rogers' Rangers, was under the command of a regular army officer, Lieutenant Colonel William Eyre, who withstood the onslaught as best he could. Although he could not prevent the enemy from destroying all outlying buildings and a ship under construction on the lake, he held the fort itself until cold weather and lack of supplies compelled the French to withdraw.

The winter attack on Fort William Henry was the prelude to Montcalm's successful summer campaign. Before the end of July, he brought together at Ticonderoga an army of 6,000, reinforced by 2,000 Indian allies, and was ready for an advance on the English fort. Ferrying his troops down Lake George in barges and canoes, Montcalm completed the envelopment of Fort William Henry by August 3. Lieutenant Colonel George Monro, in command at the fort, had only about 2,100 men to resist the army of French and Indians. Although

Brigadier General Webb, with headquarters at Fort Edward, had inspected Fort William Henry a few days before the arrival of the French, he had sent only inadequate reinforcements, and after the French began their siege, he took no action to aid the beleaguered fort. Webb contented himself with notifying Monro he could not send relief from Fort Edward, since he had only 2,500 troops in that garrison, and reinforcements of colonial militia were not yet forthcoming. He suggested Monro might surrender on the best terms he could get from Montcalm.

On August 9, outnumbered and outgunned, Monro accepted Montcalm's offer for surrender. The members of the garrison would be allowed to keep their arms, and, to protect them from the Indians who were eager for scalps, French troops would escort them to Fort Edward. The French were unable to control the Indians, who that night killed more than 200, including several women and wounded troops. The Indians carried away 400 others to Canada.

After destroying Fort William Henry and leveling the neighboring entrenchments, the French withdrew to Ticonderoga and Crown Point without attacking Fort Edward. Troops from New York and New England were by this time converging on Fort Edward, and Montcalm was unwilling to risk the laurels of his recent victory in an attempt to take this stronghold. He already had dealt a blow to English prestige and had kept many Indians from allying themselves with the English. Meanwhile, the prestige of France in North America was never higher.

While disaster was overtaking the English in New York and other frontiers, Loudoun received orders from London to proceed against Louisbourg and at once began organizing a land force to operate with the Royal Navy. In the meantime, transports embarked troops in England and Ireland. By mid-July, more than 5,000 soldiers had reached Halifax to increase the number of trained soldiers in Nova Scotia to nearly 15,000.

But the French had not been idle, and their naval force at Louisbourg now numbered eighteen ships. Before the end of July, four more warships sailed into Louisbourg harbor to strengthen the French flotilla. When British intelligence brought news of the naval and land forces ready to repel an attack on Louisbourg, Loudoun decided that the British had no hope of success and that the attempt to attack Louisbourg would have to be abandoned. Leaving sufficient troops in Nova Scotia to prevent a counterattack by the French, Loudoun left with the remainder and sailed for New York and New England ports. The British fleet encountered a hurricane on September 24. One ship was lost, many were damaged, and some had to throw their cannon and heavy supplies overboard to survive. The worst-battered ships struggled to England, but eight remained in American waters on orders from Loudoun. Thus ended Loudoun's dream of striking at the heart of French strength in Canada. On December 30, 1757, William Pitt recalled the Earl of Loudoun and appointed Major General Abercromby in his place.

William Pitt was committed to reversing the long sequence of disasters to British claims in North America, and he began to build a force to crush the French. Pitt authorized the arming and payment of provincial troops by the British government; he gave orders that regular army officers should recognize the rank of provincial officers; he ordered to America thousands of regular troops; and he brought pressure on the provincial governments to raise a militia numbering at least 25,000.

Though Abercromby was nominally commander in chief of all troops in North America, Pitt specified he was to concentrate on an invasion of Canada, after the capture of Ticonderoga and Crown Point, and leave the direction of campaigns against Fort Duquesne and Louisbourg to others. Brigadier General John Forbes, whom Abercromby placed in charge of the southern provinces, was given the responsibility of marching on Fort Duquesne and avenging Braddock's defeat. Colonel Jeffery Amherst, a British aristocrat and a soldier who served on the continent under the Duke of Cumberland, was named a major general and instructed to take Louisbourg. He was to lead the land forces and coordinate the campaign with a naval attack led by Vice Admiral Edward Boscawen. Pitt assigned to Amherst's command a talented young brigadier general, James Wolfe.

The force sent against the French in Louisbourg was unprecedented. By the end of May 1758, an armada of 157 warships and transports headed toward Nova Scotia. On June 8, General Wolfe led a landing party that gained a foothold on Cape Breton Island at Gabarus Bay and began the siege of Louisbourg. For the next seven weeks, the English bombarded the French fort from land and sea. Defending French vessels were sunk, burned, or blown up. English shells destroyed storehouses, hospitals, and barracks inside the fort. Though the great stone walls withstood blasts of the artillery, the British fire eventually knocked out all but four guns in the French batteries. On July 26, with the town in ruins, and with many of the defending troops dead or wounded and the rest exhausted, the French commander had to surrender. With this victory, the tide turned, and British morale rose.

While Amherst and Boscawen were besieging Louisbourg, General Abercromby was making an effort to advance his campaign against Canada. But provincial troops were slow in responding to his call, and supplies and arms from England were delayed in reaching him. By July 1, he had only 12,000 men concentrated on Lake George instead of the 27,000 Pitt had planned for him to use in the attack on the French forts at Ticonderoga and Crown Point. By July 5, additional troops arrived to increase his force to 16,000. Embarking his men and artillery in a vast armada of boats, rafts, and whaleboats, Abercromby crossed Lake George on the night of July 5 and landed in a cove three miles southwest of Ticonderoga. An advance party under Lord Howe encountered and routed a group of French scouts who had been sent out to explore, but Howe was killed in the first burst of fire. The army moved up the next day and camped near Ticonderoga.

Abercromby learned from captured French soldiers that Montcalm had only 6,000 troops to defend the fort but that reinforcements of at least 3,000 men were expected. Abercromby did not wait to bring up all his artillery from the rafts or to mount guns on a hill commanding the fort. In his haste, the British commander ordered an attack on French troops entrenched some distance in front of the fort, protected by freshly cut trees felled so that their sharpened limbs faced the attackers and made a barrier difficult to climb through, even without fire from soldiers hidden in the trenches beyond. With artillery preparation, the British could have demolished this barrier, but Abercromby neglected to use his weapons.

Regular troops, including Scottish Highlanders, charged against the tangle of sharpened tree limbs and died by the hundreds in the murderous fire as they tried to crawl through the maze. Some of the colonial soldiers, particularly the militia from Connecticut, fought, but others retreated. Soon the retreat was a rout, and the British force, which in the beginning outnumbered the French five to one, fell back to the site of ruined Fort William Henry. Abercromby had had enough and did not attempt to renew the fight, though one officer complained that Abercromby had men and equipment sufficient to march through Canada if he had made proper use of them. He reported the loss of 464 killed, 29 missing, and 1,117 wounded.

General Amherst notified Abercromby that he was sending six battalions so that a second attempt on Ticonderoga could be made, but this attack was postponed, and the troops went into winter quarters. This defeat overwhelmed Pitt. He ordered Abercromby home and gave supreme command of British forces in North America to Amherst.

Lieutenant Colonel John Bradstreet's move to capture and destroy the French stronghold at Fort Frontenac eased the humiliation of the defeat at Ticonderoga. Bradstreet assembled a flotilla of ships, whaleboats, and rafts, recruited more than 3,000 men, and quietly ferried his force across the lake. Unlike Abercromby, he brought up his artillery and began to bombard the fort before attempting an assault. So effective was his fire that on August 27, the French surrendered. Fort Frontenac was an important supply depot for the Northwest, and its warehouses were loaded with munitions, foodstuffs, and furs. Bradstreet's men took what they could carry away and destroyed the rest, along with the fort itself. No longer would this fortification protect the entrance to the St. Lawrence and serve as a distribution and supply point for the French. Slowly the English were drawing a noose around the French.

Braddock's defeat before Fort Duquesne at the forks of the Ohio still rankled, and Pitt was determined to extract revenge. Early in 1758, he ordered Brigadier General John Forbes to begin preparations to move against Fort Duquesne. Forbes was methodical, understanding the value of careful planning. After studying Braddock's route from Fort Cumberland to the Ohio, Forbes concluded that a shorter and safer way led across Pennsylvania.

Making Raystown on the Juniata River his supply base, he gradually built a string of fortifications across the province until he felt his communications were secure. After much persuasion and some threats, he managed to pressure Pennsylvanians to supply sufficient wagons and horses to transport supplies, munitions, and artillery. And his frontiersmen hacked a road through the wilderness toward Fort Duquesne.

Forbes had as his second-in-command Lieutenant Colonel Henry Bouquet, a Swiss officer. Bouquet served as Forbes' executive officer, and he was in charge of cutting the road through the wilderness and building forts along the route, an activity that consumed the summer and part of the autumn. In early September, the British had started construction on a fort at Loyalhanna, to be named Fort Ligonier, and Bouquet decided to send ahead an advance party of Scottish Highlanders under Major James Grant to explore the vicinity of Fort Duquesne. He was anxious to discover, among other things, the strength of the Indian allies of the French. Grant's Highlanders with a body of provincial militiamen reached the outskirts of the French fortified area before the enemy discovered them, but they made the mistake of beating their drums to stir their men to action. This alerted the French, who made a sortie from Fort Duquesne with sufficient numbers to surround Grant's men. Grant was captured, and of his 800 men, 275 were either killed or captured.

But conditions favoring the British were taking shape. Indians who until now had cast their lot with the French were becoming disenchanted. The destruction of faraway Louisbourg and the British interception at sea of French supply ships were affecting the French relations with the Indians. The French were unable to deliver goods as promised. The Indians learned the English were more reliable trading partners. Gradually the French found that their allies were deserting.

By November 2, Forbes had concentrated 5,000 men, including Washington and his regiment of Virginians, at Loyalhanna ready for a final advance on Fort Duquesne. In pursuit of a French raiding party ten days later, Washington brought in prisoners who revealed the Indians had deserted the French and that the Canadian militia also had departed. Forbes pushed forward slowly and on November 24 was readying his men for a final attack when the French blew up the fort and vanished in the direction of Canada. Before departing, Indians still loyal to the French had killed prisoners from Grant's detachment. Outside the ruined fort, they placed a row of poles on which they stuck the heads of the Scots with their kilts attached to the bottoms of the poles.

Forbes, gravely ill at the time of the fall of Fort Duquesne, died in March 1759. General Amherst appointed Brigadier General John Stanwix to replace him and ordered him to fortify the forks of the Ohio by rebuilding Fort Duquesne. The new stronghold was called Fort Pitt. Washington, engaged to Martha Custis, had been elected to the Virginia House of Burgesses. He resigned his commission and was succeeded by Colonel William Byrd III.

Though British successes had forced the French to retreat, they had not given up. They still held forts in the West and North that remained a threat to the British. Near the western end of Lake Ontario they retained Fort Niagara; Venango, between Pittsburgh and Lake Ontario, was a potential staging area for offensive action in the Ohio Valley; Ticonderoga and Crown Point were dangerous strongholds in northern New York; Quebec, of course, remained unassailed and, the French thought, invincible. The capture of all these French strongholds was Pitt's objective for 1759.

The elimination of Fort Niagara as an outpost protecting French trade routes to the western Indians would cripple French influence in that region. British relations with the Indians had profoundly changed since 1757, when even the Mohawks, the most loyal to the British of any of the Six Nations, had wavered. Now William Johnson could assure General Amherst that the greater part of the Iroquois would rally to an attack upon Fort Niagara, or upon almost any other objective he selected. The Iroquois, as well as other Indians, were considering the future. They all wanted to be on the winning side, and British victories over the French made the future look promising.

The rebuilding of Oswego began in the spring of

1759 under the direction of Brigadier General John Prideaux. Prideaux let the French and Indians believe his interest at the moment was in the restoration of that British post. But he was also busy assembling men and boats for a descent upon Fort Niagara. During the first week of July, leaving 1,000 soldiers to defend Oswego, he moved 2,000 troops and 1,000 Indians up Lake Ontario to within three miles of Fort Niagara. By July 6, he was in position to lay siege to the fort, and for the next nineteen days the British maintained constant artillery fire upon the French fortifications. On July 17, Prideaux was accidentally killed by one of his own gunners, and Sir William Johnson assumed command.

The French at Venango had been planning to march against the British at the forks of the Ohio River in an attempt to recover ground they had lost at Fort Duquesne. But after a desperate plea from Captain François Pierre Pouchot, commander at Niagara, they sent 600 French soldiers and 1,000 Indians to blunt the siege. This diversion forced the French to abandon the effort to counterattack on the Ohio. Sir William Johnson learned about the approach of the relief column in time to fortify his rear with a barricade of fallen trees. The French found that their Indian allies, fearful of antagonizing the Iroquois with Johnson, deserted rather than attack the tribesmen from the Six Nations. Although the 600 French made a desperate charge upon the British hidden behind the fallen trees, musket fire mowed them down, and they were forced to flee, with the Iroquois in hot pursuit. The Indians killed many, but the British saved some 100 prisoners, including seventeen officers. With the relief force defeated, Captain Pouchot surrendered. Ontario was an English lake. Since regular officers did not like to take orders from Johnson, whom they regarded as merely a leader of Indians, Amherst sent Brigadier General Thomas Gage to command all the Lake Ontario operations.

Gage began to rebuild the fort at Oswego, but he reported to Amherst that he did not have the manpower to move on the French stronghold of La Galette, on the site of modern Ogdensburg, New York. For the time being, the French would hold that fort. In the meantime, Amherst was leading an army against Ticonderoga and Crown Point. Since the French had only a few hundred men left in the Lake George area, on July 26, they destroyed Ticonderoga and retreated to Crown Point, which they also evacuated and reduced to rubble five days later.

The fortress that had been the goal of colonial and British hopes in all previous wars, Quebec, remained a bulwark that had to be taken before victory could be complete. In February 1759, Pitt ordered General Wolfe and Vice Admiral Charles Saunders to proceed to Halifax to begin the campaign. The army and navy would begin moving transports down the St. Lawrence as soon as the spring thaw allowed.

Wolfe would command the forces mobilized to take Quebec. Because of poor health, he had returned to England after the fall of Louisbourg and was not pleased to return to America, even in so responsible a post, and he complained he was "cursed with American service." To support Wolfe, Pitt assigned to him a number of young officers, so young, in fact, that old heads called it "the boys' campaign."

The fleet and troops gathered at Halifax and Louisbourg, and by June 4, the flotilla moved into the Gulf of St. Lawrence preparing to descend upon Quebec. Wolfe had an army of 9,000 regulars and four companies of American rangers (whom he regarded as ill-disciplined and uncertain soldiers). The flotilla consisted of some 200 vessels, including warships, transports, and supply ships. Included in the armament was a heavy train of artillery. With captured French pilots to guide them, the ships neared Quebec on June 26 and the next day cast anchor within five miles of their objective.

On the night of June 28, the French attempted to send fireships against the closely packed English transports, but the wind was not favorable. One ship blew up, others went aground, and British sailors fought others and towed them away.

On the last day of June, Brigadier General Robert Monckton made landing on Point Lévis, on the opposite side of the river from the town, and began placing artillery high enough to throw shells into the city.

Montcalm had his army strongly entrenched downriver from the town all the way to the falls of the Montmorency River. Up the St. Lawrence, he had thrown a barrage of logs across the St. Charles River and had thin defenses between the Plains of Abraham and the city walls. To make a frontal attack on Montcalm's entrenched army by assault from the beaches below was unthinkable. Consequently, Wolfe decided to try to reach his flank by landing troops below the Montmorency, which plunged through a chasm to the St. Lawrence, but could be crossed farther inland. Accordingly, he landed troops across the chasm from the French trenches and began firing into their lines. Through the month of July, the British kept up a bombardment from the batteries across the river and from artillery on the other side of the chasm of the Montmorency. Monckton's artillery destroyed many houses and the cathedral inside the town, but shells alone could not conquer Quebec.

Meanwhile, the French had fortified the crossing of the Montmorency to prevent a flanking attack by Wolfe. Despite the devastation caused by Monckton's and Wolfe's artillery, Montcalm would not take the offensive. Instead, he declared he would follow the tactics of Fabius and let the enemy wear itself out. It was Wolfe, on the last day of July, who attempted an assault on the French lines from the flats where the Montmorency empties into the St. Lawrence. At low tide, soldiers could wade through the mouth of this stream, and Wolfe attempted to lead his men across the river and up the embankments beyond. At best, this was a desperate undertaking, and the intrepid Wolfe was depending on the superior courage and discipline of his regulars to overcome the French militia and Indians who, he believed, held this portion of the French lines. But the assault failed. The French counterattacked in force, and a rainstorm wet the powder of both forces. The British were forced to withdraw with the loss of 443 either killed, wounded, or missing. Each side claimed the storm had saved the other from a decisive defeat. The French were so elated they boasted that Quebec never would be taken.

Through the month of August, the two armies lay watching each other. The British destroyed portions of the countryside, but Montcalm would not venture out of his fortified positions to attack marauders. The destruction of houses inside Quebec was distressing but not sufficiently disastrous to be decisive. The scarcity of food was becoming critical and might in time force surrender, but a few supply boats continued to get through British vessels.

If anything, the morale of the British troops was lower than that of the inhabitants of Quebec. Wolfe had been ill during the last days of August, and the troops were aware of it. Furthermore, autumn was coming, to be followed by freezing weather, and Admiral Saunders and his ship captains were getting anxious over the delays. Both soldiers and sailors were talking about the failure of the campaign and the need to halt the siege.

Wolfe studied the shoreline for a possible landing place. Sweeping the north shore with a telescope, he observed a path up the river from Quebec, leading to heights that seemed to be thinly defended. The path led from a little cove called Anse au Foulon, known ever since then as Wolfe's Cove. Legend says that Major Robert Stobo, who had earlier been held prisoner at Quebec, pointed out the path to Wolfe; at any rate, Wolfe decided this trail up the slope might offer a chance for a surprise attack.

On September 7, Wolfe sent transports loaded with troops up the river to Cap Rouge, some distance beyond the Anse au Foulon, to make a false attempt at landing. Night came, and for the next two days rain prevented further efforts. British troops landed on the south shore and took up quarters in the village of St. Nicholas. For the next few days, their vessels cruised the river well above the Anse au Foulon pretending to look for a landing spot. The French, confused by these tactics and not knowing where the enemy might attempt to come ashore, were forced to march back and forth to be ready to repel them.

On September 12, Wolfe quietly launched the troops that were resting at St. Nicholas and issued a general order for all soldiers and sailors prepare for action. The first troops to reach the opposite shore were to drive directly upon the enemy's outpost and attempt to hold it while reinforcements with artillery could come up. Wolfe planned to force Montcalm to leave his positions and commit to battle on a site where the French commander had not intended to fight. Wolfe had some 4,800 men. Montcalm had nearly twice that number, but Wolfe counted on surprise. Furthermore, he had little respect for French provincials who were part of Montcalm's army.

On the night of September 12, the British sent warships to bombard the shoreline at Beauport, downriver from Quebec, where the French had their strongest entrenchments. This ruse gave the impression that the British were going to attempt another assault, perhaps at the mouth of the Montmorency. Montcalm was fooled and massed troops to repel an attack there.

Then, about 4:00 a.m. on September 13, Wolfe, with 1,800 men, landed along the shore in the vicinity of the Anse au Foulon. A sentry heard noises and inquired who was there, and the reply was made in French that supply boats were trying to evade the British. That answer was satisfactory, and the landings went on without opposition. A group of Scottish Highlanders scrambled up the path and again a sentry inquired. Again a French voice answered, explaining that the detachment had been sent to protect the heights and that the sentry should notify the guard of that fact. The ruse worked. For a brief time - long enough for British troops to gain the top of the cliffs - they were undisturbed. But soon the little French garrison at the top realized what had happened and opened fire. Within a few minutes, Wolfe's men overpowered them and secured an area from which they could protect the ascent of the remainder of the troops.

Wolfe gave the order for troops in the boats to disembark and advance to the cliffs. He scrambled up, followed by battalion after battalion. When morning came, a red-coated army held the Plains of Abraham, a fairly level tract of grass and cornfields, named after a river pilot, Abraham Martin, who had once owned part of the land. Wolfe carefully chose his battlefield. Between him and the walls of Quebec, about a mile to the east, stretched a low, bush-covered ridge, which obscured the view of the town. Wolfe deployed his men facing Quebec in three ranks. Although the plateau at this point is less than a mile wide, with the cliffs of the St. Charles River on the north side, Wolfe did not have enough men to stretch across the whole plateau.

He sent two battalions toward the St. Charles to station themselves at right angles to the main battle line, should the French push toward their left flank. To protect his rear from the army under Louis Antoine de Bougainville that had been watching the movements of the British transports up the river, Wolfe stationed light infantry detachments behind the lines to intercept Bougainville's troops should they appear. Worn out by marching along the river watching the transports, Bougainville's men were resting several miles up the river near Cap Rouge.

Montcalm, who had been expecting an attack from Admiral Saunders' ships downriver at Beauport, heard the ominous news of the British landing early on the morning of September 13. At first, the French did not believe these reports. A fugitive came into camp in the early hours of the morning with a tale of the English landing, but Montcalm's assistant dismissed him as crazy. The noise of gunfire in the first encounter was plainly heard, but everyone thought the British were firing on supply boats. Not until after daylight was the British occupation of the heights confirmed. Montcalm ordered a general alarm and dispatched his men to defend the city. Mounting his horse, he rode through the town, stopped to discuss the development with the Marquis de Vaudreuil, governor general of Canada, whom he awoke, and then rode off to the scene of action. From high ground, he could see lines of red-coated soldiers, supported by Scottish Highlanders in tartans, with their bagpipes already sounding.

Montcalm had to decide whether to order an immediate assault before the British entrenched themselves more thoroughly or to wait for Bougainville to attack the rear. The French commander had 4,500 men on the field, while his opponent had 4,000. As yet Wolfe had brought up only two small pieces of artillery, but Montcalm knew Wolfe could land more fieldpieces and would soon be entrenched solidly. He decided to attack at once without waiting for Bougainville's army of 2,000 men or for reinforcements that the Marquis de Vaudreuil had promised to bring out of Quebec, along with artillery.

Believing his troops were more than a match for the British, Montcalm ordered them to charge the enemy's position. With cheers from the French and war cries from Indian allies and provincial woodsmen, the army charged, firing as they ran. The British waited in their triple ranks and then slaughtered the advancing men with musket fire. Unused to such massed firepower, the French began a disorderly retreat. The Scots with their broadswords swinging went after the fleeing Frenchmen and wreaked havoc. Montcalm, on horseback, falling back with his troops, was shot but managed to stay seated. Troopers supported him on each side until he was within the gates of the city, but he was mortally wounded. Wolfe too received fatal wounds as he led a charge on the right wing. Soldiers carried him to the rear. As he lay on the ground, he refused to have them send for a surgeon, for he said it was "all over with him." When messengers reported that the French were in full retreat, he remarked to one of his officers, "Now, God be praised, I will die in peace."

Wolfe had premonitions of his death before the battle. Telling a former schoolmate, John Jervis, he did not expect to survive, he gave him a small picture of his fiancé and asked him to return it to her. As he and some of his officers waited in the boats before the landing, he recited lines from Gray's "Elegy Written in a Country Churchyard:"

> The boast of heraldry, the pomp of pow'r,
>
> And all that beauty, all that wealth e'er gave,
>
> Await alike th' inevitable hour:
>
> The paths of glory lead but to the grave.

"Gentlemen," he said, "I would rather have written those lines than take Quebec."

The Battle of the Plains of Abraham was won by the audacity of the commanding general and the discipline of his troops. Wolfe risked everything and won. He easily might have lost and seen his men decimated. Had Montcalm waited until

Bougainville came up with his elite army of 2,000 well-trained soldiers to attack Wolfe while Montcalm made a frontal assault, supported by artillery available in Quebec (which he did not wait to use), the battle almost certainly would have been a French victory.

But Quebec was still in French hands. The British, like their opponents, had lost their commander. Since Monckton, the second-in-command, was disabled by wounds, Brigadier General George Townshend took charge. He immediately ordered the army to fortify its camp and prepare for further action against Quebec. Guns were readied for action. Admiral Saunders stood by with his warships to continue the attack.

Inside Quebec, the French were in a state of panic. Vaudreuil believed the last advice he received. The provincials had had enough of English musket fire, and their commanders claimed they could not be driven into action again. Food was scarce, and refugees from the countryside were pouring into the city demanding to be fed. After a council of war, Vaudreuil agreed to retreat around the English by crossing the St. Charles River; they hoped to make a stand on the Jacques-Cartier River. Quebec would be abandoned to its fate.

While these discussions were taking place, Montcalm lay dying. When the surgeon told him he had some twelve hours to live, he replied he was glad he would not live to see the surrender of Quebec. One of his last acts was to send a message to the British commander, General Townshend, asking him to protect French prisoners in the tradition of humanity that the English customarily displayed. Montcalm died early on September 14.

The command of the French armies passed to the Chevalier François Gaston de Lévis, whom Vaudreuil recalled from Montreal. The responsibility of surrendering Quebec would fall to Jean Baptiste de Ramezay, whom Vaudreuil had appointed commandant of the city. Vaudreuil fled with the retreating troops and met Lévis near Three Rivers. The new commander, hearing Quebec had not yet fallen, urged Vaudreuil to turn back and march with the reorganized troops to protect the city. The army was on the way when Lévis received news that Ramezay had surrendered Quebec. The fate of New France was sealed.

Although Vaudreuil condemned Ramezay for surrendering, he had no choice. The army - and Vaudreuil - had deserted the capital, leaving the commandant with only garrison troops and a few provincials who refused to fight. General Townshend had pushed his entrenchments closer to the walls, and his heavy guns were trained to begin a bombardment. The people inside the town were panic-stricken, hungry, and ready to surrender. When Ramezay asked for terms, Townshend promised military personnel could surrender with the honors of war and be transported to France, that civilians and their property would be protected, and they would be free to exercise their religion without interference. Under these terms, on September 17, 1759, Ramezay ran up a white flag; on September 18, Townshend marched in. The capital of New France, was now under British control.

Although 1,800 soldiers and sailors - comprising the garrison at Quebec - had surrendered and were shipped to France after the surrender, the French still had a formidable army. Bougainville's battalions were encamped at Cap Rouge. Lévis, an able commander, had reorganized the troops who had retreated to the Jacques-Cartier and begun the construction of a fort there. The French had some ships of war on the upper St. Lawrence. Vaudreuil had fled to Montreal, where he established the new capital. The French would try to recapture Quebec, and the British hurried to strengthen its fortification. Admiral Saunders, eager to leave before ice made the St. Lawrence impassable, sailed away with his men-of-war on October 18. The British garrison at Quebec would have to hold out until spring against any siege the French might mount.

Since Townshend was eager to return to England, General Monckton, now recovering from his wounds, appointed Brigadier General James Murray to be governor of Quebec and commander of the troops there, with Colonel Ralph Burton as lieutenant governor. Murray was left with 7,000 men to hold Quebec and southern Canada.

The winter was cold, food and fuel were scarce, and the garrison was riven with rumors that the French were mounting a surprise attack. Indeed, Lévis and Vaudreuil were planning a winter advance on Quebec; they had requisitioned quantities of long ladders and were training their troops in scaling operations. But they, too, suffered severely from lack of food and eventually decided to delay the attack. During the late winter and early spring, disease struck the British in Quebec, and before the return of warm weather, more than 1,000 died.

The French attempted to retake Quebec in late April. Lévis had sent an urgent message to France requesting 10,000 fresh soldiers with supplies and munitions before the British could send relief to Quebec or blockade the entrance to the St. Lawrence, but neither troops nor supplies arrived. Nevertheless, the French commander organized an expedition of 3,900 regulars and 3,000 militia to advance on the former capital. On April 27, they reached St. Foy on the outskirts of Quebec, not far from the battlefield where Wolfe and Montcalm had fought the previous September. Although Murray had fewer than half as many men fit for action as Lévis commanded, he, like Montcalm at the Plains of Abraham, chose to attack. He believed his superior artillery would give him the advantage. Accordingly, early on the morning of April 28, he sent 3,000 men against the French. The French crushed his flanks, and the British had to take refuge within the walls of Quebec; nearly one-third of Murray's troops were killed, wounded, or captured, and he was left to defend Quebec with the remnant of his army. Everything depended on whether the British or the French navy first swept up the St. Lawrence.

The British navy succeeded in denying the river to the French, and by mid-May relief ships arrived in the basin opposite Quebec. Their arrival ended Lévis' hopes of taking the city, and, with little food left and gunpowder scarce, he had to fall back toward Montreal.

The final conquest of Canada depended upon crushing the remaining French forces on the upper St. Lawrence in the region around Montreal. To this end, General Amherst devoted his energies. He chose to lead an advance down the serpentine St. Lawrence from Lake Ontario; Murray would push up the river from Quebec; and Brigadier General William Haviland would lead a force from Lake Champlain against Fort Ile-aux-Noix. With these three attacks, the French not only would be defeated, but no corridor would be left for the escape of troops to wilderness retreats.

The colonial governments had received instructions from Pitt early in 1760 to recruit militia to aid in this final campaign. From the colonies north of Pennsylvania, Amherst received 15,000 men, but other colonies raised fewer than 4,000 troops for the Canadian expedition because the southern colonies had troubles nearer at hand. The Ohio Valley had to be held, and the Cherokees were carrying on a war on the southern frontier.

The advance against Montreal moved slowly but inexorably. By late August, Haviland had reached Fort Ile-aux-Noix, now defended by Bougainville; with supplies and munitions for only two days left, Bougainville concluded he could not hold out. Evacuating the fort on August 28, he retreated with most of his men toward Montreal; he left gunners to run up the white flag when the rest of the soldiers were clear of the fort. During the same days, Murray was advancing from Quebec, and Amherst was moving down the rapids of the St. Lawrence from Lake Ontario. The defenses of the upper St. Lawrence - Fort La Galette and a hastily erected structure on an island, Fort Lévis - fell to Amherst. By September 6, he had his army in sight of Montreal. Murray had marched past Three Rivers and had secured the surrender of the French in each parish as he advanced. Haviland arrived from the south. The French were cornered. Although Lévis still breathed fire and brimstone, Vaudreuil knew the end had come, and on September 8 he signed a treaty that surrendered all Canada on condition that his troops would be treated as prisoners of war, that the persons and property of civilians would be safe, and that individuals would be guaranteed freedom of worship.

The years of war for possession of North America had ended. France, it is true, still held the lower portion of Louisiana, but the final dispersement of that territory would be made around council tables, not on the battlefield. The British were supreme from Florida north to the Arctic Ocean and west to the Mississippi River. To be sure, the frontiers were not yet safe, nor would they be for years, for brush-fire wars would break out with the Indians; but the mortal conflict with France was over, and Pitt could look upon his handiwork and take pleasure in the outcome.

12

SOCIAL AND
INTELLECTUAL LIFE

By 1760, the thirteen British colonies in North America had settled governments, a well-established citizenry, and a degree of economic strength. Only Georgia, the last colony to be settled, remained an exposed frontier, but by the Treaty of Paris in 1763, England took possession of Florida and removed the Spanish threat from the south. The same year, Georgia made a treaty with the Creek Indians and established its borders to include most of the territory later incorporated into the states of Alabama and Mississippi. With rich lands beckoning, settlers from older colonies and overseas began to immigrate to Georgia.

In other colonies, settlers were pushing farther into the interior of the continent. Indian wars in the

1760s and British efforts to preserve Indian hunting grounds beyond the Alleghenies temporarily halted the European drive west. With the French threat removed from Canada, and the Spanish no longer a danger in Florida, frontiersmen felt they only had to contend with conflicts with the Indians and such restrictions as Parliament in London might try to enforce.

Although postwar adjustments caused a temporary depression, the thirteen colonies continued to make advances in the decade-and-a-half preceding the outbreak of hostilities with Britain. The colonies included a wide variety of peoples, trades, skills, and occupations. No longer were the inhabitants of British North America homesick Englishmen, eager to make money out of the products of the New World and return home. They were Americans, with few ties to the mother country. Many families in Virginia, Maryland, New England, New York, New Jersey, Pennsylvania, and the Carolinas had been there for several generations. They farmed the land, sailed the seas, fished commercially, and engaged in many businesses, crafts, and trades.

Although economic planners in London might imagine they had created a closed mercantilist empire, with overseas possessions supplying raw material, and the mother country furnishing manufactured products, the economic picture was not as simple as that. Despite restrictive regulations and official disapproval, manufacturing on an increasing scale was flourishing in most of the colonies. For example, the manufacture of beaver hats was so successful in Boston, New York, Newport, and Philadelphia that it threatened the hat industry in England and resulted in orders to customs officers to monitor hats that were being shipped to the West Indies, manufactured in defiance of regulations.

Some manufacturing in the colonies was conducted in violation of the Acts of Trade; British authorities encouraged others. The production of pig iron, for example, was favored, but in 1750 Parliament forbade the colonies to establish mills for making nails and iron rods, or forges for making steel or iron products. This law, however, was rarely obeyed. The production of raw iron increased to such an extent that in 1775, the colonies produced 30,000 tons, or about one-seventh of the world's iron.

The colonies were not economically independent, but they had developed substantial economic resources of a wide range and variety that promised prosperity. Farseeing individuals in all colonies realized the undeveloped potential; a few already had taken advantage of the opportunities, while others were preparing to reap the benefits of the vast natural resources before them.

The colonies were still essentially rural, even those whose lifeblood was trade. Cities were small, and farm country lay just beyond their outskirts. A man could live in the center of Boston, New York, or Philadelphia and easily operate a farm nearby. The largest city in the American colonies was Philadelphia - which was one of the largest cities in the British Empire - yet Philadelphia's population in 1760 was only 23,750. In the same year, New York had a population of 18,000; Boston, 15,600; Newport, 7,500; and Charles Town, South Carolina, 8,000. By 1775, these populations had increased so that Philadelphia had 40,000; New York, 25,000; Boston, 16,000; Newport, 11,000; and Charles Town, 12,000. No other towns in the colonies numbered as many as 9,000 inhabitants before the revolution. With two exceptions, all towns that had shown material growth were ports. The largest landlocked town was Lancaster, Pennsylvania, with between 5,000 and 6,000. The population of the thirteen colonies in 1760 has been estimated at 1.7 million; by 1775, it had grown to an estimated 2.8 million.

Immigration into the colonies increased rapidly with the coming of peace in 1763. The wars with France had made sea travel more hazardous than usual; furthermore, passage across the Atlantic was not easy to get when transports were required for troops and military supplies. The end of the wars caused economic adjustments in Europe, a depression, and unemployment, all of which led to emigration to the New World. England had many unemployed who saw no future at home. Scotland, a country poor in natural resources but rich in courageous men, had eager emigrants ready to try a new life overseas. Ireland had surplus populations of both native Irish and more recent settlers who had come from Scotland to occupy Ulster. In the Rhineland and other areas of Germany, prospective emigrants had heard of the opportunities many of their countrymen had found in Pennsylvania.

The emigration of Scots was particularly significant, for they had a far-reaching influence upon the civilization of the new land. Three strains of Scots came to America: Ulster Scots from Northern Ireland, Lowland Scots, and Highlanders. The first to make an impression were the Ulster Scots, who began emigrating in large numbers in the early eighteenth century and continued to come until the end of the colonial period.

These Scots, described in American histories as "Scotch-Irish," were Presbyterians who had occupied much of Northern Ireland, lands earlier confiscated from the rebellious native Irish. They had developed a thriving linen and woolen industry, and many maintained herds of cattle. Their diligence was their undoing, for their linen, wool, and cattle offered such competition to the English that Parliament passed acts to restrict production in Ireland. Added to these restrictions was the so-called Test Act of 1704, which required all officeholders to subscribe to the Established Church, something Presbyterians were not willing to do. Depression and bitter resentment among Ulster Scots forced them once more to set out in search of a better life, this time in America. They came with a hatred of the English they retained until the revolution gave them an opportunity to vent their hostility in overt rebellion.

The number of Ulster Scots who came to America in the colonial period is difficult to ascertain, but one of the most thorough investigators of this movement estimates they numbered approximately 200,000. The emigration from 1763 until the beginning of the revolution was particularly heavy. During three years, from 1771 to 1773, 28,600 left Ireland for the colonies. By the first census in 1790, slightly more than 14 percent of the European population, something approaching 450,000, were Scotch-Irish.

The propaganda that William Penn and his agents published convinced early emigrants that Pennsylvania offered greater opportunities for fertile land and for freedom of worship than any other region. The experiences of the first Ulster Scots confirmed this, and they urged their fellow countrymen to come to Pennsylvania. Philadelphia, Chester, and Newcastle became the principal ports of entry, but they could not settle in the region around Philadelphia, already occupied by earlier arrivals. Nor could they settle on the rich lands that Germans had taken up in the Lancaster and York areas. Consequently, they had to push on beyond the settlements into frontier zones.

Thus, the eighteenth-century Ulster Scots became frontiersmen. Hardy and courageous, convinced they had God on their side, they equated the Indians with the Amalekites of the Old Testament and were eager to take their land. Although the Pennsylvania Quakers had made treaties with the Indians that they tried to observe meticulously, the Ulster Scots showed no concern about squatting on Indian land. In time, the land became theirs by right of occupation.

Ulster Scots, initially welcomed by Pennsylvania, soon became a problem for the Quaker colony. They did not get along with their neighbors of other stocks, either in Pennsylvania or elsewhere. The Germans disliked and avoided them. The English and the Welsh in Pennsylvania found them troublesome. They showed little regard for land patents and simply settled where no authority could keep them out. By the end of the colonial period they were found in clearings on the frontiers of most of the colonies, but chiefly from Pennsylvania to Georgia. Clannish, they kept to themselves and did not mix easily with others.

An Anglican preacher, Charles Woodmason, journeyed in the back country of South Carolina in

1766 and commented on the Scotch Presbyterians there. One region on the Pee Dee River he described as "occupied by a set of the most lowest, vilest crew breathing - Scotch-Irish Presbyterians from the north of Ireland." Hostile to other faiths, Woodmason admonished efforts of the South Carolina assembly to attract immigrants from Ulster instead of thinking of the interests of the Church of England: "Hence it is that above £30,000 Sterling have lately been expended to bring over 5 or 6000 Ignorant, mean, worthless, beggarly Irish Presbyterians, the Scum of the Earth, and Refuse of Mankind, and this, solely to ballance the Emigrations of People from Virginia, who are all of the Established Church."

These Scots from Ulster, for all of Woodmason's invectives, played an important role in the colonies. They spearheaded westward expansion and helped to open the frontier. They were the most ardent patriots when war broke out with England. Although narrow-minded men such as Woodmason accused the Scots of shiftlessness, they produced educational leaders who established schools in order to ensure an adequate supply of Presbyterian preachers.

As for the Highlanders, a few arrived after the Jacobite rebellion of 1715, but their numbers began to increase after the rebellion of 1745 and their defeat at Culloden in 1746. Then thousands of Highlanders accepted the king's offer of a pardon to rebels who would take the oath of allegiance and emigrate to America. Most refugees came to North Carolina and settled in the Cape Fear Valley. (The town now called Fayetteville originally was named Campbelltown because of its Scottish settlers.) Highlanders who had arrived in North Carolina earlier largely were responsible for persuading late-comers to settle in this region. This movement, continuing until the revolution, gave North Carolina the largest body of Highlanders in the thirteen colonies. Other Highlanders, veterans discharged from Scottish regiments in the wars against the French, settled in upper New York. Most colonies had some Scottish Highlanders. At the revolution, many Highlanders remained loyal to Great Britain, and Scots on both sides almost entirely fought the Battle of Kings Mountain in North Carolina.

Of the third group of Scots, the Lowlanders, many settled in towns and became traders and merchants. Few colonial towns in the second half of the eighteenth century were without Lowland Scots engaged in trade, either in their interests or representing merchants in Glasgow. After the mid-eighteenth century, much the tobacco processing industry of Great Britain centered in Glasgow, and many agents came from Glasgow to Virginia and Maryland and established tobacco-buying stations at Norfolk, Annapolis,

Baltimore, and at such inland points as Tappahannock. Scottish merchants and traders were an important element in the economic life of New England, New York, Pennsylvania, the Carolinas, and Georgia in the period prior to the revolution. Some Lowland Scots settled in the back country and became farmers, but they are hard to trace, for they soon mingled with the Scotch-Irish and cannot be easily distinguished from them. The Scots, because of their tenacity, industry, and intellectual qualities, had an influence upon the colonies that transcended their numerical strength.

The immigration of English settlers, as one could expect, increased enormously after the Peace of Paris in 1763. These immigrants were of all classes, but most were workmen, artisans, and farmers who helped to swell the labor force in those colonies where African slavery had not taken hold. Among the other increments of population arriving in the decades just prior to the revolution were large numbers of Germans (chiefly Lutherans but including some Moravians), a few Swiss, Italians, French, and Jews.

Slavery had become an institution in agrarian colonies of the South and supplied the principal body of unskilled labor, but every colony had some slaves, even Georgia, where slavery at first had been outlawed. By 1770, out of a population of some 2.3 million, African slaves numbered 462,000. The greatest number were in the South, where they worked on tobacco and rice plantations.

In addition to slaves from Africa, the colonies received large numbers of white bondsmen, known as indentured servants. Many came in the seventeenth century to the agrarian colonies, and until the end of the colonial period they continued to arrive by the shipload. Most of these immigrants could find no other way to pay their passage except to agree to serve a master for a stated period, usually four years but sometimes longer. At the expiration of a servant's period of servitude, he received certain specified benefits, which varied from time to time and from place to place. These might consist of money, clothes, tools, or a piece of land.

Another kind of indentured servant was the redemptioner, one who got to a port bound for America and could not raise sufficient money to pay for his passage. Captains would take such passengers aboard and land them at an American port with the proviso that if they could not find friends or relatives who could raise the balance due on their passage, the captain could indenture them to a master to reimburse the passage money.

An unwilling type of indentured servant who came to America was the convict, male or female, condemned to transportation. These immigrants were unwelcome - Benjamin Franklin suggested sending back cargoes of rattlesnakes in retaliation. Though from time to time colonial legislatures passed laws to prevent convicts being shipped to them, London disallowed the laws. The northern colonies were relatively successful in keeping out convicts because they could provide less employment than agrarian colonies. Although some convicts were sent to New Jersey, Pennsylvania, the Carolinas, and occasionally to other colonies, Virginia and Maryland received the greatest number. According to shipping returns, more than 9,000 convicts arrived in Maryland between 1748 and 1775. But, weak from disease and malnutrition, the death rate among them was high.

The indentured servants who served their time usually acquired land and became farmers or took up a trade or craft; if they survived their indenture, ample opportunities beckoned. Many who arrived as indentured servants started families and prospered. Little or no stigma was attached to this means of getting across the Atlantic. The tide of immigration of servants of this type, chiefly Germans and Scots, greatly increased after 1765 and continued until the revolution. It has been estimated that between 1750 and 1775, Pennsylvania received more than 50,000 indentured servants.

Scottish schoolmasters were common in Virginia and in other colonies. Indeed, planters were accustomed to buying indentured servants for this purpose, to the disgust of competing tutors. Jonathan Boucher, a Virginia tutor, complained in 1773 that "at least two thirds of the little education we receive are derived from instructors, who are either INDENTURED SERVANTS, OR TRANSPORTED FELONS. Not a ship arrives either with redemptioners or convicts, in which schoolmasters are not regularly advertised for sale, as weavers, tailors, or any other trade; with little difference, that I can hear of, excepting perhaps that the former do not usually fetch so good a price as the latter."

Because so many Scots served as tutors in Virginia, planters complained their children learned to speak with a Scottish accent. On April 6, 1774, Philip Vickers Fithian, a Princeton graduate who served as a tutor in the household of Robert Carter of Nomini Hall, noted in his diary that Carter told him he preferred "a Tutor for his Children who has been educated upon the Continent [American], not on a supposition that such are better Schollars, or that they are of better principles, or of more agreeable Tempers; but only on account of pronunciation in the English Language."

Throughout the colonial period, skilled labor was in short supply, and talented artisans and craftsmen enjoyed steady employment and good wages. In the more industrialized northern colonies, a wide variety of craftsmen flourished. Shipbuilding, for example, one of the most important industries in New England, required many specialties: carpenters, joiners, sailmakers, shipwrights, blacksmiths, ropemakers, caulkers, and painters. The iron industry needed both foundrymen and subsidiary artisans: stone diggers, miners, limestone workers, charcoal burners, furnacemen, forgemen, and drivers. Flour milling, which flourished in wheat-growing areas, particularly in Pennsylvania and Delaware, required millers, watermen, mechanics, millrace tenders, and warehousemen. Every region needed carpenters, joiners, cabinetmakers, plasterers, masons, sawyers, and painters.

In the South, some slaves became craftsmen, and their competition discouraged free white craftsmen - and caused considerable hostility among competing white labor. Even in New England, competition with white labor created hostility. The threat of skilled slave labor was largely responsible for the virtual elimination of slavery in New England. John Adams said in 1795, "If the gentlemen had been permitted to hold slaves, the common white people would have put the slaves to death, and their masters too, perhaps."

Some colonial craftsmen were as talented as those on the other side of the Atlantic. American silversmiths turned out excellent silverware in most of the principal cities of the coast. Although Paul Revere is perhaps the one most widely remembered today, other silversmiths from Boston to Charles Town, South Carolina, gained fine reputations. Silver served as a sort of savings bank for colonials who invested money in plate that could be identified by its markings and served both useful and ornamental purposes.

The prosperity of colonial craftsmen depended on the increase of wealth and demand for their services. By the mid-eighteenth century the colonies had some families who lived in fine houses, had servants, and could afford the same luxuries available in Europe. Although Robert Beverley could complain that Virginians imported everything, even woodenware, conditions in the next few decades altered materially. Philadelphia developed into a center where many crafts flourished. Philadelphia sent journeymen trained to carry on their trades in other colonies. Benjamin Franklin sent a printer to Charles Town to start a printing office and newspaper. Cabinetmakers in Charles Town, advertising their skills, recommended themselves as "from Philadelphia." At Newport, some of the finest cabinetmakers plied their crafts. Furniture made in the colonies ranged in quality from crude puncheon benches to imitations of Chippendale. The best craftsmen were in the larger cities, but hardly a town of consequence in the later eighteenth century lacked skilled workers.

Many folk arts flourished. Even in frontier cabins, women developed distinctive styles for quilts and coverlets. The Pennsylvania Germans decorated pottery, produced elaborate needlework, and carved and painted distinctive furniture.

One of the most important contributions of the Germans was the long squirrel rifle, manufactured by gunsmiths at Lancaster and elsewhere in the German districts of Pennsylvania. These rifles, sometimes with decorative elements carved on the stocks or engraved on steel panels, showed precise technical skill. The Germans also were responsible for building Conestoga wagons, which served as a great land fleet conveying farm products from the interior to the port of Philadelphia.

Colonial Americans took pride in their houses and built as well as their resources permitted. Not even the most fanatical Puritan could condemn a man for erecting an expansive house for an ever-growing family. By the late eighteenth century, many Boston merchants lived in substantial mansions on Beacon Hill, furnished with handsome furniture, waited on by black slaves better trained than servants in most southern plantation houses. The houses of lesser folk in New England were compactly built. Tradition and weather demanded sturdy buildings, and the country had carpenters and masons capable of this work. The majority of houses were of wood, the most plentiful building material, although from time to time, because of the fire hazard, municipal authorities tried to discourage wooden structures in favor of brick.

The Quakers, for all their talk about simplicity, built impressive mansions in Pennsylvania. James Logan, as early as 1728, erected a magnificent brick house he named Stenton in the country outside Philadelphia. It was three stories high and had a great parlor and state dining room in addition to a smaller family dining room, living rooms, and a library. Isaac Norris, another wealthy Quaker, built an imposing country house, Fair Hill, not far from Logan's estate. One influence that helped foster significant architecture in Philadelphia was the establishment of the Carpenters' Company, a guild of master carpenters which established high standards of construction.

The citizens of Philadelphia, the wealthiest colonial city, took pride in their public buildings, which followed the style now called Georgian. The American Philosophical Society building, the State House, and Carpenters' Hall exemplify the best of this style of architecture.

Professional architects generally were not available, even for the most imposing public buildings. Peter Harrison, an English ship captain who settled at Newport in the mid-eighteenth century, has been called the first American architect. Harrison was responsible for designing King's Chapel in Boston and the Redwood Library and Touro Synagogue in Newport. William Buckland, who eventually settled in Annapolis, was another early architect. He was responsible for designing and building George Mason's house, Gunston Hall, which was completed in 1759, and for the design of many houses in Maryland. But carpenters, with only the help of books of designs imported from England, planned and built most houses in British America before the revolution.

That so many houses from New England to Georgia were well designed and well-built testifies to the skill of master craftsmen. The best carpenters followed designs found in a number of books ranging from recent editions of Andrea Palladio of Vicenza to Batty Langley's 1740 *The City and Country Builders and Workman's Treasury of Designs*. A master carpenter, faced with a commission to erect a mansion for a Boston merchant or a plantation house on the James River, had a variety of books to help him and the owner select the kind of house desired.

Only the wealthy, however, could afford the skills of the best-trained carpenters, and they frequently complained of the lack of experienced workmen. This scarcity was greatest in the South, where slave labor tended to drive out free artisans. Slaves attained enough skill to work independently or readily learned from craftsmen brought in to teach them. They did much of the building in Maryland, Virginia, and the Carolinas.

On the frontier, and in isolated areas, buildings had to be erected by settlers with their own hands. From the Germans and Swedes, British immigrants learned the art of making log cabins, pigpen style, and by the eighteenth century, the log cabin had become the characteristic wilderness structure. With notched logs and mud caulking the cracks, it was a tight and substantial house that could be built with relative ease.

Although wars and depressions might have temporarily halted development, not even the threat of a French victory during the eighteenth century stopped the growth of the colonies or the promise of advancement and ultimate prosperity they offered settlers. Since labor was always in demand, no able-bodied man needed work. Since land was abundant and could be had on reasonable terms, every man could look forward to a time when he might be a landowner. The possession of land always has conveyed a certain status, and even though land in America was not as scarce as in Europe, its possession continued to hold both material and intangible assets.

In the South, planters, owning sometimes thousands of acres, developed a landed aristocracy that succeeded in monopolizing much of the economic and political power. In Virginia, landowners such as the Carters, Byrds, Burwells, Randolphs, Fitzhughs, and others owned the best property in the tidewater region and held the most important offices in the province. They were vestrymen in the Anglican Church - the established state church. They served as justices of the peace, sheriffs of the counties, colonels of the militia, members of the Council of State, and members of the House of Burgesses. At meetings of the council and the House of Burgesses, these aristocrats gathered in the capital of Williamsburg to attend to political business and enjoy social contacts they missed on distant plantations. They entertained each other at dinners and balls and created a lively social season. Some planters maintained houses in Williamsburg.

In their origins, these planters were usually men whose immigrant forebears had had sufficient capital to acquire land with servants enough to cultivate the tobacco that made them prosperous. Few of these families can be traced with certainty to aristocratic families in England. The Byrds, for example, started from a goldsmith, John Byrd, who married the daughter of ship captain Thomas Stegg, who was a Virginia trader. Byrd's son, the first William Byrd, came to Virginia to help his uncle, also named Thomas Stegg, in trade he had developed with the Indians. William Byrd I became a prosperous trader, inherited land and bought more, and joined the ranks of the top planter class.

These planters, intent upon getting ahead, worked hard at management. Although they enjoyed social amenities, and some wasted their wealth in gaming and horse racing, most devoted themselves to making their plantations pay. Landon Carter, who lived for years at Sabine Hall and kept a diary from 1752 to 1778, reports in minute detail the routine of a busy planter. Carter emphasizes the wastefulness of slave labor, the incompetence of overseers and their charges, the everlasting oversight required of the landowner, and the frequency of disaster and loss. No planter who achieved wealth could afford a slow pace and the ease depicted in books and films.

Maryland had an upper planter class much like that of Virginia, some of whom acquired great tracts of land and established family dynasties of power and influence. Families such as the Carrolls, Chews, Hammonds, Lloyds, Taskers, and Dulanys dominated colonial Maryland. In this colony, too, many prominent families at the end of the colonial period traced their origins to simple workmen who managed to capitalize upon opportunities to buy land and profit from trade. Some early settlers in South Carolina came from Barbados, where they had made enough money in sugar plantations to get a start in the new colony. Few families in Charles Town in the late eighteenth century exceeded the grandeur of the Manigaults. The first was Pierre, a craftsman who arrived in Charles Town in 1695, tried farming, and eventually opened a tavern. As he prospered, he established a brandy distillery, which succeeded, and he set up a shop for making barrels. Soon Manigault was the owner of a second distillery and of warehouses on the Charles Town docks. His son Gabriel Manigault added to the business and became the richest man in the province. Gabriel's son, Peter, born in 1731, went to London to finish his education, became a member of the Inner Temple, and was admitted to the English bar. One of the most prominent lawyers in South Carolina, he took his place in the provincial assembly and eventually was elected speaker.

Henry Laurens, revolutionary leader, was another self-made South Carolina aristocrat who combined business and planting. Son of a Huguenot saddler who made a comfortable fortune in his saddlery business, Henry Laurens branched out as a commission merchant exporting rice, indigo, deerskins, and furs, and dealing in imports of wine and slaves. He bought rice plantations and was soon one of the wealthiest and most influential men in the colony. Before the revolution, Laurens, who never liked selling slaves, abandoned that business and concentrated on his rice plantations.

South Carolina aristocrats of the tidewater region combined trade and farming and profited in both. Charles Town was a convenient port for West Indian traffic and for trade with the coast of Africa, which offered a good market for rice. The great planters had town houses on the riverfront known as the Battery, known for cool summer sea breezes. In the winter, they lived on their plantations, but heat, mosquitoes, and malaria made the river houses uninhabitable in summer. It was then that the planters withdrew to their town houses in Charles Town for a social season that included concerts given by the St. Cecelia Society, plays at the Dock Street Theatre, and many balls and social gatherings. Savannah, Georgia, and Wilmington, North Carolina, had a similar social structure.

All colonies developed an upper class of wealthy planters, merchants, or shippers who assumed the airs and trappings of an aristocracy. The planter aristocracy of agrarian colonies approximated English county families more nearly than any other social group in America, but the merchant aristocrats of New England were as proud of their accomplishments and status. The richest pre-revolutionary merchant in Boston was Thomas Hancock, who at thirteen was apprenticed to a bookseller. By the time he received his freedom, he was able to set up his own bookstore and later married Lydia Henchman, daughter of the leading bookseller of Boston. Hancock expanded from bookselling into other businesses, including a mercantile establishment that dealt in fish, whale oil, and rum. Hancock became a partner with Charles Apthorp, another noted merchant of the day; between them they supplied the British army in Nova Scotia under generous contracts that added to their wealth. In 1755, Hancock furnished seventeen vessels used in transporting the Acadians to their places of exile. Like many merchants of the day, Hancock looked upon smuggling as an honorable occupation and was noted for his success in evading the law.

Having no son to inherit his wealth, Thomas Hancock adopted his nephew, John Hancock, who became a vocal patriot, a signer of the Declaration of Independence, and, as the richest merchant on the patriot side, a substantial contributor to the cause of liberty. But John Hancock flaunted his wealth, lived pretentiously, annoyed John Adams, and was angry because the Continental Congress did not make him commander in chief of its army.

Boston had many great merchants who lived luxuriously, but avoided the flamboyance of John Hancock. Their ships sailed to ports in Europe, the Wine Islands, Africa, the West Indies, and to coastal ports of British America. Their cargoes were varied, sometimes legal, sometimes illegal, but usually profitable. They transported vast quantities of rum and traded some of it for slaves on the Guinea coast. Peter Faneuil accumulated a fortune and was known as a successful smuggler. He is charged with making part of his fortune in the slave trade. A bachelor, he named one of his best ships *The Jolly*

Bachelor. When news reached him of this vessel's arrival in Boston harbor with a human cargo, Faneuil is said to have gone to church to thank God for making him the instrument by which so many heathen souls were brought to salvation. Since he donated to Boston Faneuil Hall, called the Cradle of Liberty because of the many patriotic meetings held there, a current saying was that "the Cradle of Liberty rocks on the bones of the Middle Passage."

No Virginia aristocrat managed to reach such eminence as a fisherman of Kittery, Maine, William Pepperrell. His father, also named William, as a small boy was apprenticed to the captain of a fishing vessel. Pepperrell, the elder, worked hard and became a successful fish and lumber dealer. Young William became a partner in his father's business, became skilled, married the granddaughter of Judge Samuel Sewall, and was made commander of the expedition against Louisbourg. Grateful for the capture of Louisbourg, the British government in 1746 made Pepperrell a baronet, the first American to receive such a high honor. Sir William's son and heir died before his father, and for a time the title lapsed; but Sir William made his grandson, William Pepperrell Sparhawk, heir to his estate on the condition he drop his last name; and in 1774 the king of England made him a baronet.

In the later colonial era, Rhode Island had some of the most prosperous and enterprising merchants in all New England. They engaged in commerce that extended from New England to Europe, Africa, the West Indies, and the mainland colonies south to Georgia. Never meticulous about obeying the Acts of Trade, Rhode Islanders found their coast suited to evading British revenue cutters, and they managed to smuggle quantities of molasses from the French West Indies. Most of this molasses went into the manufacture of rum, in great demand on the Guinea coast, where it could be exchanged for slaves.

Newport was the first town in Rhode Island to develop an important merchant aristocracy. By the mid-eighteenth century, merchants such as Daniel Ayrault, John Channing, Henry Collins, Abraham Redwood, William Ellery, Godfrey and John Malbone, and Samuel Vernon, had created a golden age for Newport. Many made their fortunes in the slave trade.

Few mercantile dynasties in America exceeded the Browns of Providence in the diversity and the magnitude of their interest. The first of the name, Chad Brown, who arrived in New England in 1638, fathered a line that continues unbroken to present day. In the later eighteenth century, the Browns controlled fleets of vessels trading to the ends of the earth; they engaged in various mercantile and manufacturing activities including producing spermaceti candles, distilling rum, and smelting pig iron. Hardly a profitable activity in Rhode Island failed to interest the Browns. Obadiah Brown, leader of the family after 1739, was responsible for developing new enterprises, including a "chocklit" mill where he ground chocolate beans brought by shippers from the West Indies. After Obadiah's death in 1762, the business was continued by four Brown brothers under the name of Nicholas Brown and Company. Melancholy after the death of his wife in 1773, one of the brothers, Moses, disturbed by the brutality of the slave trade, withdrew from commerce to lead a contemplative life. He later became a Quaker and joined the Rhode Island Abolition Society.

Rhode Island saw the rise of a number of prominent Jewish merchants. Some were Sephardic Jews whose ancestors had fled to Holland from Spain and Portugal; others were Jews who had reached Holland from Germany. Ultimately some of these Dutch Jews emigrated to the colonies, principally to New York, Philadelphia, Newport, Charles Town, and Savannah. In the decades preceding the revolution, the Jews of Newport were among the most prosperous in North America. The leading Jewish merchant was Aaron Lopez, who had a fleet of more than thirty ships trading wherever a profit could be made; he was described by a contemporary, Ezra Stiles, as "a merchant of the first eminence, for honor and extent of commerce probably surpassed by no merchant in America."

Jacob Rivera, father-in-law of Lopez, is sometimes credited with the introduction of the technique of making spermaceti candles, though Obadiah Brown may claim that distinction. James Lucena appears to have manufactured the first castile soap in Rhode Island. Although Jewish merchants of Rhode Island were not numerous, they played a conspicuous part in the commercial development of the area.

New York had an aristocracy of wealthy and influential families, some of whom held large tracts of land, while others depended on Indian trade and other commercial activities. From the time of the Dutch occupation of the Hudson Valley, a few individuals had carved out great estates, and wealthy families frequently intermarried and consolidated fortunes already substantial. The Van Cortlandts, Livingstons, Schuylers, De Lanceys, and several other families lived extravagantly and exerted considerable political influence. Their interests included developing commercial enterprises, acquiring more land, and adding to their wealth. Philip Schuyler traveled to England on business in 1761 and returned eager to live like an English country gentleman. He acquired thousands of acres of land in the Mohawk Valley and erected grist mills, flour mills, and the first water-powered flax mill in the country.

The Livingston clan (descended from a well-born

Scot, Robert Livingston, who was the first of his family in New York) wielded great power in the province. In the legislative assembly of 1759, out of twenty-seven members, four were Livingstons. As Presbyterians, they led a popular faction opposed to Lieutenant Governor James De Lancey, head of the Episcopal party. Philip Livingston, one of the signers of the Declaration of Independence, was not only a man of wealth, but he also had many cultural and intellectual interests. In 1737, he had received an A.B. degree from Yale, and he retained a concern for higher education throughout his life.

With opportunities for land and a chance to participate in profitable trade, a few enterprising men in all the colonies managed to outmaneuver their less energetic or less fortunate contemporaries. They rose to positions of power, had the status of aristocrats, and were sometimes proud, autocratic, disdainful of the multitude, and forgetful of their origins. But many in the colonies, both in New England and the South, had a keen sense of social obligation and a belief that privilege carried with it responsibility. That concept helps to explain leaders who had a part in creating a nation after 1776.

The prominence of men of wealth, the houses they built, the furniture and silver they left for posterity, and the records of the grand life they lived tend to obscure the fact that the bulk of the population in the colonies were hard-working people who plied their trades, farmed their land, sailed their fishing craft, and owned no slaves. These were independent people, some of whom would save, invest, and improve themselves economically and socially. Others were content to live their lives in the stations to which they felt God had called them, getting satisfaction out of their skills, crafts, farms, and trades. Not every colonial aspired to be a great planter or a rich merchant. But while many were satisfied with the simple life in which they found themselves, others were ambitious. The colonial expression of this ambition for self-improvement can be found in the works of Benjamin Franklin, who set forth prescriptions for advancement in his *Autobiography* and in *Poor Richard's Almanack.*

Franklin's advice on how to get ahead in the world was written in 1757 for the *Almanack* of 1758 and is known as "Father Abraham's Speech," or by its more usual title, "The Way to Wealth." Few if any other writings by an American have been so widely disseminated and so often quoted. Under the fiction of an old man delivering an impromptu bit of advice at an auction sale, Franklin gathered up his best proverbs and wove them into a fable full of sly humor and shrewd counsel. There, crystallized for all time, are adages that are still common in American thinking: "Sloth, like Rust, consumes faster than Labour wears, while the used Key is always bright. . . . The sleeping Fox catches no Poultry. . . . Early to Bed, and early to rise, makes a Man healthy, wealthy and wise. . . . Industry need not wish. . . . At the working Man's House Hunger looks in, but dares not enter. . . . God gives all Things to Industry. Then plough deep, while Sluggards sleep. . . . Three Removes is as bad as a Fire. . . . Keep thy Shop, and thy Shop will keep thee. . . . A Ploughman on his Legs is higher than a Gentleman on his Knees. . . . Pride breakfasted with Plenty, dined with Poverty, and supped with Infamy. . . . The second Vice is Lying, the first is running in Debt. . . . Tis hard for an empty Rag to stand upright." These proverbs and others in the same crisp idiom are a part of the little narrative of Father Abraham's speech, which warns near the end that "this Doctrine, my Friends, is *Reason* and *Wisdom*: but after all, do not depend too much upon your own *Industry*, and *Frugality*, and *Prudence*, though excellent Things, for they may all be blasted without the Blessings of Heaven; and therefore ask that Blessing humbly, and be not uncharitable to those that at present seem to want it, but comfort and help them. Remember Job suffered, and was afterwards prosperous."

This tract, which combined worldly prudence with piety as a proper formula for success, gained an international audience. Franklin was astonished, and proud, of its reception. As he pointed out in the *Autobiography*, English newspapers printed it widely, householders bought broadside versions and stuck them up in their houses, the clergy and gentry distributed large quantities to their parishioners and tenants, and publishers in France printed two translations. "In Pennsylvania, as it discouraged useless expense in foreign superfluities," Franklin observed with satisfaction, "some thought it had its share of influence in producing that growing plenty of money which was observable for several years after its publication." The popularity of *The Way to Wealth* gained momentum from that day. More than 1,000 editions have been recorded in English, and 300 in other languages. Franklin's essay, which served as a manual of success, sums up the American belief that an ordinary man, by his own efforts and merits, can become captain of his fate. This doctrine, derived from experience and observation by one of the wisest of colonial Americans, profoundly influenced the social attitudes of many Americans in Franklin's time and ever since.

From Maine to Florida, conditions of colonial life bred an independence of spirit and a sense of freedom previously unknown to Europeans. No tenant fell bound to the land; no artisan thought himself confined to one employer or to one locality. If he or his family did not like life as they found it, they could go elsewhere. All the colonies had groups among their population who were on the move in search of conditions more to their liking. For example, men of wealth and power in tidewater regions did not easily govern or influence the hard-bitten Scots, who moved into the back country of the Carolinas, Virginia, Maryland, and Pennsylvania. These Scots had come to America to escape poverty and tyranny, and they refused to be subservient to any established class.

A quality that most back-country folks displayed, particularly those of Scottish derivation, was a determination to maintain their freedom and to resist encroachments upon any rights that the new country offered. Political acumen was not a monopoly of the wealthy and the privileged; backwoodsmen developed political skill and utilized these talents in a continuing contest with the powers in authority. In Pennsylvania, Virginia, and the Carolinas, the division between seaboard society and an interior group that grew steadily more discontented and aggressive is particularly marked in the three decades preceding the revolution. The readiness of frontiersmen to demand their rights and fight for them, to insist upon equality of representation, and to protest the encroachment of vested interests represented by older, more conservative elements had an important influence in the colonies from Pennsylvania south. Lines drawn between the people living in the country and conservative groups in tidewater regions persisted for generations after independence. Most people in the back country in the 1760s and the early 1770s were less concerned about the tyranny of King George than about the oppression of their own lawmakers, who paid little attention to their complaints about taxes and fees exacted for every legal transaction.

So acute was the unrest in North Carolina in 1768 that the dissidents, calling themselves Regulators, formed an organization to resist high taxes, unjust laws, and exorbitant fees. A petition presented to the legislature by thirty citizens of Orange and Rowan counties declared that the "poor Petitioners" had been "continually squez'd and oppressed by our Publick Officers both with Regard to their fees as also in the Laying on of Taxes as well as in Collecting together with Iniquitous appropriations, and wrong applications." "Money is very scarce," they added, and though "to gentlemen Rowling [rolling] in affluence, a few shillings per man, may seem triffling yet to Poor people who must have their Bed and Bed clothes yea their Wives Petticoats taken and sold to defray these charges, how tremendious." They could come by neither paper money nor coins with which to pay taxes, and they craved restitution from the legislature, which gave no relief.

The Regulators at first tried to influence the provincial government with petitions and pamphlets, but when protests proved vain, they openly rebelled. On May 16, 1771, Governor William Tryon and his militia met more than 2,000 Regulators a few miles from Hillsboro in the Battle of Alamance, from the name of a nearby creek. Each side had nine men killed, and a number wounded. Later, twelve Regulators were tried for treason and six hanged. The Regulator movement broke up, but discontent remained. Although the resistance of North Carolina's back-countrymen was more overt than elsewhere, similar animosities had developed in interior regions of most of the colonies.

Yet it would be an oversimplification to say - as some historians have attempted to argue - that the American Revolution was an internal conflict between classes, as well as an external struggle against British rule. Social relations in all colonies were complex, and they varied from colony to colony. A generalization for North Carolina will not exactly describe conditions in New York. Nevertheless, no colony was without groups unhappy over the status quo. The British missed a chance to capitalize on frontier antagonism toward well-to-do groups of the provincial ruling classes.

The modern concept of class structure is easy to overemphasize in discussing the stresses in colonial society. If we read into the complaints of artisans in Philadelphia, New York, or Boston in the 1760s the developing unrest of a proletariat, we misinterpret the facts of colonial life. Nor were discontented back-countrymen necessarily the precursors of Western radicals. Indeed, frontiersmen were more conservative in some respects than those dwelling near the tidewaters. Cultural conservatism is often more manifest in frontier societies than in older settled regions. Nowhere is this more evident than in efforts in frontier communities to reproduce the best of the older societies that settlers had known. Preachers and teachers labored to re-establish religious observances, a sense of decorum, and opportunities for education.

Few were more concerned about education than the Presbyterian ministers who carried both the gospel and literacy to the Scotch-Irish on the frontier. Although one modern historian has termed the Scotch-Irish shiftless because of their restlessness and mobility, they were responsible for some of the most significant educational developments in the back country. The Reverend William Tennent, Sr., a graduate of the University of Edinburgh, founded, as early as 1726, an institution of higher learning at Neshaminy, Pennsylvania, which became known as the Log College. Here he turned out Presbyterian preachers, trained in Greek and Latin, for it was a cardinal belief of Presbyterians that the password to heaven must be uttered in one of the classical tongues. John Blair and Samuel Finley, two early presidents of Princeton, were graduates of the Log College. Princeton, founded in 1746, produced a steady stream of preachers and teachers who carried not only a message of Calvinistic theology, but also instruction in the elements of literacy and often contact with classical culture.

For Americans, education always has been regarded as the road to social advancement. Faced with the disintegrating forces of the frontier, settlers in America very early began to establish schools or otherwise provide for the education of their children. They established the doctrine that education supplied a way to improve one's station in the world. Not every father, of course, eagerly sought to send his children to school; many were content that their children help in the fields or be bound out to work at a trade. Few communities, however, were without influential citizens concerned over the need for educational facilities. Boston and the Massachusetts Bay area set an example from the seventeenth century onward by establishing tuition-free schools to those unable to pay. Even in rural North Carolina, some effort was made to provide at least minimal instruction in reading and writing for those who wanted to learn.

But the acquisition of rudimentary learning was not easy in areas where settlements were sparse and people poor. Parents had to ensure their children learned to read and write. If parents were illiterate, children might face the same fate, unless they acquired knowledge from a passing circuit rider or itinerant schoolmaster.

The story was different in the older, more sophisticated regions. Here were schools and opportunities for association with educated people. Philadelphia could offer instruction in a wide range of subjects, from surveying and navigation to draftsmanship and painting. Benjamin Franklin's description in his *Autobiography* of the interest of young craftsmen and businessmen of Philadelphia in book-learning - and the practical use to which they apply it - has become part of the American canon. Franklin organized a club "for mutual improvement," the Junto, and later the same group established a subscription library for the purchase of improving books - the mother of all the North American subscription libraries," Franklin declared. And he added: "These libraries have improved the general conversation of Americans, made the common tradesmen and farmers as intelligent as most gentlemen from other countries, and perhaps have contributed in some degree to the stand so generally made throughout the colonies in defence of their privileges."

Franklin's words are significant. By the beginning of the controversies with Great Britain, the colonies could boast a mature citizenry, many of whom were well read and well educated for their day. Opportunities for higher education existed at Harvard College, the College of William and Mary, Yale (established in New Haven in 1716), Princeton (founded in 1746 as the College of New Jersey), Columbia (chartered in 1754 as King's College), and Pennsylvania (first called the College, Academy, and Charitable School of Philadelphia under a charter revised in 1755). Two other colleges were chartered in the colonial period but took longer to establish themselves: Brown (created as Rhode Island College in 1764) and Rutgers (chartered as Queen's College in 1766).

Every colony also had booksellers, book collectors, and libraries. Cotton Mather in Boston and William Byrd II in Virginia accumulated significant private libraries, each consisting of more than 3,600 volumes. No two individuals could have been more different than Mather and Byrd, yet both bought and read many of the same books: the classics, scientific treatises, political tracts, legal works, philosophic works, practical manuals, sermons, and devotional books. Byrd, worldly and sophisticated, was an inveterate sermon-reader: "In the evening I read a sermon in Mr. Norris but a quarrel which I had with my wife hindered my taking much notice of it," he observes in his diary for December 25, 1710. Not many book buyers of the eighteenth century could boast libraries like those of Mather and Byrd, but demand for books increased as the century wore on, and by the end of the period, the book trade was flourishing, particularly in Boston and Philadelphia. The best book market in the South was Charles Town.

Interest in science became more widespread. Americans accepted the Baconian belief that in science, one could find a means for the relief of man's estate. Benjamin Franklin was instrumental in founding a scientific society "for the promotion of useful knowledge," which in 1744 took shape as the American Philosophical Society and in 1769 merged with another organization, the American Society, which had developed from the old Junto.

Franklin's study of electricity, which had the practical result of encouraging the use of lightning rods, gave him an international reputation. The first account of his experiments, *Experiments and Observations on Electricity, made at Philadelphia in America, by Mr. Benjamin Franklin*, was published in London in 1751. Translations into French, German, and Italian attracted widespread attention.

Scientific contacts between the Old World and America were not new, for colonial observers had reported their findings conscientiously to the Royal Society in London and to other scientific groups. Botany, zoology, and mineralogy were subjects of greatest interest; many Europeans believed that cures for the ills of mankind might be found in plant, animal, or mineral materials from the New World. Eighteenth-century collectors appointed agents in America to search for specimens and material of interest, beauty, or utility. Peter Collinson, a London merchant and member of the Royal Society, made arrangements with Philadelphia Quaker John Bartram to collect botanical specimens and seeds for him. The letters between them, which continued until Collinson's death in 1768, reveal the keen observations of the Quaker naturalist, who established a botanical garden on the banks of the Schuylkill River. A self-trained scientist, Bartram learned Latin so he could study the work of European contemporaries such as Carl Linnaeus, the Swedish botanist. Bartram's fame was so great that Linnaeus sent one of his research students, Peter Pehr Kalm, to Philadelphia to study with him.

Naturalists, physicians, and amateur students of natural philosophy became prominent in the second half of the eighteenth century. Dr. Alexander Garden, a physician from Charles Town, for whom the gardenia is named, typifies the community of scientific interest that existed in the colonies. In 1754, he traveled to New York, where he met Dr. Cadwallader Colden, who had written on botany, anthropology, physics, mathematics, and various medical problems including yellow fever, cancer, and diphtheria. Returning from New York, Garden stopped in Philadelphia to see Bartram and his plants. Soon Garden was corresponding with Colden, Bartram, John Clayton of Virginia, and the leading scientists in Europe: Linnaeus, Jan Frederik Gronovius, and others. In 1763, Garden was elected to the Royal Society of Uppsala and in 1773, to the Royal Society of London.

Although colonial colleges followed traditional curriculum closely, they did not neglect science; in a few instances, distinguished scientists flourished within academic precincts. For example, John Winthrop IV, Hollis Professor of Mathematics and Natural Philosophy at Harvard from 1738 until 1779, encouraged the study of theoretical science and mathematics and gained an international reputation for observations in physics and astronomy. His excellence was rewarded with an honorary degree from the University of Edinburgh and election to the Royal Society.

Ezra Stiles, one of the most learned men in New England, who became president of Yale in 1778, had wide-ranging scientific interests - often with a practical focus. He was a close friend of Jared Eliot, clergyman and physician, who in 1762 published an *Essay on the Invention, or Art of Making Very Good, If Not the Best Iron, from Black Sea Sand,* which was impressive enough to win a medal from the Royal Society. Eliot encouraged Stiles in scientific pursuits. Stiles made many scientific observations; one of the most interesting was an experiment with silkworms to test the feasibility of silk culture in New England. During the summer of 1763, while preaching at Newport, he hatched about 3,000 worms - two of the fattest and most voracious he named General Wolfe and Oliver Cromwell - and kept detailed notes on their progress. Stiles and his slave spent a part of every day except Sunday foraging for mulberry leaves to feed the worms. The summer's work produced less than a pound of raw silk and showed the difficulties of silk production in New England.

Because of the activities of the American Philosophical Society and the intellectual curiosity of many enterprising young craftsmen, Philadelphia became a center of lively scientific interest and of the application of new techniques. In 1730, Thomas Godfrey, a glazier by trade and a member of Franklin's original Junto, invented a navigating instrument called a quadrant that came to be known as Hadley's quadrant because of the simultaneous invention of the instrument by James Hadley in England. James Logan, a wealthy Quaker official and scientist, wrote to the Royal Society in 1734 to establish Godfrey's claim to the invention.

David Rittenhouse was one of the most versatile and talented of the self-taught scientists of Philadelphia. Brought up on a farm near Germantown, he taught himself mathematics and physics and acquired a remarkable knowledge of astronomy. In 1751, he opened an instrument shop on his father's farm. In 1768, he presented a paper before the American Philosophical Society on the transit of the planet Venus that was to occur in 1769. His calculations and his later observations of this phenomenon made him famous and are still regarded as remarkably advanced for their time. Rittenhouse became a professor of astronomy at the University of Pennsylvania.

A group of physicians in Philadelphia established a school of medicine in 1765 at the College of Philadelphia (later the University of Pennsylvania). The two chief promoters of this enterprise were Dr. John Morgan and Dr. William Shippen, Jr., graduates in medicine from the University of Edinburgh. In 1769, Dr. Benjamin Rush, who later became one of the foremost teachers of medicine, was elected professor of chemistry in the new medical school.

In the later colonial period, scientific speculation consumed many of the best minds of the day, as theological speculation had dominated thinking in the previous century. Many an eighteenth-century theologian combined scientific investigation and theological writing, and occasionally a scientist turned his mind to theology. Since the time of Cotton Mather and Jonathan Edwards, theologians had found science attractive, and by the second half of the eighteenth century, science attracted many people, from preachers to apprentices.

The way in which scientific-minded people stayed current with the experiments and observations being made throughout the colonies indicates the improvement that had occurred in intercolonial communications in the eighteenth century. In the early days of settlement, little direct communication was possible between colonies. South Carolina found it easier to communicate with London than with Boston. But by the mid-eighteenth century, conditions had changed. In 1756, Charles Town cheered the arrival of the first regularly established postal carrier from Boston, the beginning of an official service. Already Benjamin Franklin and William Hunter, who had taken over the post office in 1753, were improving the service between northern cities and the South as far as Williamsburg. An increase in coastal shipping made communication by water easier.

The means of communication between the colonies and with Europe continued to improve. Military needs had stimulated the institution of a regular packet-boat service with England. Packet boats connecting the principal American ports improved intercolonial mail service. One packet service between New York and Florida advertised in 1767 accommodations for both passengers and slaves. Overland mail service between Charles Town and Boston still took ten weeks, but the time between New York and Boston by 1764 had been reduced to six days. A network of private carriers encouraged travel and the delivery of mail and parcels. Inspired by the action of British agents who opened private mail, the Sons of Liberty instigated the establishment of a subscription postal service that bore the name "Constitutional Post." Begun in August 1774, by William Goddard of Baltimore, it was an immediate success.

The relative ease of communication during the years of controversy made it possible for agitators to promote propaganda with an efficiency that would have been impossible a half century before. Newspapers flourished, and few regions were so backward or so distant that they could not be reached by paper or pamphlet. Even in the interior of North Carolina, the Regulators had carried on much of their agitation through the printed word. From Charles Town to Portsmouth, printers prospered. Benjamin Franklin made a good living in the printing trade, as did some of his competitors. Between 1761 and 1776, the printing presses of the British colonies turned out 5,862 titles. The printers were busy, and they had a vast influence on developing political events. Furthermore, between 1763 and 1775, the number of newspapers in the colonies doubled, a fact that indicates the demand for news and commentary on politics. Americans already had become insatiable consumers of newspapers. British America had produced a reading public that eagerly bought the latest books from Europe as well as the most recent pamphlet from the local printer.

13
EVE OF REVOLUTION

With the fall of Quebec and Montreal, the war with France in North America had ended for the mainland colonies, and citizens from Maine to Florida believed life would be easier. French flags were furled, and a British regime was taking control of Canada and the western outposts. The Seven Years War in Europe had more than two years to run before it ended, and the British Navy still maintained a strong presence in the Caribbean and the Pacific. Except for a brief interval, the citizens of the thirteen colonies were at peace. Or so they believed. Speculators already were counting the profits they hoped to make from land grants in the Ohio Valley.

King George II, who had waged war against the French and had led his army in person at the Battle of Dettingen, lived to see the fall of Canada, but on October 25, 1760, while walking in his garden, he had a heart attack and died. His son Frederick Louis had died nine years before, and Frederick Louis' son, George III, was crowned. The new king, a man of strict morality, was determined to give his country an efficient and honest government. He also was determined to strengthen the authority of the sovereign and to rule without allegiance to any political party. His personal views on government ultimately would have a profound effect on his empire across the seas; in less than a decade and a half, the sovereign who was hailed on his accession as a patriot king would be a pariah to his American subjects. Convinced of his wisdom, stimulated by his mother's injunction "to be a king," and unwilling to listen to advice, George III became an arbitrary ruler and unnecessarily alienated his subjects in the colonies, who at the time had no aspirations for independence.

The Seven Years' War was the costliest war in Great Britain's history. By 1766, its national debt amounted to more than 133 million pounds. It was logical that George III should consider the money spent to protect the colonies and conclude they should help pay off the debt accumulated on their behalf. Although these taxes might seem just to the king, the efforts to procure revenue from the colonies helped to bring about the ultimate fall of the empire the war had won.

The colonies had flourished during the war, and authorities in London were aware that they could afford to contribute to the imperial revenue. The colonies could not deny their prosperity, but they found reasons to label all revenue measures as unjust. From the beginning, the legislative assemblies of the several colonies had asserted their right to tax, and the colonials maintained that only their own legislative bodies had the right of taxation. Although the cry of "no taxation without representation" was to come later, the idea was implicit in these early controversies. The colonials were determined not to admit the right of any external government to impose taxes upon them.

The end of the North American phase of the Seven Years' War plunged the colonies into an era of readjustment that soon dispelled the calm that peace had brought. Colonials soon realized peace did not mean much; that wartime prosperity was vanishing; that the departure of British soldiers and sailors, whom they had not always welcomed, would cause the loss of trade. As frequently happens after a war, a depression followed in the 1760s; it did not affect all regions with equal severity but was sufficiently widespread to upset the economic progress of all the colonies to some degree.

Most port towns in the years immediately preceding 1760 had enjoyed unusual prosperity. Soldiers and sailors spent money freely, and the British government paid for housing, food, and such equipment as the colonies could provide. Shipyards struggled to supply the demand for craft of all sorts - the army required a collection of supply vessels of every type from dinghies to ocean-going ships. Farmers in the back country found a ready market for grain, hay, hogs, cattle, flour, and cured meats as army contractors sought supplies for men and horses. Hardly a trade failed to respond to the demand for goods and services during the years immediately preceding the fall of Canada. The economy was inflated, and the end of the war and the departure of troops to other areas resulted in less demand for commodities and services. The collapse was neither immediate nor general, but the boom was over.

Merchants and shipmasters from Boston, Newport, New York, and other port towns had never hesitated to trade with Britain's enemies, and the focus of the war after 1760 drove many to illicit trade. Cargoes of grain, flour, meat, fish, and even guns, powder, and lead found their way from the colonies into French hands.

One of the favorite ways of trading with France was for a shipmaster to obtain a flag of truce to sail to a French West Indian port, apparently for the exchange of prisoners. Frenchmen sometimes were hired to pose as prisoners in order to make the application for flags of truce more credible. But Governor William Denny of Pennsylvania did not bother to inquire into the details if a shipmaster could pay twenty pounds for a blank flag of truce. Other colonial governors were equally corrupt. The ships, which outward bound had carried foodstuffs, returned with sugar, molasses, tea, wine, silk, and other French luxury goods - but no British prisoners. Sometimes ships made for one of the neutral islands controlled by the Dutch, Danes, or Spaniards. Monte Cristi, on the northern coast of Spanish Santo Domingo, commonly called the Mount, was a favorite haven for illicit trading ships. A report to the British government in February 1760, asserted that as many as 100 British vessels had been counted at one time at Monte Cristi. In the summer of 1760, Pitt wrote to governors of the British colonies urging them to do all in their power to curb the "illegal and most pernicious Trade . . . by which the enemy is . . . supplyed with Provisions, and other Necessaries, whereby they are . . . enabled to sustain, and protract, this long and expensive war."

Colonial governors, however, found cutting off a lucrative source of profits difficult. So widespread was the traffic, and so entrenched were the traders, that when news got around New York that George Spencer was about to expose their practices, he was thrown into jail. In a complaint to General Amherst, Spencer claimed he was kept in prison because he had information about the illegal business of two justices of the New York Supreme Court.

Authorities in London were not as lax as they were in the days of George II, however, and they began taking a more disciplined approach to the administration of colonial affairs and keeping a sharper watch over colonial legislation and the actions of colonial governors. No longer would the colonies profit from lack of oversight. The British Navy would do its utmost to stop trade with France, and both the navy and customs officers also would enforce the Acts of Trade and Navigation.

Great Britain, like other nations in the seventeenth and eighteenth centuries, regarded colonies useful if they could supply raw materials and absorb manufactured products of the mother country. This mercantilist viewpoint resulted in regulations under James I and Charles I that later, under the Commonwealth in 1651, culminated in the first of a series of Acts of Trade and Navigation. These acts, added to and amended until the eve of the revolution, were designed to bring prosperity to British shippers and merchants and at the same time to provide a market for the products of American fields, waters, forests, and mines.

The early Navigation Acts were aimed primarily at

the Dutch, who had developed a vast carrying trade. The laws made it illegal for foreign ships to trade with the British colonies unless licensed to do so. All goods from the colonies had to be transported in British-owned ships (colonial vessels, of course, were included), with crews at least 75 percent of whom were to be of British or colonial birth. The Navigation Act of 1660 specified that certain enumerated commodities, including tobacco, sugar, and indigo, could be shipped only to England or to other English colonies. Over the years, as production of profitable commodities increased, the list of enumerated items grew longer until it included things such as rice, beaver pelts, deerskins, naval stores, copper ore, molasses, pig iron, and hemp. The Navigation Act of 1663 tightened restrictions to make it illegal to import into the colonies all except a few specified commodities from foreign sources unless they first had been transported to England and a duty had been paid there. In 1673, Parliament passed an act levying a duty equal to the duty charged in England on listed articles shipped from one colony to another. At the same time, exceptions were made over the years to encourage colonial commerce. For example, fish and barrel staves could be shipped to the Madeira and the Canary Islands and wine imported from them directly. Salt could be imported directly from Spain to benefit Newfoundland fisheries. Fish, grain, rum, barrel staves, woodenware, and a few other non-enumerated articles could be shipped to any market.

One of the purposes of the Navigation Acts was to ensure England maintained a favorable balance of trade, and that it did not have to export currency to pay for raw products. The export of British coins to the colonies was illegal, and since the colonies were forbidden to coin money, the lack of hard money was a serious problem in every colony. Foreign coins found their way into the colonies, frequently through illegal avenues. The most common form of this foreign money was the Spanish dollar, usually referred to as a piece of eight. Because coins were hard to come by, Virginia and Maryland established a system of payments in tobacco. Each colony had a system of legalized money of account, referred to as lawful money, which meant money based on bookkeeping. Actual transactions were conducted with bills of exchange, warehouse receipts, personal notes, and sometimes by barter of commodities.

In 1690, after the futile effort to capture Quebec, Massachusetts issued paper money to pay her soldiers. This was the first paper money issued in British North America, but other colonies soon followed Massachusetts' example. Some loan banks were established in the early eighteenth century and issued money based on land mortgages. South Carolina, for example, had for a time a flourishing Land Bank, and Massachusetts had another, which was suppressed in 1741 by Parliament under the so-called Bubble Act of 1720, a measure passed to correct the abuses of the South Sea Bubble. One of the soundest of colonial paper currencies was that advocated by Benjamin Franklin and issued by Pennsylvania.

But throughout the colonial period, the scarcity of hard money created a serious economic problem. The colonies' imports exceeded their exports, and the balance of payments was always against them. Planters in the tobacco colonies might be rich in land, and merchants in New England might do a flourishing business, but they were hard-pressed for coins required for the payment of debts that could not be settled in colonial currencies or by credits accumulated with their factors overseas. The shortage of hard money plaguing the colonies became particularly acute after the war against Canada in 1760.

Scholars today lean to the view that the Acts of Trade and Navigation benefited the North American colonies. They gave the colonies a monopoly on a number of raw materials, such as tobacco from Maryland and Virginia, sold to England, which processed them and exported them to the rest of the world. Some industries flourished as a result of the restrictions of the Navigation Acts. For example, New England shippers and shipbuilders profited enormously from the requirement that ships in the British-carrying trade had to be of colonial or British construction. By the revolution, it is estimated that approximately 30 percent of all commercial ships Great Britain owned were of colonial construction.

Although the Navigation Acts burdened some elements of colonial society, the officials responsible for their enforcement until the succession of George III kept them from becoming hindering trade. The passage of the Molasses Act of 1733, designed to protect the British West Indies from competition of the French sugar islands, placed a tax of six pence a gallon on foreign molasses and taxed foreign rum and sugar. If the law had been strictly enforced, rum distilleries in New England would have suffered, trade in fish and barrel staves would have declined, and merchants in New England and elsewhere would have gone without Spanish and French money they needed. Trade with the French, Spanish, and Dutch islands suffered little interference.

Colonial shipmasters sailed to Amsterdam and other European ports where they exchanged American goods for luxury products in demand at home. Boston shippers, British officials charged, supplied the colonies with contraband European goods that should have been imported from England. Honest Quaker merchants in Philadelphia, respectable Baptists in Newport, and earnest Puritans in

Boston made a handsome profit from illegal traffic. They eased their consciences by arguing that the laws were unjust, and that they had to raise cash by foreign trade in order to pay their debts, since Parliament would not allow the export of English money to the New World. Whatever benefits the colonies may have reaped from the Navigation Acts, most colonials thought the acts oppressive.

And however right British authorities may have been in insisting upon the enforcement of the laws, the new policies under George III inevitably lit a firestorm. One of the most aggravating measures was the use of writs of assistance - general warrants without the name of any informing witness - granting customs officers the right of search and seizure. A Massachusetts court had authorized these writs in 1755 as a means of combating the flag-of-truce ruse for trading with the enemy, and in 1769, they were again employed in an attempt to run down smugglers, for Pitt had ordered the strict enforcement of the Molasses Act of 1733. Incensed when the king's officers broke down their warehouse doors and opened casks and cases of suspected goods, Boston merchants hired lawyer James Otis to defend them against such tyranny. Otis was the king's advocate general in the Boston court of the vice admiralty, and normally it would have been his duty to prosecute offenders against the Navigation Acts who were required to appear in the admiralty courts. Instead, Otis resigned his lucrative office and in February 1761, argued against the legality of the writs of assistance. He lost his case, but five years later the attorney general upheld his position.

Otis argued that the law governing all Britons was based on natural law, which contradicted acts of Parliament. He maintained that British subjects in America had the same rights as Englishmen in their home country. These arguments were frequently repeated in the next fifteen years. Concerning Otis' eloquence in arguing against the writs of assistance, John Adams declared: "Otis was a flame of fire! . . . American independence was then and there born; the seeds of patriots and heroes were then and there sown."

While the king's officials were struggling with rebellious merchants in Boston and other towns in the colonies, the king's navy and army elsewhere in the world were continuing the fight against France. Belatedly, in 1761, Spain had agreed to come to aid France, and on November 3, 1762, by the secret Treaty of Fontainebleau, France ceded to Spain all the Louisiana territory, an act that would have important later repercussions for America. But the Spanish alliance was of little help to France. Everywhere the British were victorious. Within two years, most French and Spanish islands in the Caribbean were under British control, and the Philippines had fallen to a British naval force. On the continent and in India, the British continued to add to their victories. By the end of 1762, the allies had to sue for peace, which was settled by the Treaty of Paris, signed February 10, 1763.

By terms of the treaty, France surrendered to Great Britain all Canada and all lands it previously had claimed east of the Mississippi River, except New Orleans. Unrestricted navigation of the Mississippi River was guaranteed to British subjects. Great Britain allowed France to keep two small islands in the Gulf of St. Lawrence, St. Pierre and Miquelon, so fishermen in Newfoundland waters might have a place to dry their nets. But French ships were forbidden to approach British possessions in the Gulf of St. Lawrence or Cape Breton Island. Although some English merchants would have willingly traded French Canada for the sugar island of Guadeloupe, Great Britain restored this island and Martinique to the French. Spain was obliged to cede to Great Britain East and West Florida, and in return the British gave Cuba and the Philippines back to Spain.

With the war settled, and with a vast empire under its control, Great Britain could turn to the business of solidifying its position and welding all the parts together. That task proved beyond the power of the king's ministers. Instead of acceding to what London regarded as reasonable demands, the colonies resisted every assertion of imperial authority. Self-interest that had kept them obedient to imperial authority during the long periods of war no longer operated with the same validity. Now the leaders of the colonies found their self-interest did not always coincide with the interests of the empire.

Two interrelated problems brought on crises soon after the Treaty of Paris had proclaimed peace. They concerned the appropriation of the western lands and the readjustment of Indian affairs. From London, it appeared that a simple formula establishing mutually exclusive territories for Indians and white settlers might be a satisfactory solution to repeated complaints from Indians about interlopers in their hunting grounds. Restlessness and open warfare from Indian tribes formerly loyal to France indicated that drastic action was required. Some headway already had been made. In October 1758, Pennsylvania made an agreement with the western Indians in the Treaty of Easton to respect their hunting grounds west of the Alleghenies and to keep settlers east of the mountains. But, despite the treaty, emigrants swarmed into the region around Fort Pitt, on the site of Fort Duquesne. So numerous were these intruders that Colonel Henry Bouquet, military commander in the region, issued an order on October 13, 1761, requiring the observance of the Treaty of Easton.

Western Indians were increasingly disenchanted

with the British, who had replaced the French in Detroit and other western outposts. Trade goods were scarce. Powder and lead were almost unobtainable, and the Indians pointed out that they needed ammunition for hunting. Some Indian leaders accused the British of plying their tribesmen with rum, then cheating them out of their furs. More Europeans were settling across the mountains, and the Indians foresaw their land occupied and their game driven away.

Hostilities broke out in the spring of 1763. In May, an Ottawa chief named Ponteach, or Pontiac, attempted to take Detroit by treachery, but his scheme was uncovered. Members of the Delaware, Shawnee, and Seneca tribes also went to war and captured most of the British outposts between Fort Pitt and Detroit; these were the only two western outposts the Indians failed to take. Detroit held out five months before Pontiac retreated in November. Severe fighting occurred at Bloody Ridge, Bushy Run, and at other points during the summer and autumn of 1763. General Jeffery Amherst was so angry over the Indians' treachery that he wrote Colonel Bouquet suggesting he spread smallpox among the tribesmen. Bouquet replied he would be glad to distribute germ-bearing blankets among them but for the danger of exposing good men to the disease. Although the worst of the war was over by the beginning of the next year, Pontiac did not make peace until 1766.

The tumult on the western frontier and the loss to fur traders from Indian attack forced the British government to take steps to take action. In June 1763, Lord Shelburne, president of the Board of Trade, recommended that land west of the Appalachians, except for a portion of the upper Ohio Valley, be set aside for an Indian reservation, and that emigration be forbidden west of the mountains. Shelburne reasoned that this action would force settlers to move into newly created provinces of Quebec, West Florida, and East Florida, where Englishmen were needed. Before Shelburne could enact the plan, Wills Hill, Earl of Hillsborough replaced him as president of the Board of Trade. The new president revised Shelburne's plan by eliminating the provision to permit settlers in the upper Ohio Valley and issued the Proclamation of 1763, establishing the crest of the Appalachians as the line beyond which emigrants could not pass. Hillsborough ordered settlers already on the west side of the mountains to leave immediately.

The Proclamation Line, which the British government considered temporary, succeeded in angering all Americans. Although emigrants disregarded it and continued to push across the mountains, they could not be certain of their rights to land, for they were seen as squatters. The land companies and speculators had little recourse. Since the 1740s, speculators and investors had looked upon western land as a source of wealth waiting to be exploited. Governors of colonies such as Virginia, which claimed land all the way to the Pacific Ocean, had been accustomed to authorize surveys and issue patents to western lands. The Proclamation of 1763 removed this authority from the governors and transferred it to the king, acting through the Privy Council and Board of Trade, a longer, more cumbersome procedure. The western land problem was left in a state of confusion.

Land speculators, however, did not lose hope. Many land-hungry Virginians, Pennsylvanians, and others continued to explore the trans-Appalachian country and survey territory they hoped to make their own. Dozens of land companies, often composed of wealthy merchants or planters, were organized to establish settlements west of the mountains. A few individuals sought to carve out estates for themselves, among them George Washington, who kept emissaries busy investigating lands in the Ohio Valley, and George Croghan, Pennsylvania Indian trader and agent.

For a decade after 1763, land fever raged. Between 1764 and 1765, George Croghan organized a group known as the Suffering Traders - Indian traders who had suffered as a result of Pontiac's conspiracy - and other prospective landholders (including Benjamin Franklin) into the Illinois Company, which sought more than a million acres bordering the Mississippi River. Croghan and Franklin were involved in another syndicate known as the Indiana Company, which tried to get a tract just west of the Proclamation Line between the Monongahela, Little Kanawha, and Ohio rivers. Hunter and explorer Daniel Boone lent his services to a North Carolinian, Richard Henderson, who was attempting to secure land for himself and associates in Kentucky. These were only a few of the organizations seeking western land despite the prohibitions of the Proclamation of 1763. Pressure from speculators and land companies soon forced the British government to alter the line of demarcation and shift it west.

Shifting the line involved politics, for the boundaries affected investments of members of Parliament who had speculated in land, territories that the Board of Trade had promised land companies, tracts that powerful speculators hoped to get once a new line was established, and the interests of several Indian tribes whose lands had to be avoided or purchased. To placate the Indians, speculators gave them presents and made promises of continued gifts. Many Indians gave up their lands believing the Europeans would subsidize them forever. Finally, in a series of treaties negotiated at Hard Labor Creek with the Cherokees in October 1768, at Fort Stanwix with the Iroquois and other northern Indians in November of the same year, and the Treaty of Lochaber with the Cherokees in October 1770, the British shifted the line west and provided new territories for settlement. Despite the goods they received as gifts, farsighted Indians were not pleased. They realized their days in ancestral hunting grounds were numbered.

In an effort to bring order to British relations with the Indians, the Board of Trade in London tentatively adopted George Croghan's plan in July 1764 that provided for maintaining a division already made into a northern and a southern district separated by the Ohio River. Sir William Johnson was superintendent of the northern region (with Croghan as his second in command), and Colonel John Stuart was superintendent of the southern region. The Plan of 1764 called for the establishment of many small trading posts among the various tribes south of the Ohio. An interpreter would be available to help both traders and Indians. The resident agent at each post would set prices and arbitrate disputes between traders and Indians. This plan broke down because the governors of Georgia, South Carolina, and Virginia licensed many unethical traders, who swarmed into the back country and cheated the Indians.

In the Northwest, Sir William Johnson decreed that all trade must be concentrated at two main posts, Detroit and Mackinac, an inconvenient arrangement for Indians and traders. Illegal French traders and unlicensed Americans traveling among the tribesmen bought furs and conveyed them down the rivers to profitable markets in St. Louis and New Orleans. The British fur companies saw their profits dwindle as trade fell off by more than a third in the years between 1764 and 1768. The British attempt to eliminate the French from the fur trade and to make new regulations called for many adjustments that were overdue. In the meantime, the Indians were discontented, and many traders were losing money and grumbling over interference from London. The imperial effort to settle the twin problems of western land and the Indian fur trade alienated thousands of colonials.

The restlessness of the Indians - and, it was whispered, the growing rebelliousness of the colonists - influenced the British government in 1763 to establish a military force of 10,000 soldiers in the colonies. In the government's view, the incapacity of the colonies during the Seven Years' War to unite in their own defense or to provide support for a war on the frontier had made this necessary. Some observers complained that the establishment was primarily designed to provide soft assignments for British officers. But the official assertion was that the soldiers were needed to defend the country against the Indians or a foreign aggressor. And since it was for the defense of the thirteen colonies, George III's government thought the colonists might pay part of the upkeep.

Logical and reasonable as this viewpoint appeared

in London, it was despised on the American side of the Atlantic, and the revenue measures put into effect in the next few years drove the colonies further along the road of opposition to Parliament. The actions of George Grenville, first lord of the treasury and prime minister from 1763 to 1765, particularly antagonized colonists. Grenville pushed through Parliament the Revenue Act of 1764, commonly known as the Sugar Act, which imposed new taxes and provided for the enforcement of the Navigation Acts. Although it reduced the tax on molasses, in effect since 1733, from six pence to three pence a gallon, provisions were made for the collection of the new tax, something that had not occurred with any regularity. Enforcement made a difference, and importers proclaimed they were ruined.

The next year, Grenville pushed a more unpopular act through Parliament, the Stamp Act of 1765. If Grenville had intended to devise a measure to antagonize the colonists, he could not have found a better means than the Stamp Act. No one could escape the new law, the first direct tax levied on colonists, because every document required for any transaction had to be written or printed on paper embossed with the tax stamp, and the paper could only be procured from stamp tax offices. Furthermore, stamps had to be paid for in sterling rather than colonial currency, and sterling was worth a third more than most colonial money. Hardly a scrap of paper used in the colonies escaped the tax. Every legal paper, every paper in commerce, licenses of every kind, newspapers, almanacs, diplomas, playing cards, and even dice required a stamp, which might range in cost from four pence for an almanac to four pounds for a liquor license. Not only were stamps costly, they were inconvenient, for no business could be transacted until someone had gone to the stamp office and got the right paper embossed with the right stamp. Since the stamp tax affected everyone, all could unite in condemning it. And since the most outspoken members of society, lawyers and the newspaper publishers, suffered the most expense and inconvenience, their protests were loudest.

The Revenue Act of 1764 had been a precursor for the furor that the Stamp Act caused, for the new duties in the Revenue Act raised prices and attempted to change the habits of men and women in the interest of English merchants. For example, colonists had developed a taste for Madeira wine, which from the beginning they had imported duty-free from the islands. The new act placed a prohibitive tax on Madeira in an effort to make wine drinkers in the colonies turn to port or sherry, which had to be imported from England. The act also put a heavy duty on French fabrics, particularly silk and linen.

The Revenue Act of 1764 and the Stamp Act

of 1765 created a furor such as the colonies had never before seen. Newspapers published diatribes against the king's ministers, whom they blamed for the iniquity, and agitators began to clamor for repeal of the detested acts. Hardly a town of consequence failed to organize a group who took the name Sons of Liberty. In most towns, the Sons of Liberty were respectable citizens determined to circumvent laws they regarded as violating the rights of Englishmen. Mobs in New York, Newport, Charles Town, and elsewhere stormed the stamp tax offices, burned the embossed paper, or forced officials to destroy paper and stamps. Never had the colonies seen such unity of purpose and action.

The Stamp Act brought two leaders into prominence, Massachusetts' Samuel Adams and Virginia's Patrick Henry, who were firebrands of revolution. Both were concerned about encroachments upon what they considered constitutional rights granted to colonists no less than to native residents of Great Britain.

Samuel Adams, a distant cousin of John Adams, who was to become the second president of the United States, was born with a genius for politics - and for political agitation. Throughout his life, he was always ready to neglect his business for the public good. After earning a bachelor's and master's degree at Harvard, he went to work at his father's brewery, where, a historian has commented, "he did little good for lack of capacity, and little harm from lack of responsibility." By 1763, he was expressing his talent for local politics as a member of the Caucus Club, a group of Boston politicians who met in Tom Dawes' attic. He had found his element, and the enactment of the Stamp Act gave him an opportunity to foment resentment against the governing establishment in Massachusetts.

In Virginia, Patrick Henry, a prosperous planter in a backwoods county, gained prominence in 1763 in a famous case known as "the Parson's Cause." The clergy of the established church in Virginia had traditionally received its pay in tobacco. But after poor crops in 1755 and 1758, the House of Burgesses fixed the rate of pay for the clergy at two pence a pound of tobacco, and salaries would be paid in cash at that rate instead of in tobacco. The clergy complained it was unfair not to receive its pay in high-priced tobacco during years of scarcity, and members carried their cause to the Privy Council, which overruled Virginia law. In a suit brought in Hanover County by a clergyman asking for back pay in tobacco, Patrick Henry argued the case for the clergy. With flaming oratory, Henry argued that the action of the king's Privy Council in vetoing a law passed by the House of Burgesses was tyranny. Moved by Henry's eloquence, the jury awarded the clergyman one penny. From this time on, Henry's reputation as a spokesman against the king's prerogative grew. In May 1765, as a member of the House of Burgesses, he argued the Stamp Act was illegal and unconstitutional, and he offered seven resolutions that asserted, with rising indignation, that Virginia's legislative assembly alone had the right to tax Virginians. In the course of the debate, Henry made his famous declaration: "Caesar had his Brutus - Charles the First, his Cromwell - and George the Third" - and he paused dramatically - "may profit by their example." On May 30, the House of Burgesses passed the first five of Henry's Resolves, and all seven were published in newspapers. They helped to stir other colonies to action.

The legislative assembly of Massachusetts, prodded by Samuel Adams and other Sons of Liberty, passed a resolution in June that called upon all mainland colonies to join in a congress to protest the new tax. The Stamp Act Congress convened in New York City from October 7 to October 25, 1765, and representatives attended from all colonies except Virginia, New Hampshire, North Carolina, and Georgia. The Congress passed fourteen resolutions that stated the position taken by Virginia in Henry's Resolves, namely that the colonists had all the rights and privileges of any of the king's subjects, that no taxes could be imposed legally without representation, and that since the colonies could not be represented in Parliament, their assemblies had the sole constitutional right to tax them. Since the Stamp Act provided that violations should be tried in the admiralty courts without juries, the resolutions complained of this violation of the rights of British subjects.

The language of the resolutions was not revolutionary, but it characterized colonial thought. Opinion was crystallizing around the doctrine that traditional liberties were in danger and that colonists should be vigilant to defend the constitutional rights enjoyed by British subjects anywhere. Soon scores of writers would cite examples from republican Rome and quote tracts written during the Glorious Revolution of 1688 to justify their opposition to tyranny. The Stamp Act Congress, having passed its resolutions and drawn up petitions to the king and to Parliament, adjourned, and delegates went home to continue their arguments against a law they were convinced undermined their freedom.

No village or settlement in North America was too far away to escape the propaganda against the Stamp Act, the most unpopular measure affecting the colonies that Parliament had yet passed. Town meetings in New England and county courts in the agrarian colonies of the South argued about the injustice of the law. Contributors to newspapers wrote about the iniquity of the tax, and several went so far as to describe the law as the beginning of enslavement of free men.

From Maine to Georgia, the public clamor against

the Stamp Act resounded until Whitehall heard. Resolutions aside, a colonies-wide boycott of British goods alarmed British merchants. A drop in exports to the colonies frightened London merchants into petitioning the House of Commons on January 17, 1766, to repeal the act, "in order," they declared, "to secure themselves and their families from impending ruin [and] to prevent a multitude of manufacturers from becoming a burthen to the community." The petition of the merchants made an impression, and the House of Commons began an investigation. Sitting as a committee on February 3, and for the following ten days, the House of Commons called witnesses, many suggested by merchants, to testify on the effect of the Stamp Act. Among these witnesses was Benjamin Franklin, who was in London as agent for the colony of Pennsylvania. Franklin made a reasoned defense of the American opposition to taxation by pointing out the huge amounts the colonies had spent in their own defense. He argued that Americans were entitled to the "common rights of Englishmen" guaranteed by the Magna Carta and set forth in the Petition of Right. In answer to a question about the attitude of Americans toward British goods, he declared Americans no longer took pride in wearing British garments but now wore "their old clothes over again till they can make new ones."

In July 1765, a ministry headed by Charles Watson-Wentworth, Marquess of Rockingham replaced Grenville. Faced with opposition to the Stamp Act at home and abroad, Rockingham moved for repeal in March 1766. The House of Commons was willing, but the House of Lords opposed this action because, they maintained, repeal would display a weakness and lack of authority in Parliament. Finally, after pressure from the king, a bill repealing the act passed both houses and received royal approval on March 18. To preserve its dignity, Parliament felt obliged to pass the Declaratory Act on the same day, which asserted Parliament's superiority over colonial legislative assemblies in all matters. Any laws passed in the colonies "whereby the power and authority of the Parliament of Great Britain to make laws and statutes as aforesaid is denied, or drawn into questions, are, and hereby declared to be, utterly null and void to all intents and purposes whatsoever."

Overjoyed by the repeal of the Stamp Act, most colonials were in no mood to quibble over face-saving declarations of Parliament. William Pitt, who had opposed the act, was a hero, and even King George, who had used his influence to end the law, again was hailed as a noble sovereign. The New York assembly went so far as to vote to erect statues of Pitt and the king. Bells rang, and people celebrated the annulment of a measure that had stirred all thirteen colonies and had come closer to uniting them.

But a number of dissidents took no joy in the celebrations. The fundamental issues affecting the liberties of the colonies remained unchanged. The Declaratory Act firmly announced the subjection of the colonies to Parliament. Sam Adams, displeased at the glee of his townsmen over the repeal, fanned the embers of discontent to ensure the colonies not grow complacent and forget the dangers of tyranny.

If wisdom had ruled Parliament, the damage done by the Stamp Act and the Revenue Act of 1764 might have been repaired. But wisdom was not evident at either Westminster or Whitehall. The pride of Englishmen could not curtail the boldness of colonials who chose to flout the king's authority, question Parliament's right to control them, and set themselves up as philosophers and students of the ancient laws of England.

The Rockingham ministry fell in August, 1766, and the king again turned to William Pitt (now the Earl of Chatham) to form a government. This turn of events might have changed the course of American history had not Pitt's illness soon afterward forced him to relinquish the leadership of the government to young and incompetent Augustus FitzRoy, Duke of Grafton. Grafton allowed Charles Townshend, chancellor of the Exchequer, to push through Parliament a new set of revenue laws known as the Townshend Acts, which became effective November 20, 1767.

Colonists had complained that the Stamp Act imposed a direct internal tax contrary to their constitutional rights; by implication at least they had indicated that indirect external taxes in the form of duties were less objectionable. Acting on this hint, Townshend put import duties on glass, lead, paint, papers, and tea and revised laws to enforce the collection of duties. Under the Townshend Acts, judges again were instructed to issue writs of assistance to enable customs officers to search suspected premises. The new laws expanded admiralty courts, where offenders against the customs ordinances were brought to trial.

While these actions were being taken by Parliament, conflict was emerging in New York as the result of the Quartering Act, which had become effective on March 24, 1765. This act, passed at the request of General Thomas Gage, required colonies to provide housing and supplies for British troops on station, and in 1766 added a provision permitting commanders to requisition quarters in inns, alehouses, and unoccupied dwellings. When General Gage, who had headquarters in New York, demanded the legislative assembly of that colony implement the act providing for necessary lodging for his troops, he met with only partial approval. Long-held disagreements between English troops and the citizenry led to rioting. When the legislature continued to refuse to authorize proper quarters and supplies, the royal governor suspended its functions, an action Parliament later affirmed.

The dismissal of a colonial legislative assembly by administrative and parliamentary action supplied ammunition to radicals who rallied against tyranny and oppression. The indignation aroused by the Townshend Acts, combined with uneasiness produced by the suspension of the New York assembly, resulted in a fresh wave of propaganda against the British government. In Massachusetts, Sam Adams, seeing an opportunity to take action, helped organize the Nonimportation Association of 1768 and maintained voluminous personal correspondence with leaders in the other colonies. In principal ports, organizers of the boycott held demonstrations and worked to sway public opinion to support the ban on British goods. John Dickinson of Pennsylvania condemned the action of the British. By nature, temperament, and social influence, Dickinson was conservative, but he could not tolerate the contempt of the British government toward American colonists; in time, he came to believe the English conspired to suppress freedom in America. In November 1767, he began to publish the first of fourteen essays in *The Pennsylvania Chronicle*, which he titled, "Letters from a Farmer in Pennsylvania to the Inhabitants of the British Colonies." By the end of the following year, these letters, reprinted as pamphlets, were being widely read throughout the colonies and in Great Britain. Dickinson marshaled his eloquence to show the iniquity of the Townshend Acts and the dangers implicit in the suspension of the New York assembly.

The drumbeat of propaganda against British tyranny continued to rise. In 1768, Sam Adams composed a Circular Letter approved by the Massachusetts House of Representatives to be sent to legislative assemblies of the other colonies. This letter condemned the Townshend Acts and called on other colonies to unite for the common defense of their liberties. The letter particularly warned against attempts by the crown to make the royal governors and judges independent of colonial authorities. When the Earl of Hillsborough, secretary for the colonies, read the letter, he renounced it as rebellious and ordered colonial governors to suspend any legislative assembly that approved it. But several colonial legislatures had already endorsed the letter. Governor Francis Bernard of Massachusetts ordered the General Court (the legislative assembly) to expunge the letter from the record; when it refused, he suspended it in compliance with Hillsborough's orders.

The lives of customs agents were troubled and difficult. Every device was used to deceive and circumvent them, and occasionally violence occurred. When Boston customs officers in 1768 asked for armed help in enforcing the laws, the

Admiralty ordered the ship *Romney* sent from Halifax. On October 1 of that year, two regiments equipped with artillery landed in Boston. This show of force created further unrest in the city.

Throughout the colonies, sentiment for the boycott of British goods increased. The nonimportation agreements were so effective that the value of British imports fell from 2,157,218 pounds in 1768 to 1,336,122 pounds by the end of 1769. Since Parliament understood this argument, even by members who wished to punish American upstarts, in 1770, the government, led by Frederick Lord North, moved to modify the Townshend Acts.

In April 1770, all duties were removed except that on tea. Lord North insisted upon the retention of one duty as a symbol of Parliament's continued authority. But the Quartering Act, which had earned the ire of colonists, was not renewed. Gradually business began to improve, nonimportation was forgotten, and for a time it looked as if controversies with the mother country might be forgotten.

Indeed, the return of complacence troubled the radicals, and Sam Adams again began to keep his correspondents in other colonies alert to the danger of British usurpation of their liberties. Near riots between citizens and garrison troops in New York and Boston provided motivation for the agitators, and full-scale trouble in Boston on the night of March 5, 1770, was the sort of circumstance the radicals needed. When roving bands of rioting workers and soldiers in the streets of Boston met a detachment of troops under the command of Captain Thomas Preston, a fracas started, and someone gave the order to fire. Three civilians were killed, and two were fatally wounded.

This was the Boston Massacre that Sam Adams magnified in gruesome words and that Paul Revere pictured in an engraving. As the result of the upsurge of indignation, Governor Bernard agreed to remove the troops from the town to Castle William and to allow civil authorities to try for murder Captain Preston and the soldiers of his squad. John Adams, Josiah Quincy, and Robert Auchmuty served as attorneys for the accused and saw to it they received a fair trial. All were cleared of the murder charge, but two of the soldiers were convicted of manslaughter. When they pleaded benefit of clergy under old English law, they were freed, after being branded on their thumbs.

Despite the furor stirred by the riot in Boston, calm settled over the colonies as business responded to the removal of the Townshend duties. Merchants imported goods to replenish depleted stocks; cargoes of American grain, meat, fish, and other food products found a ready market abroad. The Board of Trade was forced to permit payment in English coins for American exports, a step that helped improve the financial position of the colonials. For two years following the repeal of the Townshend Acts, prosperity reigned, and the agitators found it difficult to maintain a sense of crisis and alarm.

But Sam Adams was equal to the situation. As historian Samuel Eliot Morison said: "A middle-class Bostonian, austere and implacable, Adams alone among leaders of the American Revolution was a genuine revolutionary, resembling in several respects the communist agitators of our time. He was certainly the Western world's first orchestra-leader of revolution. He knew that voters are moved by emotion rather than logic. A master of propaganda, he realized that the general run of people prefer drama and ritual to a well-argued exposition." So Adams did not let the colonies lapse into complacency under the influence of prosperity. He kept up incessant correspondence with kindred spirits in the other colonies and waited impatiently for some explosive incident that he could magnify into evidence of British tyranny.

Precisely what Adams wanted occurred in the summer of 1772. On June 9, a customs schooner, the *Gaspee,* ran aground near Providence, Rhode Island, and that night a mob led by a respectable merchant, John Brown, sailed out of Providence, boarded, and burned the helpless vessel, which flew the flag of the Royal Navy. This was an affront that London could not accept. When news reached

Whitehall, tempers flared, and a royal proclamation went out on August 26 offering a reward of 500 pounds for the identity of the men who had dared touch one of the king's ships. Furthermore, when apprehended, they were to be sent to England for trial. It is of interest that the king's commissioners could never discover them. Coincidental with this issue came an announcement from Governor Hutchinson of Massachusetts that henceforth he would not rely on the assembly for his salary but receive it directly from the crown, as would Massachusetts judges. Here was the beginning, thoughtful colonials decided, of complete control of executive and judicial officials from London. It was easy for Adams and the radicals to alarm even the least excitable of their contemporaries with visions of trials across the seas for infringements of the king's laws, or at best, trials at home before judges paid by the Crown.

The *Gaspee* episode and the new scheme for paying royal governors and judges were soon the subjects of conversation in taverns, inns, courthouses, and town markets throughout the colonies. In November, Adams assembled a twenty-one-man committee in Boston to spread the word throughout the colonies that American liberties faced a new and present danger. This Committee of Correspondence, soliciting help from other colonies, succeeded in organizing propaganda units elsewhere. In March 1773, the Virginia

House of Burgesses created a Committee of Correspondence with Patrick Henry, Thomas Jefferson, and Richard Henry Lee. By February 1774, all the colonies except North Carolina and Pennsylvania had active Committees of Correspondence engaged in distributing propaganda aimed at alerting the populace to encroachments upon American liberties.

As yet the colonies were not demanding independence from Great Britain; not even the radicals wanted to cut connections with the mother country. They merely wanted to prevent Parliament and the king's ministers from usurping rights they believed resided in the legislative assemblies of individual colonies. As colonial writers continued to debate their problems, a few found themselves advocating a federal union of the colonies into something approaching the dominion status enjoyed by Canada and Australia at the beginning of the twentieth century. If King George and his ministers had shown more wisdom and foresight, they might have welded the colonies into a dominion that would have been a loyal and profitable member of the empire. But political thinking had not advanced that far in eighteenth-century Britain, and Whitehall chose to treat the colonies as disobedient children that needed discipline.

One of the measures that King George and his ministers determined to retain was the three-pence-per-pound tax on tea, a commodity in great demand in colonial America. In the five years before 1772, colonies had imported some 373,000 pounds of tea annually. That figure did not take into account a vast amount of tea smuggled from Holland. At first a fashionable drink, tea had come to be regarded as a necessity. Like the tax on paper under the Stamp Act, the tax on tea affected the populace as a whole and made them conscious of British authority. That was its purpose - and that purpose played into the hands of agitators.

The British government compounded the problem with tea by a Parliamentary measure on May 10, 1773, intended to assist the East India Company, which was facing financial difficulties. The Tea Act remitted all duties on tea imported into Great Britain and granted the East India Company what amounted to a monopoly of tea exports to the colonies. Previous to the Tea Act, the East India Company had been required to sell its tea at auction. British merchants then exported the tea they had bought to merchants overseas. After the passage of the Tea Act, the East India Company was permitted to export tea from Great Britain directly to favored agents in the colonies. That enabled the East India Company to undersell other tea exporters, and it eliminated all tea merchants in the colonies except those selected by the East India Company. Not even smuggled tea could compete with the reduced price of East India Company tea.

In the autumn of 1773, the East India Company was preparing to ship 500,000 pounds of tea to agents in colonial ports including Philadelphia, New York, Boston, and Charles Town. Merchants in these towns, incensed over the monopoly the East India Company had on the colonies, held protest meetings, and the Sons of Liberty wrote and published indignant letters. They began a movement to boycott tea and to substitute cider and other beverages.

Feelings ran high, and when word reached the colonies of the dispatch of tea ships, the Sons of Liberty began to make plans to turn them back. In Philadelphia, a mass meeting forced the tea agents of the East India Company to resign and decline to accept shipments. In New York, the Sons of Liberty published a statement demanding pilots refuse to bring into the harbor any tea ship. In Boston, two impassioned meetings were held, and resolutions were passed that no tea must be landed. The Bostonians demanded that the tea ships must return to England without discharging their cargoes. But Governor Hutchinson, whose two sons and a nephew were agents for the East India Company, declined to permit any tea ship to clear the harbor unless it could show that its tea had been landed and the duties paid.

Overt trouble over tea occurred in Boston on the night of December 16, 1773. The tea ship

Dartmouth, with Captain Rotch commanding, had been docked in the harbor since November 27. Customs regulations required that the duty must be paid within twenty days after arrival, or the cargo would be subject to seizure. Since time had run out, customs authorities could seize the tea, which Boston citizens said must not happen. Another public meeting was held, and Captain Rotch and Sam Adams faced each other. The captain explained that the governor would not permit him to sail without delivering the tea, which was now liable to seizure. Sam Adams gave a signal, and a band disguised as Mohawk Indians rushed to the wharf, boarded the *Dartmouth* and two other tea ships, and dumped 342 chests of tea overboard. This was the famous Boston Tea Party, but Boston was not alone in refusing the East India Company's tea. Philadelphia and New York turned back tea ships because no one there dared receive the cargoes. Charles Town allowed the tea to be delivered, stored it in a damp warehouse, and later, after the break with Great Britain, confiscated it.

The destruction of the tea was not applauded universally in the colonies. Conservatives thought the Boston radicals had gone too far, and even some who had denounced the Tea Act were uncertain that violence was the best tactic. The men and women of the colonies waited to see what the British government would do. They were not kept long in suspense. The king was furious at the insult to his authority and demanded action of Lord North, his chief minister. English newspapers raged against the rebellious colonists. Finally, beginning with the Boston Port Bill passed by the Commons on March 25, Parliament enacted a series of laws designed to punish Boston for its defiance. These laws, known as the Coercive or Intolerable Acts, alienated moderates who had at first condemned the Boston Tea Party.

A crisis over tea had brought to a head all the smoldering frustrations of the colonials and all the vindictive pride of the home government. From this time on, the controversies ceased to be a debate over traditional rights of Englishmen and developed into a power struggle between the colonies and the British government. The immediate effect of the Coercive Acts was to enlist sympathy for Boston.

The Boston Port Bill, which became law on June 1, 1774, closed the harbor to all shipping except military transports and vessels carrying supplies for soldiers. Some latitude was left to the hated customs officers, who at their discretion could clear ships bringing in food and fuel. To prevent local pressure, customs officials moved their headquarters to Salem. To make it easier for other officials of the king to carry out punitive actions against the local citizenry, Parliament on May 20 passed the Administration of Justice Act, which provided that the royal governor, with consent of the council, could authorize the trial in Great Britain of any official charged with a capital offense incurred in quelling a riot or enforcing the king's laws. This act raised an outcry, not only in Massachusetts, but in the other colonies. Radicals maintained that murderers of honest citizens would be taken to Britain and freed and that no one could be sure of life or property. Even moderates had misgivings. Various colonies took steps to aid Massachusetts. South Carolina sent a shipment of rice, and others aided with food and funds.

But Parliament had worse medicine in store for Massachusetts and, by implied threat, for the other colonies. On the same day it passed the Administration of Justice Act, it approved the Massachusetts Government Act, which abrogated the Massachusetts Charter of 1691 and gave its royally-appointed governor wide-ranging powers, controlled from London. Members of the governor's council, formerly elected by the assembly, now would be crown appointees who could be dismissed at the pleasure of the king. The attorney general, judges of the lower courts, justices of the peace, and sheriffs would be appointees of the royal governor and would hold office at his pleasure. The superior judges and chief justice would be royal appointees made on recommendation of the governor. The sheriffs would pick the juries. And the governor would control that most typical of Massachusetts' institutions, the town meeting.

All these measures were designed to punish Massachusetts, and Boston in particular, for flouting the king's laws. Massachusetts would be a lesson to other colonies, and all would learn that their masters were the British Parliament and the king.

Not all Englishmen were as confident as the Earl of Hillsborough, Lord North, and King George that this punishment would improve the colonies. Nor were all Englishmen pleased over the tightening authority King George and friends exerted over their own liberties. For more than a decade, John Wilkes, a Parliament member and in 1774 Lord Mayor of London, fought the king with satire and invective to defend the colonies. Though Wilkes' character was questionable, colonists made him a hero, and the South Carolina assembly sent 1,500 pounds to help pay his debts. Other Englishmen more respected than Wilkes continued their opposition to policies they foresaw would lead to disaster. Lord Chatham remained a friend of the colonies, and Edmund Burke eloquently defended them.

In the debate in the House of Commons over the Massachusetts Government Act on May 2, 1774, Burke declared: "If you govern America at all, Sir, it must be by an army; but the Bill before us carries with it the force of that army; and I am of opinion they never will consent without force being used. . . . Repeal, Sir, the Act which gave rise to this disturbance; this will be the remedy to bring peace and quietness and restore authority; but a great black book and a great many red coats will never be able to govern it. It is true, the Americans cannot resist the force of this country, but it will cause wranglings, scuffling and discontent. Such remedies as the foregoing will create disturbances that can never be quieted." Burke's words were truer than he knew.

American moderates had struggled to persuade Englishmen that a little understanding, a demonstration of good sense, and a modicum of forbearance would ease a situation rapidly moving toward catastrophe. One of the most persistent of these Americans was Benjamin Franklin, who had many friends in Great Britain and who had served as agent of the province of Pennsylvania in London. In 1768, Georgia appointed Franklin to serve as its agent, and by 1770, he was serving as agent for New Jersey and Massachusetts, a series of appointments that gave him almost the status of colonial ambassador. He tried to bring about reconciliation and understanding. Until 1774, he continued to believe moderation on both sides would result in resolution of the problems plaguing both Great Britain and the colonies, but after the passing of the Coercive Acts, he began to feel hopeless.

Franklin had suffered enough personal abuse

in England to convince himself of the arbitrary arrogance of those in authority. One episode was enough to sour even this benign man. In 1772, he had seen six letters written by Governor Hutchinson to an unnamed English friend, believed to be Thomas Whately, secretary to Grenville, in which Hutchinson had urged "an abridgment of what are called English Liberties" of the colonists. Franklin obtained these letters in confidence and sent them to Thomas Cushing, speaker of the Massachusetts House of Representatives, with the understanding they would neither be copied nor printed. But they fell into the hands of Sam Adams, who, in June 1773, read the letters before a secret session of the House. They were soon printed far and wide, even in London. The disclosure of Hutchinson's views, and the manner in which the letters had come to light, caused a sensation, and Franklin found himself in an embarrassing predicament. At a hearing before the Privy Council in London on January 29, 1774, the solicitor general called him a thief and a rogue, and he lost his post as deputy postmaster general of the colonies. Other abuse was heaped upon Franklin until finally, on March 20, 1775, he sailed for America.

During this time, Parliament enacted other measures that further exasperated and alarmed Americans. One of these was the Quebec Act, passed on May 20, 1774, which established a highly centralized government in Canada, somewhat similar to the government Canadians had lived under during the French possession of that territory. Since under this act most of the governing authority would be in the hands of appointees of the crown, colonists to the south construed it as a sign of what ultimately was in store for them. The Quebec Act had other disturbing features. The Catholic Church was given a preferred status in French Canada, and colonial Protestants saw this as something they must resist. Worse still, the Quebec Act declared the boundaries of Canada to be on the Ohio River, which excluded Virginia, Connecticut, and Massachusetts from their long-claimed western lands.

The religious question raised by the Quebec Act was related to one that had long troubled some colonists. The connection between church and state had been a matter of contention at one time or another in most of the colonies, and the abolition of an established church would be one of the results of the revolution. Soon after the Stamp Act controversy, citizens of the colonies heard of a plan by the Anglican Church to appoint an American bishop. Previously, the affairs of the church in the colonies had been the responsibility of the Bishop of London. To colonials already excited over the threat to their civil liberties, the specter of religious tyranny, of a bishop who would work together with royal governors to impose the teachings of an established church upon them, was not to be taken lightly. The outcry over an American bishop eventually subsided, but freedom from the domination of Canterbury was one requirement of the American Episcopal Church after the revolution.

By the summer of 1774, sentiment in the colonies had reached a point of desperation and despair over the increasing authority of king and Parliament. On May 13, General Thomas Gage, commander of British troops in America, supplanted Governor Hutchinson as royal governor of Massachusetts. The change was symbolic of the determination of the crown to rule Massachusetts and the rest of America by force of arms if necessary. Just after the installation of what in effect was a military government in Massachusetts came word that on June 2, Parliament had passed another Quartering Act, this time applicable to all colonies, allowing troops to be quartered not merely in taverns and vacant buildings but in occupied houses as well.

The future course was evident for even the blindest Tory, said those who wrote pamphlets: King and Parliament were determined to suppress the liberties of Americans, and no course was left but to meet force with force. Mass meetings, town meetings, and official bodies of various sorts began to urge action against Great Britain. In Boston, the Committee of Correspondence produced a Solemn League and Covenant in which the signers agreed to boycott all British goods and avoid any transactions with Great Britain. On June 17, 1774, the Massachusetts House of Representatives sent a call to the other colonies to name delegates to a Continental Congress to be held in Philadelphia that September. Other groups elsewhere had been urging the need for a congress of all colonies. The call for the First Continental Congress was well-received except in Georgia, and the twelve other colonies named fifty-six delegates who first met in Carpenters' Hall, Philadelphia, on September 5, 1774. Twelve days later, the First Continental Congress approved a set of resolutions known as the Suffolk Resolves. These resolutions, adopted by a convention in Suffolk County, Massachusetts, on September 9, were written by Dr. Joseph Warren, an ardent patriot of Boston; they had been carried swiftly to Philadelphia by Paul Revere; and their approval by the Congress under the whip of its radical members signified the temper of the times, for the Suffolk Resolves not only declared the Coercive Acts unconstitutional and not to be obeyed, but they called upon the people to arm themselves into organized militia to resist enforcement. They also called for an embargo on British trade.

The Continental Congress' resolutions were somewhat less belligerent, but clearly indicative of a determination to resist the enforcement of laws violating the fundamental rights of colonists.

Congress enumerated these rights, including a statement "that they are entitled to life, liberty, and property, and they have never ceded to any sovereign power whatever a right to dispose of either without their consent." They declared Americans are "entitled to all the rights, liberties, and immunities of free and natural-born subjects within the realm of England." The resolutions passed by the Congress listed their numerous grievances and demanded the repeal of the objectionable acts. In conclusion, the Congress declared: "To these grievous acts and measures Americans cannot submit, but in hopes that their fellow subjects in Great Britain will, on a revision of them, restore us to that state in which both countries found happiness and prosperity, we have for the present only resolved to pursue the following peaceable measures: 1st. To enter into a non-importation, non-consumption, and non-exportation agreement or association. 2. To prepare an address to the people of Great Britain, and a memorial to the inhabitants of British America, & 3. To prepare a loyal address to his Majesty, agreeable to resolutions already entered into."

Negotiations were a possibility, but most members of the Congress secretly believed King George and his ministers would relent. Congress had declared that "for the present only" it would pursue the peaceable, but stern measures outlined. Implied was the threat of grimmer action to come. The time of debate and controversy was drawing to a close. The calling of the First Continental Congress marked the end of the colonial era. Revolution had begun.

Made in the USA
Coppell, TX
19 June 2020